Mrs Mary,
 Greetings
God. As you continue life's journey keep "just thinking" about all that God is doing around you every day. With all my love.
 Love God; Love People!!
 David M Simmons

# JUST THINKING!
## A SPIRITUAL THOUGHT ON EVERYDAY HAPPENINGS!

**DAVID M. SIMMONS**

WESTBOW
PRESS®
A DIVISION OF THOMAS NELSON
& ZONDERVAN

Copyright © 2024 David M. Simmons.

All rights reserved. No part of this book may be used or reproduced by any means, graphic, electronic, or mechanical, including photocopying, recording, taping or by any information storage retrieval system without the written permission of the author except in the case of brief quotations embodied in critical articles and reviews.

This book is a work of non-fiction. Unless otherwise noted, the author and the publisher make no explicit guarantees as to the accuracy of the information contained in this book and in some cases, names of people and places have been altered to protect their privacy.

WestBow Press books may be ordered through booksellers or by contacting:

WestBow Press
A Division of Thomas Nelson & Zondervan
1663 Liberty Drive
Bloomington, IN 47403
www.westbowpress.com
844-714-3454

Because of the dynamic nature of the Internet, any web addresses or links contained in this book may have changed since publication and may no longer be valid. The views expressed in this work are solely those of the author and do not necessarily reflect the views of the publisher, and the publisher hereby disclaims any responsibility for them.

Any people depicted in stock imagery provided by Getty Images are models, and such images are being used for illustrative purposes only. Certain stock imagery © Getty Images.

ISBN: 979-8-3850-1850-5 (sc)
ISBN: 979-8-3850-1849-9 (e)

Library of Congress Control Number: 2024902391

Print information available on the last page.

WestBow Press rev. date: 02/08/2024

# CONTENTS

Dedication ..................................................................... vii
Foreword ........................................................................ ix
Preface ............................................................................ xi
Introduction ................................................................ xiii

Chapter 1   Just Thinking…About The Family! ...................... 1
Chapter 2   Just Thinking…About Sports! ........................... 30
Chapter 3   Just Thinking…About Birthdays & Holidays! .... 59
Chapter 4   Just Thinking…About The Weather! ................. 95
Chapter 5   Just Thinking…About Secial People! ............... 124
Chapter 6   Just Thinking…About The Church! ................. 154
Chapter 7   Just Thinking…About Health! ......................... 185
Chapter 8   Just Thinking…About Ministry! ...................... 219
Chapter 9   Just Thinking…About Everyday Life! .............. 253
Chapter 10  Just Thinking…About Something Funny! ........ 281

# **DEDICATION**

This book is dedication to a very special person in my life. Her name is Peggy. I was fortunate enough to get her to marry me in 1982. She has been my rock and my security and the best helper a man could ever hope. She has probed and prodded me to get this book finished and now that it is I dedicate it to her. She was a huge motivation behind me getting it done. So, thanks Peggy. You have always had me Just Thinking!

# FOREWORD

Read this book, listen to Pastor Simmons's words, and pay attention to his pragmatic applications at the end of each chapter. Your life will be richer for doing so.

Just Thinking is written by one of my favorite friends and pastors – David Simmons. I met David in 2008. He had arrived in Travelers Rest, South Carolina, to be Senior Pastor of Reedy River Baptist Church. He is a role model, encourager, and an effective pastor, but most of all he and Peggy are dear friends to me and my wife.

Just Thinking is a collection of weekly articles that David began in 1983. A lot of things can happen between 1983 and 2023. This collection of articles allows you to meet David through different life experiences. You'll be able to relate to his personal stories and his scriptural applications of them. They will encourage you as you read this book.

Randy Bradley,
Member Care Consultant for the Americas
International Mission Board, SBC

# PREFACE

I grew up in Garden City, Georgia. I lived close to my Nana, my Mom's mother. We frequented her home many times as a young boy. I stayed with her when Dad and Mom were away. She had a round high breakfast table in her kitchen. It had rod iron legs that attached to a base on the bottom and a table on top. Many times, I sat at this table and ate. In between the rod iron legs she had the statue of "The Thinker," by Auguste Rodin. It was an original bronze statue with a male resting his chin on his hand as in great thought. It was believed to represent philosophy. Of course, as a child I had no idea what this statue represented or why my Nana would have it in her home. As an adult and pastor for 40 years I recognize the need for sometimes just thinking. Truly my life has been filled with many philosophical moments. I have tried to not just rely on my own thoughts, but highly relied on the movement of the Holy Spirit to guide my thoughts and my actions.

Dr. Henry Blackaby shared in his ground breaking Bible Study, "Experiencing God," this truth "God is always working." It is not our responsibility to find something to do and then ask God to bless it. It is more important that we find out what God is doing and join Him in what He is doing. You might say that is my philosophy of thinking. I love to watch people and don't mind laughing at myself. Instead of just brushing off the experiences I often with the help of the Holy Spirit put a spiritual truth to those experiences. It is amazing what God can teach us if we will just "think" a moment.

So, my desire is to share with you some of those experiences and allow you to "think" right along with me. I will share with you what I have learned and hopefully and prayerfully God's Spirit will speak to you through some of these experiences. My prayer is that as we live in this material world, we would transform our daily activities into spiritual moments. By the way all of this has got me to Just Thinking!

# INTRODUCTION

This book is all about, "Just Thinking." I have been blessed to have had many experiences over the past 40 years. Many church and ministry related. Many family and family activities related. It really doesn't matter what the experience is related too. What matters is what God can teach me from all of those experiences.

Let me explain how this all got started. In late summer of 1992, I moved to Lake City, SC., where I embarked on a 15 year stay at Calvary Baptist Church. It was my first time being responsible at writing a newsletter article every month. Computers were just becoming a needed commodity. Blogs were up and coming, but still in their infancy. Email was the new thing and people were still waiting to log on to AOL on their phone line. I began by writing out my articles on a legal pad that my secretary typed into the newsletter that she taped into the slot where it would be printed. I began writing about the upcoming events on the church calendar. One day after several months my older, but wiser secretary, Mrs. Evelyn Balton, spoke to me and said, "If you are going to rehash all that is in the newsletter in your article there is no use for me to put all that stuff in the newsletter. You need to write inspiration and thought." I took that information from that precious lady and begin in January of 1983 of writing the column, "Just Thinking!" Ever since I have been writing a monthly article entitled "Just Thinking." As most things do it has evolved. It has received many retorts from practitioners, friends, and family alike. It was once a daily minute on a local Christian radio station for about six months. It moved to a weekly article when I moved to Reedy River Baptist Church in 2008. It transformed into a monthly article again later that year. Several years ago, it began to show up in a weekly email that I send out to church members and family and friends. My prayer for you as you read is that you will allow the Holy Spirit to speak to you and you will allow yourself to "Just Think" about what He would have you learn.

# CHAPTER ONE
# JUST THINKING... ABOUT THE FAMILY!

## "REMOVING THE PLUG"
### 2 Corinthians 7:14

My family and I have moved into our new house. Needless to say, although we are sleeping in our new house there is still a great deal to do before everything is in order. One of the things I did before we moved in was to put our new appliances in place. One of those was a new dishwasher.

Now, I am no expert at anything. I remember that I had a man in one of my churches that use to say, "I am a jack of all trades and a master of none." Well, I have dabbled in a little plumbing over the years and have installed a few dishwashers in my time. I was doing really well. I connected all of the right hoses, connected the water line, wired the electricity and got the dishwasher into the cabinet with a perfect fit. Now came the real test. I turned on the dishwasher to a quick rinse cycle. The water began pumping into the machine and it ran with quiet precision. Needless to say, I was pretty proud of myself. I then hit the cancel button so the dishwasher would drain. Nothing happened.

I couldn't get the water to drain out of the dishwasher. I figured the old drain line was clogged, but just to make sure I disconnected the new drain line and placed it into the sink. I pushed cancel again and still nothing happened. I then checked to see if any water at all was escaping from the dishwasher. I could see a small amount of water going into one of the hoses, but it was not traveling the necessary distance. I just knew I had done everything I was supposed to do.

My wife was now asking questions. I was getting aggravated, so I called for reinforcements. I called a friend who stopped by only to tell me he didn't know what else to do because it seemed like everything was hooked up right.

I called a young man in my church who does some plumbing work. He agreed to stop by and after listening and doing a few things he went to the original drain hose that I had connected on the bottom of the dishwasher. He disconnected the hose and asked me for a pair of needle nose pliers. He reached into the hose connected to the dishwasher and removed a yellow plug. He told me that they tested the pumps at the factory and because they were not always able to remove all the water after testing, they plugged the hose so water wouldn't leak out. Needless to say, my wife began laughing. She said she asked me had I read all the instructions. I told her yes, but as I picked up the instructions once more, I had left out a line. It said, "…be sure to remove the plug in the drain line."

Now, all of this got me to Just Thinking! Have you ever felt in a standstill in your relationship to Christ? Have you ever felt that you were just not getting through? Maybe you are praying and it seems as if God is not listening. Maybe you are seeking God's will for your life and you just don't seem to be getting any answers. Maybe the reason you are having trouble is that you have a plug in the line of communication with God. God calls out to us and reminds us that there is a necessary action we need to take if we are going to be blessed and nurtured in His will. Here is what He said to His people: "If my people, who are called by my name, will humble themselves and pray and seek my face and turn from their wicked ways, then will I hear from heaven and will forgive their sin and will heal their land." God becomes keenly aware of our prayers when we have humbled ourselves, sought His face, and confessed and turned from our sin. Maybe your line of communication is plugged with pride. Maybe your line of communication is plugged with complacency. Maybe your line of communication is plugged with unconfessed sin. Sometimes we need a friend to point us in the right direction. If you are having trouble in your relationship with Jesus, try removing the plug and allowing God to drain your life of self and filling you up with His grace.

## "FRIENDSHIP"
### Proverbs 27:10

    This past week I located a pool table to purchase for my son. One of the things that we promised him as we moved into our new house was to provide a game room for him. We have been very frugal in purchasing of toys for this room. I was very blessed to find a good table for little cost. The problem was how would we transport the table from the house where it was located to our new home? Immediately, I felt the problem was solved. I called some friends and I asked if they were going to be busy on Saturday morning. I invited them to breakfast early on Saturday and after breakfast we headed to get the pool table.

    We were able to get the table into a moving van that I had also borrowed from a friend. We transferred the table to the game room and had it set up in no time at all. As all of my friends left the house that morning, I was struck with the appreciation of what a joy it is to have friends who will sacrifice a Saturday morning to help a friend.

    Now, all of this friendliness got me to Just Thinking! Do we take advantage of our friends? Do we really appreciate them? I am blessed to have good friends who will put off things of their own to help me out. Not a one of my friends put me off, or told me they were too busy or that they had more important things to do. All of them came through and helped me make short order of a difficult task that I never could have done by myself.

I am reminded of what the writer of Proverbs says: "Do not forsake your friend and the friend of your father, and do not go to your brother's house when disaster strikes you – better a neighbor nearby than a brother far away." To all of my friends who helped me I say thank you. Thanks for being a friend that is like a brother. I am also glad that all of my friends are counted as a friend of God. It is good to have friends that you can count on and friends that make a difference in your everyday life. I hope you have friends like mine.

## "NEVER TO OLD!"
### 2 Timothy 4:2

When they were living, Peggy's parents often came to see us about once a year. As they were getting older, those visits began not be as frequent. One special weekend, Peggy's oldest sister brought them to our home. On this visit Peggy's dad was 82 years old, but you would never have guessed it by his abilities. Having been blessed to be a part of this family for over 20 years at that time, I can say with pride that it has been one of my greatest joys.

Peggy's dad is a retired pastor. I can still remember the first time I heard him preach. His desire to have everyone understand the surpassing love of his Lord and Savior were very obvious. His passion and excitement of sharing the good news was an inspiration for me as a young preacher. Even in retirement Peggy's dad was very active in the senior adult ministry in the church he attended, but he didn't get the opportunity to preach as much as formerly did. I asked him to preach for me on the Sunday night they were visiting. Although he initially turned me down, he reconsidered and agreed to preach for me. I was not only overjoyed at his acceptance, but I was thrilled at the finished product. To have been preaching so long and to have been a little apprehensive because he was not as prepared as he would have liked to be, his delivery of God's message to us on the 23$^{rd}$ Psalm was timely and needed. Although older, his passion and excitement had not diminished as he urged us to remember the Lord who was our shepherd. He yearned for us to be grateful for a God who would protect us even as we walked through the valley of the shadow of death. He lovingly reminded us that our emphasis on our lives should not be just for today but for a time when we will dwell in the house of the Lord forever. I will be forever grateful of his willingness to heed the call of Jesus to speak for Him.

Now, this special event for my family got me to Just Thinking! Do you ever get to old to stand up and speak a word for God? So often we want to say we are unable to do certain things for God. You are unable to serve in this capacity or that because you are older and it's time for the younger generation to take your place. Well, I am all for the younger generation to stand up and take its responsible place, but I am not for the older generation bowing out of service for God. Paul exhorted young Timothy to be always ready to stand up for God. He, as a senior, was not going to stop his service for Christ, but he wanted Timothy to take a more active part in serving Christ.

What a great example for older generations. Don't stop! Exhort and encourage the younger generation to take a stand. As I think about my father-in-law, I see the example of senior Paul telling young Timothy, "Preach the Word; be prepared in season and out of season; correct, rebuke and encourage - with great patience and careful instruction."

I have been led with a kind and compassionate heart and I only hope that when I reach the age of 82, I have as much fire in my bones to express my love for my Savior as Peggy's Dad did. I truly loved him and thanked for a wonderful example.

## "SET FREE!"
### Galatians 5:1

Our last pet's name was Hawkeye. Hawkeye was a full-blooded, blond, cocker spaniel. He was temperamental and had his own way of doing things. He was house broken and loved to play. Sometimes I believed that he understood perfect English even though he didn't speak it.

One house we lived in did not have a fenced in backyard, so Hawkeye stayed in a 10 x 10 pen during the day. We would let him out every morning and he would basically stay in his doghouse until we returned the evening. Once in a while, we would take Hawkeye to a large field and unleash him to be able to run and frolic. He always seemed to enjoy the freedom of running and jumping and not being cooped up in that 10 x 10 cage.

When we moved, Hawkeye no longer had to stay in that pen. He had a large fenced in backyard to run and play in. We never came home and found him just sitting in his doghouse. He was always enjoying his freedom and the opportunity to explore new horizon - even if it is within his own territory. He seemed to be a happier, more contented dog.

Now, Hawkeye's freedom has got me to Just Thinking! How often do you feel cooped up in a pen of religion? You know, sometimes, just because we have been doing something the same ol' way doesn't mean it is the only way to do it. We get ourselves in some deep ruts and don't seem able to get out of them it. We find ourselves just accepting the same ol' things instead of trying to find new ways to be free. We may even experience something that makes us feel good and then we convince ourselves that it was just a one-time experience instead of seeking it always in our lives. And if we ever start making it a daily part of our lives, we become much happier and contented in who we are and what we've become. I believe that this is the experience that most feel when it comes to being spiritually disciplined. We take reading the Bible and praying as something we have to do a certain way or with a certain formula. We go to worship believing that it can only be one way and we, symbolically speaking, never get out of our doghouses. Listen to the words that Paul encourages the Galatians with. He says, "It is for freedom that Christ has set us free. Stand firm, then, and do not let yourselves be burdened again by a yoke of slavery."

Many times, our traditions and standards have made us a slave to not experiencing all of life that God wants us to experience. I encourage you to get out of the doghouse where God is concerned and learn the experience of running and frolicking in the wide-open spaces of God's love.

## "TIME FLIES!"
Psalm 90:12

I remember when our oldest son came home from his first year at college at the University of Kentucky. It was hard for me to believe that he was finished with his freshman year. Where did the time go? It seemed that his mother and I just took him off to college and now he was coming home after his first year. There were times when it felt like the year would never end, but now that it is over, I look back and wonder where it went. I guess that is how it is with life. Older adults have always told me that the older you get, the faster time flies. I remember thinking as a little boy that Christmas or my birthday would never get here. Now they come too often and too quick.

I remember how happy I was Joshua was home. I remember that he didn't stay with us long before he was off doing mission work that summer. Before we knew it he was headed back for his sophomore year at school. Time really does fly!

All of my reflection of that school year and how quickly time is flying got me to Just Thinking! Am I making every day count? Am I living out every day to the best of my ability and getting the most out of my life? If time is flying by, am I stopping to enjoy every moment of time or am I just trying to get by with the least amount of effort?

When I hear someone say something to the effect of "I can't wait until next week or next year or next month." I always say something like, "You better be careful wishing your life away." Sometime I think that is just what we do. We wish our life away for something that is to come later and don't enjoy the moment.

The Psalmist was going through similar thoughts as he said, "Teach us to number our days aright, that we may gain a heart of wisdom." I believe that he is telling us to look at each day as an opportunity to gain insight on the next day. Every day can and should be a learning experience for the days to come. Every day can and should be an adventure into all that life has to offer. Every day can and should be a privilege to give life our very best and cheat death until it comes. If time really is flying by, then I want to look back and be able to see where I have been. I want to enjoy every moment so that I can appreciate where I am going. I want to see the hand of God in every minute of life. It is my wish for you that you will number your days and count your opportunities and your blessings.

## "GROWTH POTIENTIAL!"
### Proverbs 23:24

I remember the day our youngest son, Caleb, turned 15. I remember very vividly the morning he was born. It was a joyous occasion for our home. That 15th birthday was also another milestone in his life as he went that morning and received his driver's permit.

We are very proud of Caleb. He has grown into a very fine young man and continues to mature and grow every day. Caleb has a great deal of fine attributes. Not only did he play three sports in high school, he is very smart and sings very well.

One of the special things that Caleb and I shared together during those years was Georgia football. We both loved the Bulldogs and although I wasn't successful in sharing that love of Georgia with my first son (remember he is a Kentucky Wildcat) I was successful in sharing that love with Caleb. We loved to talk and go see our beloved Bulldogs play in Sanford Stadium. It was truly one of the highlights of our fall.

As a dad I could not be any prouder of my son, Caleb. And although I saw him growing and maturing in worldly ways, nothing makes me prouder of his growth than when I see him maturing spiritually. Caleb is a loving and caring child. He is one of the most caring young men I have ever been associated with. I loved to watch on a Sunday morning as he went around and hugged all of the older ladies whom he knew. Their whole day was brighter because of his small effort to say hello. I knew then that God had great plans for Caleb. It was always fun saying "Happy Birthday" to my son.

Now, all of this birthday talk and being proud got me to Just Thinking! Do you remember when you were born into the family of God? I can only imagine that God was a proud father and could not wait to see you grow and mature. The question for you and me is are we making Him proud with our growth potential? Are we living up to the plans and goals that He has set for us?

Now, I know whatever Caleb does with his life will make me a proud dad, but I have to look in the mirror every day and wonder whether I am making God proud of me. I know that no matter what I do I cannot ever miss out on God's love, but I also know that even though he loves me he might be disappointed with me. I want God to be able to say how proud He is of me. I want to be a loving and caring child when it comes to how I deal with His other children. I want to find my potential and live it to the max.

The writer of Proverbs makes an important statement. He says, "The father of a righteous man has great joy; he who has a wise son delights in him." I know that not just on his birthday, but every day I delight in my son, Caleb. I want God to feel the same way about me. I hope we can all give God reason to rejoice.

## "DO YOU UNDERSTAND?"
1 Corinthians 14:9

I went to a high school graduation for my nephew in a large gymnasium with many people. The graduates entered and the commencement exercise began. Right away we discovered a problem. No one could understand the words being said from the podium. We could hear noise and, once in a while you could pick out a word or two, but all in all the words were garbled. We listen to the valedictorian and the salutatorian go through their speeches without really hearing what they said. We heard a few songs and figured out one of the songs because we knew the words. As they announced the graduates you could pick out the names only if you followed along in the program as someone was being announced. But all in all, most of the words being said to the audience were not heard. We spent several hours there but the words and speeches were not heard so they were not communicated to the audience.

Now, the fact that the communication of words did not come through got me to Just Thinking! What a waste of time worship and church would be if we did not communicate. What a waste of time and energy if the people who come to worship are not hearing the words of the hymns or prayers or the sermon. It would be a tragedy if people came to church and never heard a word from God.

Many times, our communication is garbled and people leave a worship service with nothing because we have tried to say things in a way that people just don't understand. Maybe we have tried to be so too sophisticated that we have missed our audience and their ability to understand. I remember the words of one of my mentor pastors, Rev. Carl Bates, telling us in preaching class to keep it simple. Preach so that a child can understand.

I do hope that as we tell others about Jesus that we don't make the words and concepts so complicated that we don't communicate the love of Jesus. Paul was concerned about that very thing when he wrote to the church at Corinth. He said, "Unless you speak intelligible words with your tongue, how will anyone know what you are saying? You will just be speaking into the air."

Let's make sure that we are speaking words that make a difference. Remember who you are talking and singing about. Also don't forget who you are praying too. Our words are important as we share the Good News. Let's make sure people can hear!

## "THAT IS SOME GOOD STUFF!"
Psalm 34:8

It is funny sometimes what your children will and will not eat. We laugh at our son, Caleb a great deal because we say he will eat anything. He also eats a lot of everything. Yet, every now and then he will decide that he doesn't like something because years ago he didn't eat it. Take this story, for instance.

I had some fresh tomatoes and I cooked them over the stove. I fixed a pot of rice and then mixed the two together. I had some smoked sausage and cut it up in the rice and tomatoes. As I was fixing this, Caleb entered the kitchen and asked me what I was doing. I told him I was fixing rice and tomatoes. As soon as I told him I was fixing tomatoes and rice he stuck his nose up in the air. I told him he had better try some and he said he had tried it before and didn't like it. I asked him where he had tried it and he said at school. I let the conversation end and kept on fixing my meal. He got invited to go play basketball a few minutes later and left the house.

Peggy and I sat down to our rice and tomatoes and made a meal of it. As a matter of fact, we both remarked how we wish we could have eaten more because it tasted so good. About an hour later Caleb returned home. Peggy and I were going to the store and I asked Caleb could if I could pick him something up to eat. He reluctantly said he would try the rice. He got up from his chair and went to the stove where the rice was still warm. He took one spoonful and as soon as it was down, he turned to me with a smile and said, "I'll eat this." I smiled and Peggy and I left for the store.

When we returned, I asked Caleb if he got enough and he said yes. As I went to the stove and looked at the pot where the rice had been I noticed that all of it was gone. It looked as if he had licked the pot clean.

Now, the fact that Caleb ate the rice after his first initial reaction was to turn it down got me to Just Thinking! How often do people make assumptions about church because of a bad first impression? How often do people turn away from God because of something someone else says or does? How often do people make decisions about church attendance because of the fact that as a child they were made to go? People often stay away from church and God because of some preconceived idea that was placed into their heads by some incident that will probably never take place again in the life of the church.

What I would like to recommend to you that if you have a negative idea about church or God that you give it another try. Maybe your taste buds have changed and you will find refreshing within the family of God. Maybe you need to reconsider all the reasons you don't believe and weigh them against the value of believing. The Psalmist had the right idea when he said, "Taste and see that the LORD is good; blessed is the man who takes refuge in him." I invite you to taste and I believe you will lick the pot clean.

## "A PICTURE CAN'T SAY A THOUSAND WORDS!"
### 1 Corinthians 13:12

I remember the day we celebrated my Dad and Mom's 50th wedding anniversary. We had a great time with family and friends. One of the things that my brother and sister did was to have a bunch of pictures on display from the years gone by. My brother had scanned in almost 500 photos on his computer and every five seconds a new photo would appear on the screen. We also had some photos of our graduation and my parents' wedding from years ago. It was fun to see all of the photos and to see how we have changed and to look at all of the different hairstyles and clothing styles. We laughed at some of the poses and at seeing some of the places that reminded us of days gone by.

Pictures are wonderful ways to remember. They do, as the slogan goes "paint a thousand words." Yet a picture can't say what is on the minds of those you see. There is one picture of me where I am wearing my cap and gown before I graduated from high school. I am looking at the camera and I have my arms down by my side with the palms of my hands facing outward. My youngest son asked me what I was doing. I remembered that my mom asked me to do something and I remembered turning my hands around and asking what do you want me to do. At that moment she snapped the picture. There is a great deal going on that the picture never tells.

Now, all of the photos and memorabilia got me to Just Thinking! Can you imagine just what God can see? He knows our past and our future. He knows what we looked like then, now and what we will look like in the future. God sees us for who we truly are. There are no hidden meanings or agendas where God is concerned. I can be smiling on the outside, but God knows if there is pain on the inside. I can show the world a peaceful demeanor on the outside, but God knows if there is turmoil on the inside. I can look in the mirror and see my reflection and can even fool myself sometimes, but God is never fooled with who I am.

Paul wrote about a time when there will be no confusion with who we are. Listen to his words to the church of Corinth. He says, "Now we see but a poor reflection as in a mirror; then we shall see face to face. Now I know in part; then I shall know fully, even as I am fully known." Everything will be revealed. Everything will be made bare. There will be nothing hidden from God and all will be before Him. And when it all comes to an end the only thing that will matter is did, we love God and did we love others as God loved us?

As I looked back at some of the pictures, I remembered the good ol' days, but as I look at life today, I wonder if I miss out on the best days because I fail to love as Jesus loved me. My prayer for all of us is that whether in the mirror or a picture our reflection may be one of the love of God in our lives.

## "WHO'S IN CHARGE?"
### Psalm 32:8

We arrived to enjoy a weekend for of my parents 50th wedding anniversary celebration. As we entered the house and began getting settled in for the weekend, we started to receive our instructions. My sister, Lisa, was taking charge. She let us know that at 10 the next morning we would be taking pictures. We had to have some ivy cut for the tables on Sunday and then we would need to make sure we had all of the pictures ready to take to the church. We would need to be ready to leave the house by 4 p.m. to eat on Saturday night. We would all need to be ready at 9:15 the next morning go to church together. I just nodded my head and said I'll be ready.

I appreciate my sister so much for all she did to give my mom and dad this celebration of love and life. I appreciate someone who will take charge and give instructions to help me know what

I am supposed to do. She did a great job of coordinating the activities and I know I enjoyed the whole weekend better because it was well planned.

The results of all the planning paid off. We had a great turnout. The tables were pretty, the decorations were well placed, the guest were many and when it was all over, everyone had an enjoyable time.

Now, the fact that my sister took charge of the whole weekend got me to Just Thinking! Who is in charge of your life on a regular basis? Who makes the decisions on when to be a certain place or be prepared for a certain event? Who guides you to the proper decisions and helps you in your everyday life? I will tell you that I had a great time enjoying the fruits of my sister's labor. I enjoyed not having to throw something together at the last moment and knowing that all the details had been worked out. I listened as she talked to the florist about the flowers and how she and my brother had already made the trip to the store and purchased all of the necessities. I was able to just come and enjoy all of the people and all of the celebration.

Is your life a life of enjoyment or do you constantly worry about having to throw something together? Is your life a life of anxiety or can you relax knowing someone has already ordered your steps? I like what the Psalmist says about instructions. Hear these words, "I will instruct you and teach you in the way you should go; I will counsel you and watch over you." If we could just listen to God's instructions and follow them, we would all enjoy life better. The problem we have is that we want to have our say so about things. You know I could have gone to my parents' celebration this weekend and said something to my sister like, "Who put you in charge?" or "Who died and made you king?" But for me it was a joy to be able to relax and enjoy all of the instructions that helped me to have a blessed weekend. Instead of questioning God about what He has in store for you, why not relax and enjoy the fruits of His labor? His counsel is best and He will watch over you.

## "NO VACIANCIES!"
### John 14:2

    We were taking Joshua, our oldest son, back to Kentucky for school. We had taken him and his fiancé to the World's Longest Yard Sale on the way. On Saturday night of that weekend, we began looking for a hotel room about 9 p.m. We had been traveling in Tennessee and Kentucky for most of the day. We had started out early on that morning and because we did not know where we would end up, we did not make a reservation to spend the night. We figured that we would get off the main corridor of the yard sale and find a place to stay.

    We arrived in Somerset, Ky., about 9 o'clock. We stopped at a hotel, but learned there were no vacancies. We drove around to four other hotels and got the same results. We stopped to eat about 10 and made a few telephone calls to other hotels and got the same answer: no vacancies. We decided to drive to Interstate 75, which was about 25 miles away. Surely, there would be a vacancy on the interstate.

    We couldn't figure why all the rooms were full. It wasn't a special weekend and we were miles away from the Highway 127 corridor where the yard sale took place. About 11 p.m. we arrived at the interstate. There were three hotels at the intersection and every one of them said indicated no vacancies. We got on the interstate and started traveling towards Lexington.

    As we were driving to the next intersection about 14 miles away, Peggy made the remark, "Well I guess I know how Mary and Joseph felt now!" We laughed and we plodded along to Berea, Ky. We exited and drove into another hotel. This time, I let Peggy go in and try her luck. She came out and said they had a room, but it only had one king size bed. Well, that wouldn't do because we had 4 people.

    We drove into a Knights Inn next. I got out of the car and walked into the office and, finally, the man told us he had a room. It was about 11:45 pm. We were grateful and stayed for the night.

I don't think we will try again to just luck up on a room. In fact, we made reservations the next morning for the hotel we stayed at in Lexington on Sunday and Monday nights. It was a good thing, too, because that hotel was full on Sunday night.

Now, the fact that we didn't have reservations and struggled to get a room got me to Just Thinking! Do you know there are many who do not have reservations for a room after they die? They are just taking their chances. They are just enjoying life to the fullest and say things like, "I'll make preparations at a later date." There are people who are going through this life expecting that if they wait to the last minute, they can always find a room for eternity. Yet this is not so. Jesus calls us to be ready. He tells us that we never know when our life might end and we might be called upon to leave this life and enter the next. Jesus said we do not know the day when our life might be required of us. If we are uncertain about our existence on this earth, we can be sure of our eternal place.

Jesus told his disciples an important fact about eternity. Listen to His words from the book of John, "In my Father's house are many rooms; if it were not so, I would have told you. I am going there to prepare a place for you."

If you are going through life without reservations for heaven then I want to invite you to make your reservations today. Just call on Jesus and confess your sins and be made complete in Him. He will give you eternal reservations to a place that He has prepared for you. Don't keep thinking that you can always get a room because if you find the No Vacancy sign out when you die then you will be eternally lost. Make your reservations today.

## "JUDGE NOT!"
### Matthew 7:1

I remember when school didn't start until after Labor Day. In fact, the first day I ever went to school was the Tuesday after

Labor Day, 1965. Believe it or not, but I remember that first day of school most vividly. My Mom took me around the block to Sprague Elementary School. It was within walking distance of the house. We walked into the room and I met my first-grade teacher, Mrs. Gooding. She welcomed me to first grade. She was very nice and told me to go and find my desk.

Now, these desks were those old wooden desks with a place for your things under the top. It wasn't a drawer, but an opening where you could keep you pencils and paper. Each desk had a wooden chair. The desk had the student's name in the upper left-hand corner on a hand-printed 3x5 card taped to the desk.

As I was looking, with my mother at my side, I found a student sitting in my desk. In the upper left-hand corner was the name David. I looked to my mom, upset, and exclaimed, "He's in my desk! Mom calmed me down and had to point out to her upset son that his name was David R. for Rogers and right next to his desk was one with David S. for Simmons.

I looked at the cards and realized that his name was like mine except we had different last names. I quickly settled in my desk and, as you might imagine, before long became fast friends with my desk mate, David R.

Now, remembering my first day at school has got me to Just Thinking. Isn't it amazing how quick we judge without knowing the circumstances? I was only 6 years old and was quick to judge someone for being in the wrong place. Yet, I didn't have enough information to make the proper judgement. When given the right information I could see the truth and could readjust my thinking. Yet I was only 6 years old.

How often do we as adults make snap judgements about people or circumstances without learning the truth? We jump to conclusions without finding out all of the facts. We criticize without knowing the whys and why nots. We think we know things and make judgments without finding out the truth. The words of Jesus continually ring in my ears, "Do not judge, or you too will be judged." Let us not judge people on what we hear or assume. Let's not guess or just make an assumption. Let's get to know the person. Build a relationship. Who knows? You might find a friend, just like I found in David R.

## "IT'S WORTH BRAGGING ABOUT!"
### Matthew 3:17; 17:5

Brag, Brag, Brag, Brag, the dictionary says it is when "Someone boasts of something or someone." Well, I realize that to most of us bragging is something we don't enjoy other people doing. But, hey, when you have something good happen to you or to someone you love you, just can't wait to tell someone.

As a young boy, our youngest son, Caleb was chosen to be Oliver, the lead role in the Community Theater's production of the musical "Oliver." Well, to say the least, we were pretty proud of our little man. He worked hard at talking with an English accent and we were all overjoyed at this opportunity for him. It was a great experience for him, and I knew he would do well and meet many people. We told everybody. We called parents, brothers, sisters, friends, acquaintances, strangers - anyone who would take just a minute to listen, we told. It was a pretty special day in the Simmons' family and we just wanted everyone to know about it. I know - enough already.

All of this bragging has got me to Just Thinking! Didn't God brag about His son when He was born? Yes, I believe He did. He sent angels to predict the birth; angels to announce His birth, wise men to confirm His birth. At His baptism, God spoke out of the heavens as the Spirit descended as a dove and said, "This is my son, whom I love; with him I am well pleased."

On the Mount of Transfiguration, a voice from heaven spoke and said, "This is my Son, whom I love; with him I am well pleased. Listen to Him!" Jesus was going about His Father's business and getting the job done. He was obedient to all the father wanted him to do. God the Father was so proud of His son that He rewarded Jesus for His faithfulness and obedience by raising Him from the dead.

Now, there is something to brag about. How much do we brag about Jesus, God's Son? How much do we tell others about the good news of Jesus Christ? Has it become old news to us? Or do we renew its freshness each season that we celebrate His birth? My prayer for you is that you will Brag, Brag, Brag, Brag, about Jesus.

## "BIRTHDAYS!"
### Luke 15:10

I remember vividly the events of Nov. 1, 1984. I was awakened by my wife at about 2 a.m. She told me I had better call the doctor because the time had come. I spoke with the doctor, who said that since Peggy wasn't having contractions really close together, he normally would tell us to wait, but because we lived an hour away from the hospital, we probably should take our time and head on in. I took a shower while Peggy got some final things together.

We headed out to the hospital. It was a rainy, dreary day on the outside of Baptist East Hospital in Louisville, Ky., but on the inside, it was one of the brightest days of my life. After some back labor and finally getting an epidural for pain the moment was here: Joshua was born. I remember the excitement and thrill of being a father. I remember how I couldn't wait to tell everyone and share the news. I remember literally leaping for joy when the doctor said, "Its a boy!" (Joshua was born back in the days when we didn't know the gender before he was born.)

At 11:59 a.m. a wonderful ray of sunshine filled my life. I remember holding him for the first time. I remember the nurse weighing him and checking to make sure everything was OK.

I remember running out of the recovery room to greet some friends who had stopped by and jumping for joy. I remember calling my dad and mom and telling them they were grandparents, hanging up the phone and crying uncontrollably. I remember holding an original birthday party for Joshua with friends from seminary and he wasn't even in the room.

There have been many days since the birth of my son. Although there have been some good and bad days, I have been blessed and am very proud of the young man he has become. He truly makes his parents proud of him all of the time and we could not be happier for the life God has given him.

Now, the experience of the birth of our first child, our son, has got me to Just Thinking! God must leap with joy at the spiritual rebirth of every one of His children. I can only imagine that when that time happens in someone's life that He is proudly shaking His head in affirmation. God has goals and dreams and a plan for everyone. When someone is born into the family of God, Jesus said, "I tell you, there is rejoicing in the presence of the angels of God over one sinner who repents." It is no surprise to God when you make that decision, but He rejoices just the same.

Even in the good and bad days, God loves us and wants us to be the best we can be. He is proud to be called our Father and wants the best for us. Even when we fall, God lifts us up to a new opportunity and a new chance. I hope and pray that you can be proud to be one of His children.

## "HOW PROUD ARE YOU?"
### Romans 1:16

If you do not know this fact let me share it with you. My wife, Peggy, is known for one of her favorite things to do, which is to shop. One time, she accompanied me on a senior adult trip to Lancaster, Pa. Wherever we stopped, Peggy was looking to shop. She is very proud of her ability to find a bargain and she loves to share her accomplishments. While we were on this trip, she even convinced our driver to carry a group of the ladies (and coerced some of the men) to an outlet mall in the pouring rain after supper one night. There were purchases all over the bus when we arrived home on Thursday. She was not ashamed of her love of shopping. She proudly proclaimed that she was a pro. No one disputed her claim. She will often go shopping and not buy a thing. Often, she calls it retail therapy. It takes her mind off of the daily grind of work and other things. She just loves to shop.

Now, the fact that Peggy likes to shop and is not ashamed of that fact has got me to Just Thinking! If we have hobbies and interest that we proudly proclaim to the world, why is it we so often hide our claim to Jesus? Some of us like shopping, some like yard work, some like to hunt and others like cars. None of this is bad or wrong. Yet, why do we so often make excuses about our love of God? We will gladly offer a story about a good hunt or the fish that got away or a bargain that we found. We will talk about our hobbies and exploits and tell anyone who will listen.

The question becomes are we as free with the story of how God answered our prayer or protected us from evil or gave us our daily bread? Do we start a conversation with, "Let me tell you what Jesus did for me today?" Or how about, "God really came through for me today when ..." I just don't understand why we are so quick to share about our hobbies and interest, but fail to share about Jesus. I am reminded of what Paul said in his opening remarks to the Christians at Rome, "I am not ashamed of the gospel because it is the power of God for the salvation of everyone who believes..." Surely, you and I are not ashamed of Jesus. Surely, we are not ashamed to tell others how He makes a difference in our lives each and every day. My hope and prayer is that we can all be proud of our faith and promote it to everyone, that we will allow our life in Christ to be a daily topic of our conversation. I am not ashamed and I pray you are not, either.

## "GO ALL THE WAY!"
### Acts 3:19

One summer the family and I vacationed in the mountains of South Carolina. On Tuesday afternoon we traveled into North Carolina and had fun sliding down a natural "sliding rock" and splashing into some very cold water. Not far down the road from the rock was Looking Glass Falls. We walked down some steps and were amazed at the falls. The water was falling approximately 110 feet into a pool of very cold water. The boys and I took the plunge, and swam into the cold water and propped ourselves on a rock to experience the water falling on our heads. It was a most exhilarating experience.

Many people made the trip down the stairs to see the falls, but they all had different experiences. Some just watched from a distance. Some moved closer and felt the mist from the water's plunge into the pool. Some walked up to the edge of the water and even stepped in. Others waded out knee deep. Some swam in the pool, but never made it up to the falls. And some swam under the falls and stood on a ledge behind the falling water.

Now, the experience of swimming in the pool and going to the waterfall has got me to Just Thinking! Many of us treat God like the people who visited Looking Glass Falls. Some don't even stop to see God. Some stop, but they stay back and just observe. Some move towards God, but they barely get their feet wet. Some will wade in to their knees, but they are not willing to commit everything. Some will take the plunge and go all the way to allow God to pour over them with refreshing waters.

How far are you willing to go with God? Where are you now? Are you willing to give God everything and submit to His will? All too often we allow sin in our life to keep us from seeking and knowing God.

After Peter healed the man at the gate called Beautiful a crowd gathered and Peter preached to them. He finished his sermon with these words, "Repent, then, and turn to God, so that your sins may be wiped out, that times of refreshing may come from the Lord…" My prayer for all of us is that we will swim all the way in so that God can refresh you with living water.

## "NO PLACE LIKE HOME!"
### Revelation 21:3

Have you ever just been somewhere having so much fun that you didn't want to leave? You just want to have the ability to stop time. You look at the time and wish that it wasn't so late or that you didn't have to be anywhere tomorrow so that you could just continue doing what you are doing and that it would never end. Well, that is my feeling every time I make a trip to Morehead City, NC. My father was raised in a little town near there called Newport.

I gathered up my wife and children and we drove 8 hours to go to a family reunion. My boys were a little skeptical. Joshua was especially trying to figure out what we were going to do while we were there. I keep reassuring him that we would not be bored. And, sure enough, when the day was over and we were traveling back on Sunday, all he could talk about was when could we get the chance to go back. It is hard for me to explain the feeling I get while I am in that area of the country. I idealized my papa. He died in 1986. My granny died in 2000. Yet, today there are still eight of their 13 children still living. I got to see five of my aunts and, of course, my Dad was there. I met people who I wasn't sure I had ever met and got to reacquaint myself with others. My family and I spent Saturday evening at my Aunt Lauretta's house with my cousin, Dewayne, who I ran around with as a kid. His family was there, along with others, and we just sat around and told old stories and laughed a lot. I just didn't want it to end.

Now, the experience of this weekend got me to Just Thinking! I think I know a little of what it will feel like in Heaven. When I breathe the air in Carteret County, N.C., it just feels me with a sense of belonging. I always leave there feeling better than I did when I got there. It feels like home. I just never want to leave.

Heaven has got to be like that. It will give you a sense of belonging. You will be with the people you love. You will never want to leave. And the one that has made it all possible will be there with you. I can't think of a better place. In that final book of the Bible, John writes, "Now the dwelling of God is with men, and he will live with them. They will be his people, and God himself will be with them and be their God."

I know that is a place I never want to leave when I get there and thanks be to God I won't want have to leave. I hope you are there with me.

## "FINDING THE RIGHT PLACE"
### Matthew 7:13-14; 21-23

My wife Peggy and I went up to Asheville, N.C., one Saturday evening to meet our son and daughter-in-law, Joshua and Laura, for supper. We had some time before we met them, so we stopped a few places to wait for the appointed hour. We stopped at the Farmer's Market, a furniture store and a car dealership. With still a few hours to spare, Peggy started looking up places on the GPS. I wasn't sure what she was looking for so, I was just driving. She began to direct me down several side roads and we were listening to the directions of the GPS.

Finally, it said we had arrived. We were looking for a place that was called "Lush Life," I think it was supposed to be some kind of flower nursery. To tell you the truth all we found was a house in a residential neighborhood with a makeshift green house in the side yard. We didn't stop. I drove to the next stop sign and waited. She finally got the GPS directing us to another place. She did not inform me where we were going, so I just followed her and the GPS instructions. We finally pulled into some strip mall only to find out the place that we were looking for (supposed to be a place to buy bird houses) was no longer in operation. Of course, as all this was going on I was giving her a hard time and we were having a great laugh.

This journey through the streets of Asheville got me to Just Thinking!! You can have all the right equipment and all the right directions, but you can still end up in the wrong place. We had names and addresses of the places we were looking for. We had a GPS device and a person (Peggy) who is good at directions. We had a driver (me) who was willing to follow the directions to the letter and not waver from the intended destination. Yet, we still ended up nowhere. The places we were looking for were either not what they were supposed to be or no longer in business.

As Christians, we must always remember to make sure we know that our intended destination is founded on God's plan for our lives. We cannot just go off seeking our own way. To follow our own way is a good way to end up nowhere. We must be careful as we read the Bible not to inject our desires or presuppositions into the text. We must be careful not to be selfish is our request to God, but to be open to His desires for our lives.

In the Sermon on the Mount found in Matthew 7, Jesus points us to several important concepts that we must always remember as we seek to follow Him. It says, "Enter through the narrow gate. For wide is the gate and broad is the road that leads to destruction, and many enter through it. But small is the gate and narrow the road that leads to life, and only a few find it."

He also warns us that our intentions must be to always follow Him and His directions. The verses say, "Not everyone who says to me, 'Lord, Lord,' will enter the kingdom of heaven, but only he who does the will of my Father who is in heaven. Many will say to me on that day, Lord, Lord, did we not prophesy in your name, and in your name drive out demons and perform many miracles' Then I will tell them plainly, 'I never knew you. Away from me, you evildoers!'"

So, as you live out your life searching for the right path to follow, make sure that you are tuned in to the right voice of direction. Jesus said, "My sheep listen to my voice; I know them, and they follow me." Let's all listen to the right voice and end up at the right place.

## "IT IS BEAUTFUL!"
### Psalm 8:3-4

At one time we owned a 1997 Harley Davidson Road King. We loved to ride it and enjoy the surroundings. We loved to ride it in the mountains and see the sights. One day, Peggy and I rode up Highway 276. It was overcast and we did get a little rain after we left the town of Brevard, N.C. After the rain, the sun came out and we had a beautiful ride through the Blue Ridge Mountains. I cannot express how nice it is to ride up the mountains, around the curves, through the narrow streets of little towns and see all the beauty that God has made. I am always astounded at the sheer beauty of mountain ranges and the peaks and valleys of the countryside. The trees were in full bloom, the flowers were blossoming all around and everyone we saw seemed to be enjoying the beauty of God's creation.

We even saw the wonder of God's creation of people. We saw laughs and smiles and families spending quality time together. We saw people picnicking on the side of the road, families and friends tubing down the river and many fellow bike riders cruising the landscape of mountainous roads.

We did not leave our son's house in Canton, N.C., until after dark. We skirted Interstate 40 and drove down I-26 until we got to Highway 25 in Hendersonville, N.C. As we traveled the road in the dark, we watched an electric light show in the southern sky put on by the lightning behind the clouds. It was as if someone were making broad and narrow strokes with a brush and the images were unexplainable.

Now, all of this beauty that we got to see has got me to Just Thinking! With all of this wonder around me it is hard for me to realize that there are those who do not see it the same way that I do. There are those who do not recognize God's handiwork. There are those who see all of this amazing art work as happenstance or chance. I am amazed when I look at all that God has created and realize there are those who do not recognize God. To you Oh, Lord, I ask forgiveness for all of those who are so narrow minded that they do not see God in all things that you have made. And I ask you to forgive me for not pointing it out to them more.

I echo the words of the Psalmist, "When I consider your heavens, the work of your fingers, the moon and the stars, which you have set in place, what is mankind that you are mindful of them, human beings that you care for them?" I am so grateful for all that you have created. Thanks for giving me a place in your creation.

## "PARENTS!"
Exodus 20:12

Well, here I go again. I know you are probably tired of me talking about my family. I just can't help it one more time. I will put my Dad and Mom up against any in the business. I simply marvel at all they do and all they can do. I know that as a child and probably mostly as a teenager that I gave them much to worry about and probably had them asking the question, "Why in the world did we have children?"

But God did a fine job when He blessed me with my parents. I am overwhelmed at their desire to serve. My parents have gone above and beyond the call of duty when it comes to doing for others and working to see the Kingdom of God grow. They do all of this with joy in their hearts and a smile on their face. I hope that as I get older and wiser that I can just have the faith and courage and fortitude that my parents have.

My dad is getting up in age. Most people do not know that he is about 95% blind. He doesn't hear as well either. He could easily just throw up his hands and say "enough is enough" and quit. But that is not in my dad's vocabulary.

And how about my mom? She makes it her life to care for her husband. She shadows him and makes sure he has what he needs. She drives them wherever they need to go. One time in their life she drove a huge 40-foot motor home. I can't tell you how many times I heard, "How does she do that?" Well, I'll tell you she did it out of faithfulness and love. The love of God emits from their lives and I am so proud to be called their son.

Now, all of my rambling about my parents has got me to Just Thinking! God said, "Honor your father and mother!" There is not enough gratitude and praise that I can speak or even think about when it comes to saying how honored I am to have them as my parents. They have showed me God and taught me His love and about His Son. They have lived it in their lives and made it a priority in their lifestyle. They have allowed God to make a difference in their lives. Are we allowing God to make a difference in us? Are we living out an example of Jesus every day? Are we being models to our children and grandchildren about how we are to honor and serve God all the days of our life? Hey, I know my parents are not perfect, but I believe they seek to do what Jesus call us to do. Even in their old age they haven't stopped serving and living for Him. I pray that can be said about all of us.

CHAPTER TWO

# JUST THINKING... ABOUT SPORTS!

## "THE RIGHT EQUIPMENT"
Psalm 34:11

Both of our sons played baseball in little league and high school. My oldest son, Joshua, was a pitcher and my youngest son, Caleb, was a catcher.

One Saturday, Caleb caught two games. He has always liked catching. As many of you know, the catcher has gear that he wears. He has a helmet, a chest protector, and leg guards. He also has a special glove called a mitt. I have watched Caleb catch many games, but on this Saturday, I began to notice something. With him catching 10 innings, I was amazed to find out just how insignificant the catcher's equipment was. We kept the scorebook, and I can tell you that Caleb probably caught an average of 15 pitches each inning. Now, if my addition is correct, that means that he caught about 150 pitches.

Now, one of the reasons that he wore the equipment was to protect him in case the ball was to hit him. Yet, of all the pitches, there was only one that actually hit the equipment and not the mitt. Early in the first game a boy fouled off a pitch and it hit Caleb in the mask. It glanced off the mask and went to

JUST THINKING!

the screen. Caleb never flinched. He just got up, went to the backstop and retrieved the ball. Actually, it happened so quickly that no one really ever noticed. I figured it up. If only one ball out of 150 hit Caleb, he probably would have been OK without the equipment. I mean, the percentages were in his favor. If I figured it correctly that is only a 0.6% chance of him getting hit and injured. If I were figuring that in other matters, I probably wouldn't even consider that significant at all. Yet, we would never let any child get behind the plate without their equipment.

Now, all of that equipment got me to Just Thinking! My Sunday School director gave me some statistics the other day. Let me share with you some of them:

- You can increase the average life expectancy of your children by 8 years.
- You can significantly reduce a child's use and risk of alcohol, tobacco, and drug abuse.
- You can dramatically lower their risk of suicide.
- You can help them rebound from depression 70% faster.
- You can dramatically reduce their risk for committing a crime.
- You can improve their attitude at school and increase their school participation.
- You can reduce their risk of rebelliousness.
- You can reduce the likelihood that they would binge drink in college.
- You can improve their odds for a very happy life.
- You can provide them with a lifelong moral compass and you can get them to wear their seatbelts more often.

Now, I am not making this up. This research is supported by Duke University, Indiana University, the University of Michigan, and the Centers for Disease Control and Prevention, the Barna (research) Group, and the National Institute of Health. All it takes for you to get this kind of result is to have your child or grandchildren to participate in an active Sunday School program. That's right, Sunday School is proven to make a difference in people's lives.

Now, you wouldn't send your child or grandchild behind the plate without the proper equipment. Why would you send them into the world without it? The Psalmist says, "Come, my children, listen to me; I will teach you the fear of the Lord." The word fear here means respect. When we all learn respect for the Lord, we all possess the right equipment.

## "SELECTION PROCESS"
### Romans 10:8-10; 13

March Madness!

You may not be into college basketball, but I have a son who is entrenched into the whole basketball scene. My oldest son, Joshua, is a big college basketball fan and loves the University of Kentucky. He is a very big Wildcat fan and has been for many years. The Sunday after the major conference tournaments are over is selection Sunday. This is when a committee of experts gathered together a field of 68 teams to play basketball for three weekends and determine a national champion. Of course, Joshua is proud because Kentucky is one of the favorites most years. Each year, Joshua sits in front of the TV watching for three consecutive weekends to see if his beloved Wildcats can win six games in a row to be the national champion.

The thing for me that is so interesting in the process of selecting 68 teams is that some teams that seem deserving do not get in the tournament and some that don't seem so deserving do. Someone is making a decision to allow some teams to play and some to be left out. That must be a pretty awesome responsibility to tell some teams they are not good enough. It must be a very humbling experience to get into the tournament by winning a conference tournament and not really deserve to go. Yet, all in all, there is a selection process that allows some teams in and leaves some teams out.

Now, all of this selection process has got me to Just Thinking! I believe that sometimes we think there will be a great selection process when it comes to going to Heaven; you know, that God has picked some of us to go and he has chosen some of us to not make it. There are some who believe that if they perform well enough, God is sure to let them in and there are some that believe that as long as they perform well in the end when it counts that is what matters.

Yet, all in all, our performance has nothing to do whether we get into Heaven or not. It is not by what we do or how we perform that gets us into Heaven, but in whom we believe. In the book of Romans it says, "But what does it say? 'The word is near you; it is in your mouth and in your heart,' that is, the message concerning faith that we proclaim: If you declare with your mouth, 'Jesus is Lord,' and believe in your heart that God raised him from the dead, you will be saved. For it is with your heart that you believe and are justified, and it is with your mouth that you profess your faith and are saved."

You see, it has nothing to do with us and everything to do with God. So, if you are trying to work your way into good standing with God you are wasting your time. Just believe and confess and you will find yourself a part of the selection process. For it is like it says, "Everyone who calls on the name of the Lord will be saved."

## "WHERE IS YOUR ALLIGENCE?"
Psalm 33:12

At one time I was on the Recreation Commission in the county where we lived. Because of that, I had the opportunity to do the invocation at many large sporting events within our county. Once I was asked to pray the invocation prayer at the beginning of the ISA Fastpitch Softball tournament. With 163 teams and a few thousand people in the Civic Center, we began the festivities with the murmuring at a high pitch resolution. As the welcome speaker approached the podium it was obvious that most of the people were more attentive to their own needs than they were to listening to the welcome.

As I approached the podium to pray, I felt as if I was in competition with most of the people there. There was a constant roar in the background as I prayed for God to keep them safe and make them good sports. I was convinced that most of the people there did not hear me pray and probably didn't care.

Then, a troubling event happened. A group was called to the podium to sing the National Anthem. As they began the words, "O Say Can You see," a hush fell over the crowd. People looked away from their own needs, and stood to attention and put their hand over their heart. Before the group sang, "Whose broad stripes and bright stars," the few thousand people had become silent. As the National Anthem finished the crowd roared in applause to "the home of the brave."

Now, the reaction of the crowd has got me to Just Thinking! Is something wrong with our allegiance? I am as proud to be an American as anyone. I am always so appreciative to those who have fought bravely for my freedom. I am thankful for and pray for those who are serving now in the military to keep our freedom. I pray for the leadership of our country and am proud to be an American. But when we are more concerned with giving our allegiance to America than we are to praying to the God of all, something is wrong. We have gotten our priorities messed up and confused when we put more faith in our country than we do in our God. I wish that we taught as much respect for God, as we do for our nation. I love America. I would rather live here than anywhere on earth, but America cannot take precedent over God. Maybe this is why there is so much evil and violence in America.

The Psalmist said, "Blessed is the nation whose God is the

LORD, the people he chose for his inheritance." I believe that we need to get our priorities right. We need to seek God first and then be faithful to our country. I want God to bless America, but until we as a nation turn back to God we may miss out on His full blessings.

## "WINNING IS FUN!"
### 1 Corinthians 15:57

Believe it or not, but sometimes it happens. With two sons organized little league baseball was always a part of our spring and summers. Our boys played baseball until they graduated from high school. Early on in my oldest son's beginnings we had a banner year. First of all, Joshua's team, the Padres, won the league championship by going 10-0. It was the first undefeated season we had ever been a part of as father and son. Then, Joshua made the all-star team. We began preparing for the county tournament on June 7. Who would have ever believed that on June 19 we would win that tournament and become the champions of the Small Fry League? Yeah, I know he was only 8 years old, but winning sure is fun no matter what the age.

And being able to coach those young men sure was fun for a 34-year-old. It was a dream come true for all of us. I am no Vince Lombardi and I can truly say that "Winning isn't everything," but it sure is nice once in a while.

Now, winning has got me to Just Thinking! What a great joy it is to be a part of a winning team all of the time. As Christians we have our ups and downs. We were never promised an easy life, and I can tell you that winning is not always easy. But, just remember that as long as you have Jesus as your Lord and Savior, you are a winner. There is no substitute for having Him on your side.

I am also part of another winning team. And that is my church. Yes, there are those who want nothing to do with church and organized religion, but I am glad that we are on the winning side of life. Many people try many things to find happiness and satisfaction, but fail. I know that if I work hard and do my best in my life and in my church, there will be a satisfaction that the world doesn't understand.

You who are a part of a church can be proud of all you do to make it a winning team. We experience victories in salvation, in prospects, in Bible School, and in the very spirit that you have in your church. Thank you so much for making Jesus the leader of a winning team. For without Him we can do nothing. Paul spoke to the Corinthians about the last days and he ended his talk with these words, "But thanks be to God, who gives us the Victory through Jesus Christ our Lord." Jesus has won the victory for all of us. It sure is fun to be a winner.

## "PRIDE IS NOT ALWAYS BAD"
### Acts 11:23

I am not an avid golfer. I have played on and off during my adult life. There were some years when I played a great deal. There were some years when I didn't play at all. Now, because of health issues, I don't play golf anymore. But I do like to watch golf. I have been blessed to go to several golf tournaments. One of my favorite golf events is when America faces off against Europe in the Ryder Cup matches.

The Ryder Cup is a team tournament between the best players in the USA and the best players in Europe. The United States has dominated play since the tournament's inception – originally matching the Americans and Great Britain - in 1927. But recently there has been a struggle to keep the Cup in the USA.

The tournament is played every two years and the site of the tournament is alternated between the United States and Europe. The Ryder Cup is match play and for the first two days each player has a partner. There are 28 points up for grabs. The Americans won in 1991, winning the Cup back after three years. In 1993 the USA was down heading into the Sunday singles matches. When I left for church that Sunday morning in September, I left my VCR recording the match, which was being played in England. In 1993, we defended the cup in Sutton Coldfield, England, at the Belfry Golf Club. But the victory did not come easily. As I watched my recording of the single matches on Sunday, I was stressed out with the possibility of seeing the U.S. group lose the cup. But I watched with much joy and pride as the Americans came from behind and retained the cup, 15 points to 13. It was a great tournament and I was thrilled with the outcome.

Now, all of this pride started me to Just Thinking! Of all my pride in America and its victories in sporting events and life, there is still nothing that compares with the pride I feel in serving God in my church. While the U.S. was celebrating its victory on that Sunday in 1993, we celebrate a victory of our own every Sunday of our own. It is a resurrection celebration. The church doors are open to any and all who want to come and worship our living Savior. It makes me proud when we are opening our doors to include many people in the church. It makes me proud to know that people want to join in the church and be a part of a growing and excited fellowship. It makes me proud to know that we, too, see the victories in life because of the victory that Jesus has won for us on the cross.

In the book of Acts, Luke is telling about the expansion of the Gospel of Jesus. He talks about a time when with the church at Jerusalem sent Barnabas to Antioch to see what was happening in that town as far as the Gospel was concerned. It records these words, "When he arrived and saw what the grace of God had done, he was glad and encouraged them all to remain true to the Lord with all their hearts."

It is good to see pride in the church. It is good to see the church sharing Jesus and people excited about what God is doing. I sure hope that you will have pride in your God and in your church. I also hope you will share that pride with others.

## "WE WON!"
### 1 Corinthians 15:55

On a Sunday evening in the spring of 1992, a small 7-year-old boy came to church devastated. His team, the Kentucky Wildcats, had been defeated on a last-second shot by Duke and they were not going to the NCAA Men's Basketball Final Four. Six years later the same scenario presented itself. The same two teams playing to go to the most prestigious weekend in college basketball: The Final Four. This time, the last second shot fell short and the now 13-year-old's team was going to the Big Dance.

I happened to drive up into the driveway about the time the shot fell short. I looked into the living room and saw him jump as high as the ceiling. He must have noticed the headlights because he came barreling out of the door screaming to the top of his lungs, "WE WON! WE WON!" He then set a world record (unofficial of course) for the long jump as he catapulted into my arms. He was so excited. I must admit I was excited for him. They went on to win it all in San Antonio March 30, but somehow, I'm not sure that really mattered. He was happier that they beat Duke and didn't lose again in the last second. I'll never forget how excited he was and how loud he was yelling, "WE WON!"

Now, remembering his excitement and hearing those words "WE WON! has got me to Just Thinking! Can you imagine the angels on Easter Morning? When the stone rolled away and Jesus walked out of the tomb I can only guess that they had the same feeling as that 13-year old. "WE WON! WE WON!"

Paul wrote, "Death where is your sting? Grave where is your victory?" Satan took a last-second shot, but it too fell short. Jesus defeated the death that sin brings to the spirit of mankind. True believers in Jesus Christ need not fear physical death because there is a victory waiting for those who believe. What would be so terrible about getting excited about the greatest event in human history? What would be wrong with waking up Easter morning, and shouting, "WE WON! WE WON!" We did win!

## "THE GOLD MEDAL"
### 1 John 5:14

Do you watch the Olympics? We have enjoyed watching the Olympics over the years. In 1996 the Olympics were held in Atlanta. I was living not far away. I was not happy with the television coverage that year. Here I was just some 300 miles and not more than six hours away by car and we are having to watch most of the Olympic events on tape. What was really disturbing is that the reporters didn't even tell us that is was on tape. They wanted to make us think that we were watching it live.

I could understand us seeing the events on tape if they were taking place halfway around the world. But when they are in your own backyard, it would seem that the network would try to show some of the coverage live. I guess in some would say it is good to know the outcome before the event is over. It takes out the suspense and worry over who is going to win.

Take, for example, the night when the women's gymnastics final was taking place. I had already heard on the radio that they won the gold medal. I asked my wife, Peggy, did she want to be surprised or see for herself. She chose to see for herself. But guess what - they won it again. For me, there was no surprise.

Now, knowing things ahead of time has got me to Just Thinking! How neat would it be if you could live each day and then sit back and watch it played out for everyone else later? You could know what was going to happen before it really happened. Maybe then you could fix your mistakes before they were seen before the world. You could give a perfect interview for that job you want. You could make a great impression on the boy or girl you want to go out with. You could make sure you knew all the answers on the test before you really had to take it. You could slow down before the police car pulled you over for speeding. What a way to live!

But wait a minute. That is not reality. You can know one thing before it happens. You can know what your life will be like in eternity. You can know if you have eternal life. I have heard many people say that they hope they go to Heaven. Or "I think I'm going to Heaven."

Well, John said, "These things I have written to you that believe on the name of the Son of God; that you may KNOW that you have eternal life." To know something is not to guess or hope. It is a sure thing. So, it is possible to live your life knowing what your afterlife holds. Even before you die you can know that you have eternal life.

Hey, this is better that the Olympics. Instead of a gold medal, you can have street of gold. I like knowing those results before it happens.

## "DON'T GIVE UP!"
### Romans 8:28

"It ain't over until it's over. "It ain't over until the fat lady sings" "Never give up. Don't ever give up." I'm sure you have heard all of these clichés before. Yet, how many times do we really believe them? Well, during a week of baseball tournaments, I became a believer. Never have I seen a baseball team of young boys work so hard at never giving up. They did not win the tournament, but they played very well. They worked together and everyone contributed to the victories. They won three games all in their last at-bat. They left everything on the field and even when it looked like a lost cause they went to the last inning determined to win and three times that week they did just that.

It would have been easy too just give up. It would have been easy to say there is no reason to try. It would have been easy to say it doesn't matter. But they never stopped believing that they had the talent and ability. The final loss was devastating, but they could hold their heads high because they never gave up.

Now, watching those young boys give it everything and not give up has got me to Just Thinking! Have you already given up on going to church on Sunday? Do you get up on Sunday morning and because everyone is not in a great mood give up on getting to church? Do you strive to be friendly and courteous to your fellow workers and because one of them is in a sour mood you give up on being friendly the rest of the day? Do you give up on living a Christian life one day because you have already done something that you know you shouldn't have done?

Maybe you are reading this and have given up on becoming a Christian because you have lived too much of your life and don't believe there is any reason to change now!! Do you give up on family because you and your spouse have had a fight that you don't believe you can resolve? Do you give up on friendships because there has been a misunderstanding? Do you give up on God because you see hatred, evil, and destruction in the world?

"Don't GIVE UP! Don't EVER GIVE UP!!" God is working in the world and wants you and I to believe in Him and His purposes. Paul said it like this. "And we know that in all things God works for the good of those that love him, who have been called according to his purpose." God is still working in us all. There is still plenty of time for all of us to be victorious. Go at life swinging and never give up.

## "HOW IS YOUR GAME?"
### Matthew 25:40

Sports have been part of my life since I can remember. As a little boy, I loved professional football and professional baseball.

On Sunday afternoons in the fall and winter you could find me sitting on the couch watching football games. If there wasn't one on the television, I was outside trying to find a game to play.

During the spring and summer, I was watching baseball. I couldn't wait for the Saturday Game of the Week to be broadcast on NBC. Back then, that was the only game in town. As I got older, I became more of a college football fan. At the age of 12 I made a trip to Maryland to visit my cousin and he turned me on to what I now believe to be the best sport and that is professional ice hockey.

I have watched a great deal of sports on the television and in person. After a championship game whether it is the final game of the World Series, Stanley Cup, or the Super Bowl there is a quote that is often heard. It goes something like this, "It's not whether you win or lose; it's how you play the game." I have noticed something interesting about this quote. You normally only hear it in the losers' dressing room. They might not actually use those works, but they will say something like, "We just didn't play well enough."

I'm not sure I have ever heard the winners talk much about how they won. They are just glad they won. It doesn't matter whether they played brilliantly or were lucky or a bad call helped them win. They are just happy they won. The loser is always analyzing the loss. What they could have done differently?

Now, listening to the ones who lost talk about losing has got me to Just Thinking! Often in the game of life the same is true. We talk about how we wish we would have done things differently. We say, "Well, if I had to do it over, I might change this or that."

When things are going well in life, we never talk much about fixing anything or doing something better. There is no need since everything seems to be winning. In Matthew 25, Jesus refers to those who won the game of life by giving them entrance into the kingdom of Heaven. Those who lose the game of life are cast out into eternal fire. The victors are glad and don't even realize they have played such a good game. They even ask how we did it.

They were just living life like they believed it should be lived. The losers are shocked because they have not played good enough. They don't understand what they didn't do right. Matthew records Jesus' words about what we need to do in life, "The King will reply, 'Truly I tell you, whatever you did for one of the least of these brothers and sisters of mine, you did for me.'" Jesus tells us the key to the game is treating others like you would treat Him if He were to be in need.

Do we need to work on our game? We need to care for those who are in need. We need to treat others as we would like to be treated. We need not to be selfish and miss out on what God intends for us to do. Practice so that the game you play will become a lifestyle.

## "A GOOD SURPRISE"
### Acts 4:13

My wife and I enjoy going to the World's Longest Yard Sale every August. Our favorite places to ride along Route 127 are in Tennessee. On this journey, we left on a Wednesday evening to drive some of the way toward our starting place. We set out with our goal being Knoxville, Tenn. We stayed in a motel right across from the home of the Tennessee Smokies' AA baseball team in Kodak. They were playing that night, so we decided to take in the game.

As we watched with some 3,000 other fans, a young man with a Smokies golf shirt sat down in front of us. He started a conversation and finally asked if Peggy would be willing to be the Tanger Outlet Women's Fan of the Game. Before Peggy could answer, I answered for her and told the man she would be glad to. He got her name and during the middle of the second inning he came back and made her stand up and announced her to the crowd being from a different city and state. They presented her with a $10.00 gift certificate from the Tanger Outlet Mall in Sevierville.

It was one of those funny moments in life when you are

surprised by what can happen in the strangest places. I'm not sure why he picked Peggy, but I am sure glad He did.

Because we were leaving early the next morning, we knew Peggy would not be able to use the gift certificate, so we gave it to the night clerk in the hotel we were staying. She was very appreciative.

Now, having that surprise of her being the Woman's Fan of the Game has got me to Just Thinking! Have you ever been surprised at what has happened to you where God is concerned?

Has God ever surprised you with His presence or with some grace gift He has bestowed on you? Sometimes I can be expecting nothing to happen and God shows up and does something extraordinary. I don't know why, but it seems like we are always astonished when the Holy Spirit does His work among us. I guess it's kind of like traveling six hours from your home and being picked out of 3,000 people as the Fan of the Game. It doesn't happen every day, but when it does it is really neat.

Take, for instance, when Peter and John spoke to the religious council after healing a man. The Bible records it and says, "When they saw the courage of Peter and John and realized that they were unschooled, ordinary men, they were astonished and they took note that these men had been with Jesus."

When Jesus shows up in our life, surprises happen. We need to get to the point in our lives where we expect it instead of being surprised by it. My prayer is that you will find Jesus showing up all the time. I pray that God will astonish you sometime this month with His presence.

## "A PERFECT GAME"
### Matthew 5:48

What would you believe is the rarest thing to happen in baseball? Some say it is an unassisted triple play. Others say it is winning the Triple Crown, which is leading the league in home runs, batting average and runs batted in. And the debate goes on.

## JUST THINKING!

Yet, one of the rarest things in baseball is a pitching a perfect game. In a regulation nine-inning baseball game the minimum number of batters faced is 27. That would be three outs for each half-inning. You can pitch a no-hitter, but not pitch a perfect game. A walk, an error, or some other anomaly may put someone on base and there goes the perfect game. Many times, it is not the fault of the pitcher, but unless you face the minimum you cannot call it a perfect game.

Since the beginning of Major League Baseball there have only been 24 perfect games. And, even more astoundingly, there has only been one thrown in a postseason game. It is hard to be perfect.

Now, once I was at my younger son Caleb's last baseball game. I saw a young boy pitch a perfect game. It was interesting seeing each batter come up to the plate and each batter get out. It is unusual for a pitcher not to issue a walk, but this young man kept throwing it across the plate and either they struck out or they hit into an out. Inning after inning was the same. It was literally three-up and three-down. He only got to a three-ball count on two batters. When it was all over, I'm not even sure he knew what he did. It was an awesome to see something like this in any baseball competition.

Now, watching and understanding the workings of a perfect game has got me to Just Thinking! How often do we ever live a perfect day? You know what I mean. Have you ever had a day that you said, "I was perfect today?" I doubt that any of us can say that at all. Yet, in the scriptures doesn't Jesus say, "Be perfect, therefore, as your heavenly Father is perfect."? Jesus calls us to perfection, but for most of us we are ready with the excuse that the "devil made me do it." We are setting ourselves up to fail before we even try.

I think what Jesus is teaching us is that we are to strive for perfection. We are to do our best in everything that we do and everything that we think. I do think that God wants us to do our best - not so we will get the glory, but that he will get the glory.

So, although a perfect game is rare, it is possible. And although you and I living a perfect day is rare, we need to strive for the perfection that Jesus calls us to. It is better to strive for perfection than to not try at all. Not trying would be for a pitcher to face the first batter and intentionally walk him. He would be admitting I know I can't throw a perfect game so why try? That becomes our attitude if we give up without trying. Honor and glorify God by at least trying to be perfect. Who knows? Maybe, just maybe, one day!

## "ARE YOU INVESTED?"
### John 4:23-24

PLAY BALL! Those are two words I used to love to hear. Yes, believe it or not, baseball once was one of my favorite sports. I loved watching it on television or at the stadium. I loved coaching little league and watching high school teams. I always enjoyed my experiences and although I don't watch as much as I used to, I still will go and watch a game every now and then.

You know some people think baseball on TV is boring. I just don't understand how it can be boring. I know I've heard all the excuses about how on TV it's too slow and how they need to speed up the game. And I do believe that there are probably some things that could be done to help the game along.

But to tell you the truth, when you learn the game, it is not as slow as some people think. There are strategy considerations, like when the manager has to decide whether to squeeze bunt the winning run home or let his big hitter swing for a home run, or whether the pitcher will throw an inside fast ball and try to get the hitter to swing or whether he will throw an off-speed pitch and try to freeze him for a called strike three.

I know some of you right now don't understand a thing I'm talking about, but isn't that the point. To understand and enjoy baseball you have got to know more than balls, strikes, innings, and outs.

# JUST THINKING!

Now, all of this baseball talk has got me to Just Thinking! The same goes for enjoying a worship experience. To come and feel good about church and worship, you have got to understand that worship does not take place from the pulpit. Worship takes place within a person's heart. God wants you to put something into worship. It is our responsibility to come prepared for Him to speak to us. Maybe He will use the music, maybe the prayers, maybe the offering, maybe the scripture reading or the sermon. Just maybe, He might use a friend. But if I decide to stay away from worship because it's is boring, I have cheated myself.

I have found out that to enjoy baseball I have to think like a baseball player. If I am going to enjoy worship, I have to think like a worshiper, not like a spectator. A worshiper is someone who comes to hear a word from God. Remember, Jesus said, "Yet a time is coming and has now come when the true worshipers will worship the Father in Spirit and in truth, for they are the kind of worshipers the Father seeks. God is spirit, and his worshipers must worship in the Spirit and in truth."

My prayer is that we will learn more about worship and enjoy it for what it is meant to be: a time to tell God how much He is worth to us. Let's not be a spectator, but let's be a participant in the worship in our churches. Let's allow the Spirit to have a vital part in our worship so we can receive everything we are meant to receive.

## "MAKING THE RIGHT CALL"
### Genesis 3:12-13

One year I decided to become a basketball official. I really enjoyed getting to know the game better and meeting some great people. It was interesting to me the response of fans and coaches about the officiating of a game. I have never had a winning coach complain after the game about bad calls or the fact that I didn't make a certain call during the game. They are always happy and excited for their teams. Anytime there is a close game the losing fans and coach always has questions about why I hadn't made a certain call or why I did such a bad job.

It is interesting that it always seems to be the officials' fault when a team loses a close game.

Now, I am not saying that I always made the right call. I know that sometimes I missed a call or maybe I didn't always get it right, but most of the time a team loses because it did not execute or make a free throw or they turned the ball over at the wrong time. I am not sure it is ever the officials' fault - although some would argue with me.

Now, all of this officiating this year got me to Just Thinking! Do you ever wonder why we are so quick to always blame someone else for our mistakes or problems? It is a problem as old as mankind itself. Remember when God asked Adam did he eat of the fruit of the tree that was forbidden? Here, let me show you what was said, "The man said, 'The woman you put here with me – she gave me some fruit from the tree, and I ate it.' Then the Lord God said to the woman, 'What is this you have done?' The woman said, 'The serpent deceived me, and I ate.'" Adam blamed Eve and Eve blamed the serpent. We have been following that example ever since.

I think that we are much better followers of Jesus when we just realize that we make mistakes and ask for forgiveness. Jesus is ready to forgive our mistakes. He is willing to help us clean up our messes and to restore a right relationship within us. We just need to get away from the blame game and start accepting the responsibility. When we fail to live up to the Father's game plan and we lose, don't put the blame on others.

Let's step up to the plate and be responsible. We can take our life and restore it to a work in progress as God creates in us His image.

## "RIDING THE WIND"
### John 3:8; Galatians 5:25

The sport of kitesurfing is a popular activity. We saw many people doing this on a vacation we took to the Outer Banks of North Carolina. The people participating in this sport were amazing. They would strap themselves to a huge kite, grab the handle, strap their feet into a board like a wake board and the wind would do the rest. The wind would propel them back and forth across the water and they would do awesome tricks. It was amazing to watch them jump out of the water attached to their boards and go as high as 15 feet into the air. We watched as these men and women (we saw one man who had to be 60+ years old doing this) were having the time of their lives surfing on the water in the wind.

It looked simple. The people doing it seemed to making little effort as they glided across the water. As the week wound down and the wind subsided to a slight breeze there were not as many people kitesurfing. Matter of fact, when we left on Saturday morning, we couldn't find any of the kitesurfers on the water. The wind had almost stopped.

Now watching these surfers and the wind glide them across the water got me to Just Thinking!! Have you ever noticed how some Christians have little trouble "walking with the Spirit" and how others struggle every day. Paul tells us "Since we live by the Spirit, let us keep in step with the Spirit." A problem is that I am often missing a step and falling on my face. I need to follow a simple guideline of the kitesurfers. I have to harness myself to the wind and allow it to take me where it wants me to go. Jesus explained to Nicodemus that to be born again means to allow the Spirit to take us where it wants us to go. Jesus words were, "The wind blows wherever it pleases. You hear its sound, but you do not know where it comes from or where it is going. So, it is with everyone born of the Spirit!"

Have you ever noticed how we want to be the ones guiding

the Spirit? We want to tell the Spirit what we want to do and where we want to go. Yet, Jesus says the Spirit comes from unknown places and takes us to unknown opportunities. One of our fears is that the Spirit may take me some place we do not want to go. It may ask me to do something I would rather not do.

There comes a time when my faith must trust and believe that God will always provide for me to do whatever He wants me to do. When we watched the really good kitesurfers you could tell they had spent a great deal of time on the water. The ones who were not as good hadn't spent as much time. The same goes for those who "live by the Spirit." If you want to walk without missing a step or falling on your face you must trust and practice. The more time you and I spend with Jesus, the more we will be able to trust the Spirit in every move He makes. Otherwise, we will find ourselves just sitting on the land and watching as God uses others to fulfill His kingdom work. Take my word for it. I believe it would be a whole lot more fun participating than just watching.

## "HOPE IS A GOOD THING"
### Hebrews 10:22-24

On the first weekend of college football in 2013 I was home watching the Thursday night games. I went to bed but I couldn't go to sleep so I got up and ventured back to the TV.

The last quarter of the Mississippi State-Vanderbilt game was on. I began to watch it. Mississippi State took the lead with only about 1:30 left in the game. The Mississippi State crowd was whooping and hollering and the faces of the crowd were ecstatic. The Vanderbilt crowd was subdued and sad.

Well, everything changed when the quarterback for Vanderbilt hit on a 34-yard scoring pass and with just over a minute left, the table was turned. Now the Vanderbilt crowd was whooping and hollering. The Mississippi State crowd was subdued and sad.

Well, in just a matter of seconds on the game clock everything changed again. A senior running back for Mississippi State took a handoff and ran 75 yards for a touchdown with less than a minute left. Again, the tide had turned. The Mississippi State crowd was whooping and hollering and the Vanderbilt crowd was once again subdued and sad. I sat in my chair not so much stunned at the events, but at the reaction of the crowd, the team and even the coaches. They went through the highs and lows of winning and losing in so short a time. It is amazing how quickly we can lose what we once thought we had.

Now, this game and the events of the final minutes has got me to Just Thinking! I am so glad I don't have to go through those same emotions with my belief in Jesus. Can you imagine if we were living this life and wondering each day each moment if we were on the winning team? Can you imagine waking up one day to wonder if Jesus was still sitting on the throne? Can you even think that one day the Jesus that promised you forgiveness would all of a sudden renege and take back that forgiveness because He changed His mind?

The Bible speaks of "hope" in many ways. It talks about hope as a good thing. It says we should hold on to the hope that we have. If I can quote from one of my favorite movies, "Hope is a good thing; maybe the best of things. And no good thing ever dies."

Listen to the words of the writer of Hebrews, "… let us draw near to God with a sincere heart and with the full assurance that faith brings, having our hearts sprinkled to cleanse us from a guilty conscience and having our bodies washed with pure water. Let us hold unswervingly to the hope we profess, for he who promised is faithful. And let us consider how we may spur one another on toward love and good deeds…"

Now, that is something I don't have to worry about coming and going. My attitude about my Savior never changes. No one person, philosophy, new fad, or worldly pressure will ever make me lose hope. I don't have to worry that my emotions will be on a roller coaster over what Jesus said He would do and what He will do. That is comforting for me and every Christian. I hope you feel the same way.

## "HIT IT STRAIGHT"
### Matthew 7:13-14

As I said earlier. I used to play golf. At one time I owned a set of golf clubs, but they were at my son Joshua's house in North Carolina. Joshua, at that time, was playing as regularly as possible and because it was a way to spend some quality time with him, I picked up my clubs again.

Now, after several months I guess you could say I was "hooked" again or for you golfers out there you could say I was "sliced." The reason I say that is because I cannot hit the golf ball straight. I always slice it. That means it starts off the club straight, but it curves to the right as it begins to descend. Therefore, I am playing from the rough and woods a great deal.

It is amazing to watch the pros. They do it so effortlessly. They swing, they hit the ball straight. Me, I swing and the ball has a mind of its own. One day I played with a man who had bought a new driver. He let me hit it and I actually hit the ball straight. It was called an R7 Draw. It was supposed to help a "slicer" like me to hit the ball straight.

Well, my wonderful wife went out and bought me the club. I have played with it several times and guess what? I still cannot hit it straight consistently, but every once in a while, I hit a straight shot. I have said if anyone can slice a draw club it would be me. That was just one of my many experiences with golf.

Now, all this "hook," "slice," and "straight" talk has got me to Just Thinking! Jesus was very straight in his talk about the Christian life and eternal living. He reminded us that we need to find the straight and narrow path that leads to a good life. He said to the multitudes, "Enter through the narrow gate. For wide is the gate and broad is the road that leads to destruction, and many enter through it. But small is the gate and narrow the road that leads to life, and only a few find it."

Sometimes my life is like my golf ball. It seems to have a mind of its own. I try to hit it straight and I go off either left or right. I need to concentrate, get in the right position, take proper aim and take the proper swing so that I can live each day down the center of God's fairway. He has given me the proper instruction through His word and I need to study it and spend time with my instructor, The Holy Spirit. When I am doing that I am much more likely to accomplish life like God intended. It is not easy. It is a constant work in progress. Yet, it should be my desire as a disciple of Jesus to live life the right way. I hope you will work on your game as a Christian because the game of life is much more important that golf.

## "UNDERSTANDING THE RULES"
### John 14:6

I'll admit it: I'm an ice hockey fanatic. Every time I tell someone in the south that I love ice hockey they think something is wrong with me and make a joke that goes something like, "I went to a fight and a hockey game broke out." Well, that goes to show that sometimes people make comments about things they are unsure of. I have been an ice hockey fan for many years. My cousin in Maryland, Donnie Wyatt, got me interested in 1972. We went to a game and I was hooked.

Atlanta got a National Hockey League franchise that very year and the ice hockey came to the south. I began to watch Atlanta Flames games and I learned the rules and began to experience what I still say is the most exciting game with the most talented athletes.

Now, I know many of you tell me that it doesn't make any

sense. But isn't that the reason to watch and learn? If you watch and learn then you will understand.

The fact that people will not take time to learn and understand has got me to Just Thinking! There are many times when people tell me the same thing about God. They say they don't understand or that God is too complicated. They are afraid to give God their best because they are not sure about the "rules" of the game. They say being a Christian is too complicated. It is hard to live and follow all of those rules.

Well, I believe that it is up to you and me to help nonbelievers understand the rules. We have to live our lives as a disciple so we can show the way to others. Christians need to be in the world helping others to learn and understand the "rules" of life. God has placed us here to help others understand. We need to explain that Jesus is the "only" way to God. Jesus said, "I am the way, the truth and the life. No one comes to the Father except through me."

Are you helping others to understand the "way" of life? Are you helping others learn about the greatest "truth" of life? Are you helping others live a Godly "life" by being good examples for them to follow? If people are confused about following Jesus maybe it is the followers who need to step up.

By the way, if you are interested in learning about God or ice hockey, give me a call!!!

## "PUTTING IT IN THE HOLE"
### John 14:27

Have you ever played carpet golf? Some people call it miniature golf. I would guess that somewhere along the way each of us has or tried it. The object of carpet golf is to get a ball into a hole by hitting it with a golf putter. Well, I have played carpet golf, but it is a totally different game than trying to putt on a real golf course. In golf, getting to the green is one aspect of the game, but putting the ball into the hole is an entirely different aspect.

Now, I never claimed to be a good putter. As a matter of fact, I was not even an average putter. Here is why I struggled. When you look at where the ball is and where the hole is, there is normally a break in the green's grass where the ball will either turn to the right or the left. There is also the decision of whether you are hitting the ball uphill or downhill. Then you have to decide if the greens have been cut and are fast, or they have not been cut and are slow. It also may depend on whether the greens are wet or dried out. You see, putting is not an easy task. It is very seldom that you get on a green and have a straight putt. Needless to say, I don't make many putts. I miss most of them and get very frustrated when I do. Putting is hard.

Now, all of this talk about putting has got me to Just Thinking! Trying to be all that God wants me to be is hard, too! Sometimes it is like putting. I am trying to read the way God would have me act or react, and sometimes I misread and go completely the wrong way. The Bible calls that sin. God has a purpose for me and when I "miss the mark," I sin.

I am thankful that the Holy Spirit is my teacher. In the Bible Jesus says, "But the Advocate, the Holy Spirit, whom the Father will send in my name, will teach you all things and will remind you of everything I have said to you." He helps me to better understand how to be what God wants me to be. If I continue to listen to Him, He will help me to be what God wants me to be. He will help me better understand how not to "miss the mark," and stay on course. It is a tragedy when we fail to use the resource that the Father has sent to us. The Holy Spirit is available to every Christian. We need to be attentive and listen to Him. I never became a good putter. Maybe I needed a putting lesson.

## "THE RIGHT CALL"
### Acts 2:38

As I stated earlier, we love watching the Olympics at our house. We have really enjoyed the swimming events and I love the track and field events. I have even gotten into the volleyball matches. What I do not enjoy is the gymnastics. It is one of my wife Peggy's favorite events. It is not that I don't appreciate the athleticism of the competitors. They are definitely some of the most athletic and strongest participants in the Olympics. What I don't care for is the way their sport is judged. It is too ambiguous. There is not enough black and white; there is only gray. One judge sees it one way another sees it differently. It is so up in the air. Even the commentators don't agree with the judging. Some say it is sour grapes when their favorite competitor doesn't make the medal stand. Some say it is fixed. I don't know. It just seems to me if they had a better way of judging then there would be no arguments.

Now, the vague way in which the sport is judged got me to Just Thinking! I am glad that there is only one criteria for eternal life. After Peter preached his sermon on the day of Pentecost the people cried out, "What do we do?" The Bible records the answer, "Peter replied, 'Repent and be baptized, every one of you, in the name of Jesus Christ for the forgiveness of your sins. And you will receive the gift of the Holy Spirit.'" Now I don't know about you, but that is pretty clear. That is not up for debate. There is no way that can be seen in any other light.

Yet, the world tries to make us believe that there are many ways to obtain eternal life. Some try to convince us that if we are good to our fellow man that we have an upper hand in receiving God's reward. Some believe if they belong to a service organization and participate in some worthy cause that surely God will notice. Maybe if they just don't steal and cheat that will give them an upward hand.

Now, I will admit that servanthood is a byproduct of knowing

God, but it is not the way to Heaven. Treating our neighbors well and helping out in worthy causes are good things to do also. And not stealing and cheating are always good attributes to have. But none of these will provide forgiveness for our sins. Peter said it perfectly we have to repent and allow Jesus Christ to forgive us for our sins. There is no other way!

## "ACCEPT IT"
### Romans 15:7

The world gets excited over World Cup Fútbol (football). For many of you this means nothing. Here in the good ol' USA, we call it soccer. Most of us southern folks only know one kind of football and it is played in four quarters of 15 minutes each, not two halves of 45 minutes.

I tried watching some World Cup of the games on television. The truth is that I would get bored very quickly. I cannot understand the concept of kicking the ball backward instead of moving it forward. Most of the games I did watch (I never watched an entire game) had very few scoring chances. Most games end 1-0 or 2-1. In the first round they could even end in a tie. The old saying is that is like kissing your sister. I tried - I really tried - but I just couldn't get the hang of watching fútbol.

Now, that is not true with the younger generation. Many all over this country watch soccer. I would watch our youth and youth leaders as their faces would light up when they talked about the games. They would talk about the excitement and the thrill of the matches. They knew the players by name and would talk about the different countries. They had their favorites; Germany, Brazil, and, of course, the USA. I guess the best team will win, or at least the team who gets the most, lucky breaks.

Now, this fútbol stuff has got me to Just Thinking! We assume that everyone we meet has the same thoughts about Christianity and religion that we do. We figure that most Americans should know about Jesus and the fact that He died for our sins. We live our lives like everyone should be excited every Sunday to get up, and go to church and worship God.

The truth is our world around us is changing. There are many people that we encounter every day that do not have the same ideas as we do about church. Many of them did not grow up going to church. Many of them have never been raised in church with the mindset that they need a loving and caring fellowship of believers.

Paul told the believers in Rome where Christianity was just getting started this truth, "Accept one another, then, just as Christ accepted you, in order to bring praise to God." It is important that those who don't see it like we do don't feel as if they are second-class citizens. They need to be accepted and loved.

Just as my soccer friends have tried to get me to understand soccer and encouraged me to watch it, we have to encourage our unchurched friends to give church a try. We have to convince them that church is not a place where we will put them down or condemn their lifestyle. It is a place where they can be loved and find the love of Jesus. Let us do our best to show others that church is a place of acceptance. Olé! Olé!

CHAPTER THREE

# JUST THINKING...
# ABOUT BIRTHDAYS & HOLIDAYS!

## "The Greatest Gift"
### Ephesians 2:8

My wife and I celebrate our birthdays just four days apart. Here is what happened the year we turned 60. On Friday before my birthday, Peggy told me before she left for work that she was expecting a package, I would have to sign for it and she didn't want me to leave the house until it arrived. And then, when it got there, I was not to open it.

So, I hung around the house and the package came at about noon. I signed for it and placed the box on the chair next to the door. I didn't even shake it or look at the return label to see where it came from. She got home, we ate lunch and when I came back into the den there was the box wrapped in birthday wrapping paper.

I smiled and told her I didn't think she wanted me to open it and it still wasn't my birthday. She said she couldn't wait until tomorrow, to please open it now. So, I did and am so glad I did.

I love professional Ice Hockey. That love was started in Maryland at the home of my cousin, Donnie. I was a mere 12 years old when I visited with my grandparents that summer. I'm not sure I even knew anything about ice hockey before then. I'm not sure I even knew it was a sport. I have no recollection of the sport. My sports were focused on football, baseball and basketball. I loved sports. I loved playing and watching and reading about them. Donnie helped me to fall in love with ice hockey.

Donnie had a table top hockey game with the rods that you pulled, pushed and twisted to put the puck in the net. I didn't know the rules or anything about it. Donnie began to teach me that week I spent with him in Maryland. Donnie told me about the best players to watch. That was the first time I heard the name Bobby Hull.

I came home and asked for a table top hockey game for Christmas. I got it and I was good. I beat anyone who challenged me. I even beat the opponent when two people managed the players and I would play by myself. My best scorer on my imaginary team of plastic men was Bobby Hull.

With all my playing on the game I still hadn't learned much about the rules. I took some of the money I earned and subscribed to The Sporting News, which did a great job of covering hockey. I waited each week as the paper would come and I would read every box score and every article. I especially would check to see how Bobby Hull had done and he became my favorite player.

Then, November 1971, the city of Atlanta was awarded a National Hockey League team. They began playing in the fall of 1972 and many of their games were on TV on the TBS Superstation. I began watching, since hockey was new to southerners, the announcers would explain the rules when something was called on the ice. I became more and more obsessed. I watched every opportunity I could.

The sad part about watching was that my favorite player had left the NHL's Chicago Blackhawks for the World Hockey Association in a salary dispute. Bobby Hull went to play for the Winnipeg Jets. I only got to see him play in replays, but I was able to keep up with him from The Sporting News.

Now, let's get back to me opening the wrapped birthday present. I opened the box and there wrapped in plastic was a signed Blackhawks sweater. There on the back was the number 16. On the back was also Bobby Hull's actual signature and his handwritten note "1961 Stanley Cup."

I was overwhelmed. I couldn't believe it. Peggy was afraid I would rather have someone else's sweater, but I told her she hit it out of the park. I put it on immediately. I wore it the rest of the day. I hung it up that evening. On Saturday afternoon we drove to Hendersonville to meet the children for a birthday celebration. I wore my sweater. I came home and hung it up. And then Sunday after worship service I went home and wore it the rest of the day. Someone asked me if I was going to put it in a frame and I said no, I was going to wear it. I am very proud of it and will tell you the story any time you would like to listen.

Now, the story of my love for hockey and the Bobby Hull sweater has got me to Just Thinking! The thought and gift from my wife for my 60th birthday was a highlight gift in my life. It will be one of those things that I will always remember when I got it and who gave it to me. I know I have made much of it and have shown it off.

Yet, with all of that being said, it is not the greatest and best gift I have ever received. The greatest gift I ever received came when I was 7 years old in a cabinet warehouse. Our church was building a new sanctuary and had rented a warehouse to hold our worship services during construction. There, during an evening service, I told the pastor that I wanted to receive the gift of salvation given to me by Jesus. That evening I confessed that I was a sinner and that I needed someone to forgive me of my sins. I knew that my life was not good in and of itself and that even as a 7-year-old boy there were things I did and thought that were not Godly. I surrendered my life to Jesus that night and it is the greatest gift I have ever received.

Paul said it best, "For it is by grace you have been saved through faith and this is not of yourself, it is the gift of God."

My life has never been the same. Yes, I did some things that didn't represent Jesus very well as I ventured through my teen years, but thank God for His grace that gave me forgiveness. Now I have lived 60 years and I am doing my best to become more like Jesus. I want to be loving to everyone. I want my life to be full of the fruit of the Spirit which consist of love, joy, peace, patience, gentleness, goodness, faith, meekness, and self-control.

Now, that is what the gift does for me. It gives me the greatest joy in living. I want my attitude and disposition to be something I wear everyday – not just on important occasions. I sure don't want to hang up this beautiful gift at night or when I'm not in public. I want my family, friends, acquaintances and anyone I see to be able to recognize that I have the gift of grace given to me by my Savior, Jesus Christ.

If you have received the gift, then I pray you know what I'm talking about. There is no place for subpar Christianity. Our lives need to show the world that Jesus makes a difference. It is not just a tag to wear so that you can skip hell. If you have never received the gift, I want to impress upon you that your life may be great right now, but I am telling you that you are missing out on the greatest feeling in the world: the feeling that someone loves you so much that they died to give you life everlasting. And you don't have to do one thing to receive it.

## "Leave it to a Child"
### Luke 9:48

Right before my oldest grandson, Foster, turned 9 he was at the house and we started talking about what to buy him for his birthday present. He told me he wanted an RC car. For all of you who do not know it, an RC car is a remote-controlled car. Now, he didn't want a cheap little RC car; he wanted one that was nice. We looked at a few on Amazon and I told him I would contact a friend of mine and see which one was the best. I texted a person

## JUST THINKING!

I knew who worked on RC cars. He told me that for a little more money I could buy one that if it broke - and they all do at some time - he could fix it for us.

So, Peggy and I rode to a hobby shop and, sure enough, they had the car and we bought it for Foster for his birthday.

Well, I couldn't wait for his party. He opened up the box and was excited. We were even able to buy him a blue car - which is his favorite color. As I took it out of the box for him to try, I had already charged the battery. I put the battery in and without knowing it, raced the car off the table onto the ground. It shot off the table like it was on fire. I tried to get the car to follow my commands, but I wasn't having any luck.

I told Foster how to operate it and before long he was driving the car and turning and doing jumps. He was so excited. Later that evening, Foster's dad Joshua called to tell me that he couldn't control the car, but Foster had no problem making it start, turn and stop. Foster had mastered it pretty quickly where the adults couldn't even get it to run straight and make a turn. It was all pretty funny.

On Sunday afternoon, Joshua took Foster to a large parking lot next to his school and Foster would drive the car long distances and bring it back, turning and stopping on a dime. Joshua sent me a video and Foster was just all smiles and excited.

I am glad Foster liked his present. I am glad for a friend who helped me with the purchase and got us a good product that Foster could enjoy. I am a little surprised just how quickly Foster took to the controls when his papa and dad had such a hard time. But, I guess I shouldn't be surprised that a child can handle electronics better than an adult.

Now, the fact that a child seemed to have it all figured out and his papa was perplexed has got me to Just Thinking! Several times the gospels record that Jesus took a child in His arms and remarked to His disciples, "Then he said to them, 'Whoever welcomes this little child in my name welcomes me, and whoever welcomes me welcomes the one who sent me. For it is the one who is least among you all who is the greatest.'"

Little children are the key to faith. A child believes so easily. A child doesn't have problems believing something that someone they trust tells them. Adults try to figure it out. We want to know the how and the why. We want to analyze it and understand it. Children just believe.

Foster just took the controls and started using them. I tried to understand them. He drives the car much better than I do. Jesus wants us to believe like little children. He wants us to trust Him without trying to figure it all out. He wants us to trust Him in spite of what we find out. If we understood then we would be God and that is not going to happen.

Oh, to be able to trust like a child; to have faith and believe everything that Jesus says and his promises. We say we believe, but do we act upon His truth? Jesus says do not worry, but we worry. Jesus says don't fear death, but we do. Jesus says to just trust and obey, but we don't. A child just says I will. My prayer is that Jesus will help me be more childlike in my faith.

## "A Specialty Birth"
### Matthew 1:21

Corbin is my granddaughter. She is the only girl out of four grandchildren. That's OK, because she can take care of herself.

One of the things I love about Corbin's birthdays is they are always special. She was born three days before Christmas. Her parents always make sure she has a themed party. Once I cooked pancakes for everyone because she loves pancakes. Once we had a donut party where the treats were special donuts. During the pandemic when you were not supposed to have people over, her Mom planned a drive-by party. Corbin was stationed outside in their church's parking lot and people drove by and wished her a very happy birthday party. As you drove up to speak to her, there were signs that highlighted several aspects of her life. One that really interested me was that she had never had her hair cut. It is still that way today. It is long and beautiful. When we celebrate her birthday at our house on a Sunday close to her birthday, she always requests for me to make spaghetti. She loves my spaghetti and I love making it for her.

These parties are always fun, and it is great to celebrate this little girl's life. She is always so full of energy and you just never know what she is going to come up with next. When she was very young you had to be careful that she just didn't disappear. Often when she stayed at our house she would disappear for a little while and you had to go find her to see what she was into. You just never knew with Corbin.

Now, celebrating Corbin's specialty birthdays has got me to Just Thinking! Where Jesus is concerned, we only know of one birthday. It is the day He was born. Wow, now that was special. He was born in a stable. He was laid in a manger. The angels sang to a group of shepherds who went to see him. A few days later he was taken to the temple and two total strangers proclaimed His mission. A few years later wisemen traveled to see Him and worship Him. Talk about special!

Yet, we seem to forget how special His birth was. We fail to recognize that it was a life changing birth. We fail to emphasize just how important it was to all mankind. As the angel Is talking to Joseph before the birth of Jesus he said, "She (Joseph's wife Mary) will give birth to a son, and you are to give him the name Jesus, because he will save his people from their sin."

That is pretty specialized. He was born to save. He was born to make a difference. If you have accepted Him, you have experienced the difference. If you haven't then you need to.

DAVID M. SIMMONS

## "Fearfully & Wonderfully Made"
Jeremiah 1:5; Psalm 139:14

David Reid is my third grandchild. Reid was born under a cloud. The doctors had told his parents-to-be Caleb and Sally Ann that he had a cyst on the base of his brain. They were scared about just what that meant for the little boy. The day after he was born the doctors at the hospital said that it was necessary to get him to a children's hospital and something be done. Everyone was so worried that this cyst was life threatening. No one was really sure what the outcome would be. On that second day of Reid's life, Caleb and Sally Ann finally got some news from a child neuro specialist. He told them to take their little boy home and just watch him. He told them to go to Charlotte in a few weeks for an appointment and they would see where they were.

They finally got to the child neuro specialist and after a rapid MRI they were told Reid needed surgery to relieve the pressure on the brain. So, as an infant in the next several months, Reid had brain surgery. The second surgery was to put in a shunt. The shunt would drain the cyst and, hopefully, make it smaller.

Well, as many of you know, this last procedure was a great success. Unless you knew about the incidents in Reid's life that first year you would never know that he had had two major brain surgeries.

Today he lives a full and normal life. He laughs and is so welcoming to everyone. He is a bright penny when things started off like there would be major problems. It is always a blessing to celebrate his birthday.

Now, seeing Reid and knowing what might have been has got me to Just Thinking! In the book of Jeremiah there is a passage about Jeremiah's calling that says, "Before I formed you in the womb, I knew you..." There is another passage in Psalms 139 that says, "I praise You, because I am fearfully and wonderfully made. Marvelous are Your works."

When we dedicated Reid as a child, I gave Reid Psalm 139 as

his life verse. Let's be succinct: God knows you better than you know yourself! When you and I were created, He knew just what was being born into His world. He understands you better and has a plan for your life. There is never - and I repeat never! - a mistake with God.

Now, we want to blame God for many things in our world. We ask questions like, "Why do we suffer?" "Why is there evil?" "Why do bad things happen to good people?" And on we could go. Yet we need to understand that it was never God's plan for us to be the object of sin. It is our own doing. We are the ones who ushered in sin. We are the ones who keep it alive and well, and with sin comes consequences.

Jesus came to do away with sin. He came to do away with evil. He came to give hope to a world that has lost its way. I can't explain why bad things happen. Yet, with all the struggles that we have experienced in our lives there, is one constant that never changes. God is on our side. Jesus came to show us that very fact. God has paved a way for us to usher in the New Kingdom - the Kingdom of God. He showed us how and what we needed to do.

None of us knows how many days we have here on this earth. Yet, as Christians and disciples of Jesus it is imperative that we live each and every day seeking to bring the Kingdom of God closer than it ever has been. Jesus said it. The disciples lived it. Paul preached it. The Kingdom of God is coming and what we do as ambassadors of Christ will help to bring it about.

Are you ready to be a special child in helping to bring the Kingdom of God into the presence? God has made you as you are to be that person. Let's get to it!

## "What are You Asking For"?"
### James 4:2b

Gregory James, is our last grandchild. As we celebrate his birthday it is amazing to see how fast he is growing up. He is full of life and is very head strong. He plays hard and is very independent. I love watching him grow and develop. He is constantly on the go. Like most children, he doesn't like it when he does not get his way. He will whine and cry and beg for something he wants.

As his grandfather I am pretty easily convinced when he wants something. I am quick to give in. I have to be careful not to overindulge him with snacks and candy. If his parents are there, I will sometimes tell him he has to ask them before I will give him what he wants. If they are not there, I usually just give him what he asks for.

Now, I realize that can be good and bad. Sometimes one more piece of candy is not good for you. As adults we need to know the limits of a child and not give in. With my grandchildren I am not very good at being that adult. I am too quick to give in and grant them their wish. When we celebrate his birthday, I always want him to enjoy everything he receives and be the star of the party. I always want him to have the best.

As I was thinking about James and giving him what he wants, it got me to Just Thinking! We can be like children when it comes to asking God for things. We sometimes ask for things that are not really good for us. We can whine and cry when we do not get what we want and often wonder why. Yet, God knows our needs and our wants. He understands what is good for us and what is not. As children we have to trust Him and believe that He will give us what is best for us.

That doesn't mean we shouldn't ask. The Bible says, "We have not because we ask not." Yet, we must be willing to accept whatever we receive from the hands of God. He truly wants what is best for us. Often, we go off by ourselves and get things that are not best for us and often we have to pay the consequences. When we make bad choices then we must accept the difficult consequences. God wants us to avoid those consequences. He wants us to flourish and be blessed. So, we must be willing to follow His lead and receive what He offers and be okay with what we do not receive.

As we seek the will of God in our lives, we can learn to be grateful for all the blessings that we receive. We can also learn to be content with the lives He has given us to live. As we grow older let us pray, we will become wiser and seek the good things from God that will bless our lives and give glory to Him.

## "What a Sacrifice"
### Matthew 28:6

When you grew up did you celebrate St. Patrick's Day? I have very fond memories of St. Patrick's Day. As a young boy there were not very many, if any, St. Patrick Day parades that I missed while growing up just outside of Savannah, Ga. At that time Savannah hosted the second-largest St. Patrick's Day parade in the United States. The only one that was larger was the one in Chicago. For all of you who didn't know, Savannah has a large group of Irish Catholics living in the area.

Every year our family would have front row seats as the parade came down Bay Street in Savannah. For many years I sat on the hood of our Rambler station wagon wearing a hat that said, "Kiss me I'm Irish," always hoping that one of those pretty girls marching in the parade would come over and give me a kiss. They never did!

It was at the St. Patrick's Day parade that I shook Jimmy Carter's hand when he was governor of Georgia. It was there that I remember seeing many people from area schools who marched in the parade with their bands. And, believe it or not, I even marched in the parade one year as a boy scout. We never had school on St. Patrick's Day because everyone who was anyone went to the parade, and not everyone was as fortunate as I was to get to sit on the front row every year.

Some may ask, "How were you able to pull that off every

year?" Well, I had a mom who got up very early on that day and drove our car downtown to Bay Street before the road was blocked off for the parade. A friend would follow her and bring her back home as she left our car parked in a prime spot. After she returned home and woke us up, fed us breakfast and got us ready, we would walk to the bus stop and take the bus downtown. We would get off the bus and then walk to our car. (They don't let you park on Bay Street anymore.) What great memories and what a great sacrificial mom to inconvenience herself that early in the morning to bring pleasure to her children.

The sacrificial attitude of my mom on St. Patrick's Day and many other times in my life has got me to Just Thinking! At church we watched the video of the Easter Experience. It was titled "He Knows Our Pain." We watched as Jesus was scourged and beaten by the Roman soldiers. We watched as He willingly allowed Himself to be beaten and never once opened His mouth in rebellion. We watched as His life was snatched away one lash at a time. We watched as the blood flowed from His body and He stood in His own blood to endure the pain. Anyone who was at church that Sunday had to be moved by the picture of Jesus bearing up under the load of pain.

I cannot help but to recognize sacrifice in a totally different way since that video. The fact that the video portrays Jesus as not running from the area of pain, but willingly removing His robe and placing His hands around the pole without as a fight. He did not struggle to remove Himself from pain, He voluntarily gave Himself to it. Why? Why would Jesus allow Himself to go through such a horrible beating and then a horrible death? For You and Me!!!

For me that is why Easter is such a wonderful day. It reminds me that the sacrifice was worth it. It reminds me that no matter how hard life is for me, with Jesus as my Savior there is an Easter coming. It reminds me that although I do not understand everything about why God does what He does, I can trust Him because He always does what is right. True sacrifice always brings good in the end. That is the story of EASTER!! "Do not be afraid, for I know you are looking for Jesus, who was crucified. He is not here! He Is RISEN just as he said. Come and see the place where he lay."

## "High & Lifted Up!"
### Revelation 5:13

I'm sure at some time in your life you have experienced an Easter drama. The church I was pastoring put on a drama and I don't know that I have ever felt the energy in a service as I felt during the finale of the drama. Let me give you just a little touch of what happened.

The drama was entitled "Will you Wait with Me?" It was about Mary the mother of Jesus waiting at the foot of the cross with some other women. They were all trying to figure out why Jesus had to die and what was the significance of the whole episode. Along with some Biblical women, there were some other women who chimed in about Jesus' death on the cross. Mother Teresa, Corrie ten Boom, and just an ordinary woman gave their understandings of Jesus' death on the cross.

After all of the interaction of the women and the feeling that we must all be in limbo waiting at the cross, our interpretive movement team appeared to finish off the production. As they gave us their interpretation of "Arise My Love," Jesus appeared during the singing of the song. He stood at the top of a banister and raised His hands in victory over the grave and the cross.

As the song concluded the congregation erupted with applause and the electricity of the moment charged the people. There were tears and chill bumps as the reality of Jesus's resurrection reminded us that the cross was just a temporary setback in the victory of the empty tomb.

Now, the response of the crowd got me to Just Thinking! I can't wait until I see Jesus face to face. I can't wait to see the response of His children when they gather around the throne and give Him the glory and honor that He is due. I can't wait to experience that feeling of joy and gratitude that I feel when I am just seeing a glimpse of His glory here on earth. I can't wait to be numbered among the chosen when we see the prophecy realized as told in the book of Revelation. "Then I heard every creature in heaven and on earth and under the earth and on the sea, and all that is in them, singing: "To him who sits on the throne and to the Lamb be praise and honor and glory and power, for ever and ever!"

I can't wait to see my Lord high and lifted up. If you have never experienced the feeling of the presence of God then in some way, I feel sorry for you. But do not despair. There is hope. For everyone who calls on the name of the Lord will not only be saved, but will have the opportunity and the privilege to praise Him forever and ever.

## "Every Day is Easter"
### John 20:1

When I was growing up, my mother always provided some sort of Easter basket for my siblings and I. Easter morning was waking up early to go to Sonrise service if one was provided by the community. We would return home and have breakfast and would get to see what the Easter Bunny had left us. One of my gifts was a mesh bag full of solid chocolate balls. They were wrapped in thin foil and I received this gift for several years in a row. I remember them because I would only eat one or two a night. I would twist the bag and then let it unwind and the balls would hug the outside of the mesh bag and make a circle in the middle. As each night the bag got less, the unwinding of the bag got faster.

I would indulge myself every now and then and have more than one or two. Sometimes I would eat eight or 10 at a time, but still hoping to make them last as long as possible. After about a month - or maybe even less - the bag would be empty. I would throw it away and would not have another chocolate ball until the next Easter.

Now, thinking about this candy and realizing how much I enjoyed these special treats for a season has got me to Just Thinking!! I have a feeling that most of us do the holiday of Easter like I did those solid chocolate balls. We look forward to it and really talk it up. We plan a Sonrise service and maybe a breakfast afterward. We then gather for worship with the church family and some visitors and Easter attendees. We sing Easter songs, repeat "He is Alive!" several times and then hear the message that Jesus died on the cross for our sins, but He rose again the third day to give us victory over death and sin.

We concentrate on the empty tomb. We decorate the flower cross with beautiful flowers and remember Jesus's sacrifice. We dress up and for a few hours really dedicate ourselves to Easter Sunday. We even hear about it a few Sundays following Easter and the pastor may even preach on after Easter events in the Bible that help us to focus on the resurrection.

Then, just like my chocolate balls, Easter is gone. We have finished with Easter and we will have to wait again until next year to bring out the songs, the mantra, and the message. We will worship every Sunday and go about our "regular" services and when the New Year rolls around we will mark our calendar when Easter is coming and plan our events to celebrate the resurrection.

In many ways this makes me sad. We seem to forget Easter once it is over. We seem to take it for granted and just move on. We get back to "normal," so to speak, and fail to highlight the importance of the resurrection in our lives each and every day. How sad it must be that we don't speak enough of the majesty and miracle of the empty tomb.

In the early first century after Jesus ascended into heaven, the church took off like a bullet after the coming of the Holy

Spirit. Many first-century Jews were getting confused about the difference between Judaism and Christianity. The early church decided to change their meeting day from the Sabbath – Saturday; to Sunday - resurrection day. They decided that they would meet on the first day of the week to commemorate the resurrection of Jesus from the tomb. So, the precedent was set.

John records, "Early on the first day of the week, while it was still dark, Mary Magdalene went to the tomb and saw that the stone had been removed from the entrance." We worship the risen savior on the first day of the week instead of the last day of the week. Sunday has become our gathering day. We will gather because we are who we are because of Jesus's resurrection and life that He gives. This has not changed. We gather to worship the Savior of the world on the first day of the week to remember that resurrection makes a difference. Resurrection changes everything. Resurrection gives us freedom from sin and hope for tomorrow.

Everything that Jesus did in His earthly ministry points to the resurrection. His ushering in of the Kingdom of God and establishing the church was sanctioned and grounded in the resurrection. There was no one before and there will be no one after who established His Kingdom and died and rose again.

If you believe this, then Easter should never come and go. Easter is here every Sunday. We gather to celebrate the Risen Lord! We gather to sing about the goodness and grace of the Risen Lord! We gather to worship and praise the Risen Lord! If we are true to the very essence of Easter, then Easter is celebrated every Sunday of our lives. We should never get to the bottom of the bag and have to wait until next year.

So, I offer you Easter every week. I offer you the opportunity to come expecting to experience the Risen Savior every week. I offer you the chance to have a life-changing experience every time you walk through the doors of the worship center. Jesus is Alive! It is why we do what we do! Get greedy this week. Take out more than one or two. Take a whole handful of what Jesus has for you!!

## "Are You Truly Free?"
### John 8:36

Every year in America we celebrate the Fourth of July. We should all pray and thank God for our freedom. I notice too often in this land we live in that we take our freedom for granted. We shirk the responsibility of living in a free country and take advantage of all that this country has to offer. We have forgotten what it means to be free. We have come to the place in our lives where we believe our government owes us a living. We have our hand sticking out for a handout instead of reaching out to help our neighbor.

Let me point out a couple of things that I believe show our laziness and inability to be responsible. One of the simple things is the amount of litter on the streets and on the roadsides. If you notice as you drive down the road, litter is everywhere. People will throw anything out of their automobiles. You will see scraps of paper as well as cans and bottles. I have even seen full bags of trash or a fast-food bag full of the paper waste. I have often wondered what a person thinks when they throw trash out of their car. Either they think someone else will come along and pick up after them or that they just don't care about the land they live in. It is a shame that we don't think of our responsibility to keep our land clean.

Another item that just blows me away in this great land that we live in is the lack of courtesy. People can be so rude. We will not even take a moment to say hello, to hold a door for someone or to say "excuse me." We are all in such a hurry that we can only see the fact that we are being inconvenienced by someone who is taking life a little slower than we are.

This fact can be really brought out when we get behind the wheel of a car. We can be calm, simple folks one minute and then become monsters behind the wheel of an SUV. We have forgotten how fortunate we are to have the freedom to get around in this mobile society that we live in. We take these simple free pleasures for granted.

Now, the fact that we take these freedoms for granted got me to Just Thinking! Have you ever noticed how we trash God? We will take the precious promises and urgings of our Savior and throw them away for what we believe at the time is more important.

Have you ever noticed how much of a hurry we are to get done with the things of God? We come to church looking at our watch and wondering just how long we will have to be there. We wonder how long the preacher will preach and if we will beat the crowd to the restaurant. We will scan the Bible - we don't read it - and for most of us a quick, "Thank you Lord for the meal," is the only time we address God during the day.

The Bible says that salvation is a "free" gift from God. You can't earn it, buy it or be good enough to get it. Yet don't we take advantage of the fact that God was willing to give us this gift of freedom? The only true freedom we have is gained through Jesus Christ.

John records, "So, if the son sets you free, you will be free, indeed." I encourage all of us to be more grateful for all that God has given us. We need to take more responsibility for all that God has done for us. We need to celebrate our freedom in Christ by living each day for Him.

## "Avoiding the Boom!"
Galatians 6:7-8

We have spent several Fourths of July with Joshua and the family. For many years, Canton, N.C., has had a fireworks show on the evening of July 5th. One year we stayed around late to enjoy the explosions of light in the night sky. It was a beautiful evening for the show.

As the sky lit up with beautiful colors, we were about a mile away from where the fireworks were being shot. As the sparkling lights would shower through the night, we would then hear the explosion. I'm sure at the epicenter of the fireworks the explosion came before the emittance of the colorful lights, but since we were a distance away, the explosion always followed the lights. The reason is that light travels faster than sound. There was always a delay in the boom.

The delay in the explosions has got me to Just Thinking! The Bible says we will reap what we sow. "Do not be deceived. God cannot be mocked. A man reaps what he sows. Whoever sows to please the flesh, from the flesh will reap destruction; whoever sows to please the Spirit, from the Spirit will reap eternal life."

This law of the harvest says you always reap later than you sow. If we sow to destruction, we will reap destruction. If we sow good works, we will reap good works. We may not always see the results of our sowing immediately. We will probably have to wait. If we are sowing bad seed, we may think we have gotten away with something, but ultimately, we will have to reap the bad because of our behavior.

Sin is like that. When sin creeps at our door we often think it will not affect us much. We think that disobedience can't really be that bad. Yet, often we find out later the consequences of that disobedience. When King David sinned with Bathsheba it was nine long months before the child died and King David suffered the consequences of having Uriah killed. At the time it seemed like the right thing to do, but sin against God will have to be paid for.

There are consequences in all of our choices. Those consequences can be good or bad depending on our actions.

Ultimately, the boom of sin has to be paid for. Thankfully, Jesus came to defeat sin and death, and gives us the opportunity to receive forgiveness for our sin. He came to restore to us the life that God intended for us to live. If we put our faith and trust in Jesus, we do not ever have to wonder when the boom will come.

We can be assured that Jesus has taken away the explosion in our life.

My prayer for each of us is that we are not waiting to reap destruction, but that we are preparing to reap eternal life in Jesus Christ.

## "Thank You!"
### Psalm 9:1

Thanksgiving reminds me to reminisce about "Thank You" notes I have received over the past 40 years. Some of the greatest blessings in my life have come from "Thank You" notes. I have received them after doing a wedding or funeral. I have received them after helping a family through a difficult time in their lives. I have received them after just praying for someone or being there when they were going through surgery or sickness.

Some of my favorite "Thank You" notes have come when I didn't really even do anything. I have received them from people who just thanked me for helping them to grow in their spiritual journey. Some of these have come years after I ceased being their pastor, yet have kept in touch with them in various ways.

"Thank You" notes are a warming expression of sincere gratitude from one person to another. I know through the years I have cherished everyone I have ever received. They often come at just the right time. They help to inspire me to continue on the road that God has called me too.

As I reminisce about these "Thank You" notes, it has got me to Just Thinking! Have you ever sat down and wrote God a "Thank You" note? -just words that tell Him how glad you are that He loves you and cares for you. The Bible is full of thanks to God.

The psalmist is continually thanking God. Here is one example, "I will give thanks to you Lord, with all my heart, I will tell of your wonderful deeds."

I can't imagine how empty my life would be without God. I cannot imagine where I would be right now without the guiding hand of God in my life. There is no way mere words can express my thanks, but it is a start of letting God know how appreciative for all that He does in my life.

If you have never thought about writing God a "Thank You" note, Thanksgiving would be a good time to write one. You could express your gratitude for all God has done for you. It will put a smile on His face and help you to see just how blessed you are.

## "Looking Out for Each Other"
### Philippians 2:3-4

Each Thanksgiving we have been blessed to have our boys and their families on Saturday after Thanksgiving. We gather and eat a wonderful meal prepared by Peggy. Thanksgiving feast is her forte. My parents come over and feasted on turkey, dressing, fried okra, creamed corn, mac & cheese, sweet potato crunch (provided by Mom) and rolls. There are mini pecan pies and homemade chocolate cake (again provided by Mom).

After the meal the grandchildren played in the yard and had a big time. About 4 p.m. the annual front yard football game commenced. I sat on the sideline one year and watched as Joshua, Foster and Corbin went up against Caleb, Reid and James. I must say it was worth the wait.

Many years ago, on a Thanksgiving weekend we were with some friends and Caleb was about 3. The family we were with also had two boys and the fathers and sons gathered in the front yard to play football. Every time someone was tackled, Caleb would come into the play late and fall head first on the pile. After several late tackles, he got up one time and turned around to me and said, "Tackle, I just love to say the word." We have laughed about that incident for many years.

Well, it was like Deja vu. There they were playing football in the front yard and when one of the children was tackled, James would pile on. It didn't matter whether it was his team getting tackled or the other team, he just jumped on the pile. It was fun watching the little one run for a touchdown with the help of the others allowing it to happen. They would pretend to try and tackle Reid or James, but they would allow them to run all the way and score a touchdown. The smiles and laughter were good medicine for the heart of a papa. Of course, when anyone would score, the fans in the stands (Peggy, Laura, Sally Ann and I) would cheer and call their names.

Of course, every now and then one of the little ones would get frustrated because they didn't have the football and begin to pout and cry. We would have to take a timeout and fix the problem. Once everyone knew we had to take turns and allow everyone to play, things got back to fun and laughter. Foster, as the oldest grandchild was great at allowing the little ones to have the limelight. Corbin was just uninhibited, even though she was the only girl. She would go up and jump on the back of whoever had the ball and wrestle them to the ground.

I guess the best part of the game was the fact that everyone was enjoying the game and everyone was happy. Everyone was helping everyone to enjoy themselves and no one was being selfish.

Now, the football game and the way it is played has got me to Just Thinking! What would happen if we tried life the way our family football game is played in the front yard? What if we sought for everyone to be cheered on by everyone involved? What if we did our best to encourage and promote people being successful instead of putting people down?

What if we took time to explain sharing when we see someone who is being selfish and doesn't understand the concept of being a servant? Can you imagine life - or better yet - can you imagine a church where everyone is looking out for the needs of the others?

Paul wrote to the Philippians, "Do nothing out of selfish

ambition or vain conceit. Rather, in humility value others above yourselves, not looking to your own interests but each of you to the interest of others."

Can you imagine what it would look like if we sought the best in others? The church should be the show place for selflessness. We should be the ones serving others and seeking to show them the pleasure and happiness when we consider others better than ourselves.

My prayer is that we will help each other along the way. That we will support and enhance each other's experience. The truth is that everyone's a winner when they acknowledge Jesus. Don't allow the world to drag you down. Help pick the world up with the message of the Savior.

## "Thanks-living"
Psalm 119:175

On a Sunday night close to Thanksgiving, my wife, Peggy, led us in a hymn titled "Thanksgiving/Thanks-living." I had never sung it or even heard of it before, but there it was right in the Baptist Hymnal.

As we learned the new song and did our best at singing a new hymn, I was struck by the words of the hymn, especially the second verse. Here are the words:

"A life of living thankfulness moves lifeless words to willingness;

Willingness to serve our Father.

That service born of love, demands our hearts, our minds, our strength, our hands.

All the words of our Thanksgiving fail to say what we can show by our Thanks-living."

"Thanksgiving-Thanks-living" Words by Terry W. York; Music by Dennis Allen

How often in our lives do we say thank you? I would wager

that we say thanks a great deal, but how often in our lives do we live out the thankfulness in our actions? We should be grateful for all that God has done for us. We can begin with our salvation and continue into our everyday needs where He supplies grace and mercy.

If we truly access our situations, we know that we have life and breath because of the Lord's granting us the ability to live. We have to truly acknowledge if we are honest with ourselves that everything we have is because of God and His goodness. Although we like to claim control of our lives, if we really are paying attention, we know that God is much bigger and greater than we are and we need Him and His goodness to sustain all that we have and all that we are.

The early pilgrims recognized that without God and His protection and provision they would not have survived. Therefore, they set aside a very special day just to say thanks. We now celebrate this holiday and after gorging ourselves on wonderful delicacies, family and football, we remember somewhere along the way to say "Thanks."

Now the words to this song and of course this wonderful season of the year have got me to Just Thinking! What if I began to show my thanks instead of just saying my thanks? What if my service began to be an expression of my thankfulness to God for His many blessings? What if my thanksgiving gave way to thanks-living?

The Psalmist said, "Let me live that I may praise you..." I don't want my thanks to be just one day a year, but every day of the year. God doesn't pour out his blessings on just a few days each year, but He pours out these blessings continually. So, shouldn't we conclude that our service to God should be a year-round gift of thanks to the God who gave all for me? What a way to show my thanks, my love and my dependence of the God whom I trust with all of my heart.

I want God to see in my life a reflection of my gratitude for all that He has done for me. I want Him to see me loving others like He loves me. I want Him to see my blessing others like He has blessed me. Isn't that a great way to show our thankfulness? Once more hear the words of the final phrase of the song which is repeated after each verse, "All the words of our Thanksgiving fail to say what we can show by our Thanks-living."

Let's start today and, by the way, "Happy Thanks-living!"

## "A Good Life"
### John 10:10

It is always fun to have our children and grandchildren home for the weekend after Thanksgiving. We enjoyed them as always and share time together with activities and food. One of my favorite things to do with the grandchildren is to watch and hear them laugh. Most of the time it is the simplest of things that gets them laughing. Whether it is reading a funny book, chasing a ball in the hall, or tickling them while they are in your lap, for me laughter is truly the best medicine.

They each have distinctive and noisy laughs. Foster has to be reminded not to wet his pants if he laughs really hard. When Corbin laughs, her whole face lights up with the prettiest smile. When Reid laughs, his whole body shakes with laughter. James just drops his head and laughs hysterically. They are all so full of life when they laugh and you know they do not have a care in the world.

As a grandparent, it makes you feel good to know that your grandchildren are happy and full of life. As a parent, you feel good knowing that your children are settled in their lives and doing well. As a Christian parent, it thrills you to know your children are taking your grandchildren to church and they are learning about Jesus and how much He loves them. When I think about how blessed I am as a father and grandfather, it puts a big smile on my face.

Now, the laughing and joy on my grandchildren's faces has

got me to Just Thinking! Does God have a smile on your face about your life? Is your life full of laughter and joy or are you always worried, stressed, sad and out of sorts? When God looks into your heart does He see contentment or does He see a life unsettled?

The God of the universe who sent His son into the world so that the world may find life wants His children to be happy. He is not happy when He sees His children's life in a mess. He is not smiling when His children are not satisfied with their life. He does not understand when His children are worried about things they cannot control and will not just completely trust in Him.

Jesus made this statement when He was stressing the point that He was the Good Shepherd, "The thief (referring to Satan) comes to steal, kill and destroy, but I (Jesus) have come to give you life and give it to you abundantly."

When we allow our circumstances to win the day, then we have allowed Satan to come in and steal life away from us. When we allow our mood to make us hard to live with, then we allow Satan to kill our relationships and sense of being. When we allow life to dictate who we are and what we become, then we allow Satan to destroy everything that God wants us to be.

If Jesus is the Good Shepherd, then His desire is for us to have a good life. That means we should take advantage of every opportunity we have to enjoy the life He has blessed us with.

Do not allow your circumstances or your attitude to define who you are. Allow the Spirit of God that lives in you if you are a Christian to define who you are. God has created you with a purpose. When we allow the Spirit to teach us that purpose, then we find the "good" life that God wants us to have. Do not allow your situation to define you. Allow Jesus to define you and you will experience the laughter of a good life.

JUST THINKING!

## "Light Up Your Life"
### Psalm 119:105; Matthew 5:14-16; 1 John 1:4-5

We were in Brunswick, Ga., one year and found out that the Christmas lights at Jekyll Island were still on display. So, on a Friday night we drove over to take a look. As we drove onto the island, there was a sign that pointed to a self-guided tour of the lights. We followed the tour and were delighted at the festival of lights that we saw. There was no doubt that the lights that were illuminating the trees were LED lights. When they draped them in the trees, they allowed them to fall down as the Spanish moss hangs and it was beautiful. There were several places where they had scenes. One was of a penguin sliding into the water. The lights actually outlined the penguin as it slid into the water. That was also true when it jumped out of the water. We drove down one road that had the 12 days of Christmas in lights. There were actually 12 drummers drumming and all the rest. We saw a Christmas tree that had more than 35,000 lights on it. Overall, officials said there were over 500,000 lights on the tour. It was really amazing and it was astonishing how bright the LED lights were.

At one church where I ministered, we replaced our chandelier lights with LED lights. It was amazing how much brighter the sanctuary was after the change. Someone even told me that maybe we needed to leave the recessed lights off because the others were so bright. The older I get the more light I need to be able to read. Even with glasses, light makes a big difference in my ability to see clearly. The more light, the better we see.

We know this to be true because all of us have seen the difference when the batteries on a flashlight are low. You still have a little light, but when the batteries are new the light is brighter and makes finding your way much easier.

Now, all this talk about bright lights has got me to Just Thinking! How bright is your Christian journey? Is your path well lighted so you can see where it is that the Spirit of God is leading you, or are you lost in some darkness? Are you struggling with direction because to you the pathway is not clearly lit?

The Bible talks about light. It uses it in a very positive way. In the Psalms it says, "Your word is a lamp to my feet and a light to my path."

Reading and studying God's word is a great way to have your path illuminated and directed by God. Jesus talks about Christians being light to the world. He said, "You are the light of the world. A city that is set on a hill cannot be hidden. Nor do they light a lamp and put it under a basket, but on a lampstand, and it gives light to all who are in the house. Let your light so shine before men, that they may see your good works and glorify your Father in heaven."

We need God's light to shine through us so that we might illuminate the way for others to see. John says that light overcomes darkness, "In Him was life, and the life was the light of men. And the light shines in the darkness, and the darkness did not comprehend it." When we are in Christ, we have the light of life in us and darkness cannot win.

Let's ask ourselves some questions: Are we going through life worried about the darkness? Are we going through life hiding our light? Jesus gives light to all who ask. Jesus wants us to shine bright in a darkened world. Let's allow the light of God's Spirit to permeate every situation in which we find ourselves involved. Let's let the light of Jesus shine like an LED bulb. Don't allow your light to be dimmed, but give it full exposure to make a difference in your own life and the life of others.

## "Real or Imagined?"
John 3:16; Joshua 24:15

I want to relate to you a real-life story that I witnessed:

A child came home on Christmas night to see Santa in her living room setting up a doll house. She was tentative at first as she slowly came around the corner and looked into the room. Santa's back was to her. She was followed by her parents and older sister. The older sister was hanging back, shy and a little scared.

The smaller child, about 4, walked slowly into the room and spoke very softly, "Santa Claus?" Santa stood and turned around with a great big grin on his face. The little girl rushed up to him and grabbed him around the knees. Santa reached down and picked up the little girl and they gave each other a great big hug. She said, "It is really you!"

Santa spoke very softly to the little girl and told her he hated to leave her so soon, but he had many places to go and many things to do. He told her that he hoped she liked what he had brought her. He sat her down and looked at the older sister who was now in front of her parents. He called her name and said that he had brought her some special things also. He pointed to a corner where a bicycle was sitting. The little girl ran into Santa's arms and hugged him and kissed him on the cheek. He sat her down and she went to look at the bicycle. Santa nodded to the parents and slipped out the room and out of the door.

For the next week or more, the little girls told all of their friends about finding Santa Claus in their home. They could not stop telling this wonderful news and they would tell anyone who would stop to listen. People never hesitated to listen and smile and tell the little girls how happy they were for them. These two girls are now grown women and have families of their own. I am not sure if they remember Santa being in their house that night, but it will be a night I will never forget: the excitement and astonishment in their eyes; the expressions on their faces; the very fact that Santa was holding and speaking to them. The magic of the night is etched in my mind.

Now, this story is true. It really happened. And remembering it has got me to Just Thinking!! Do you remember the time when you first met Jesus? Do you remember being astounded? Do you remember being amazed and overjoyed? Did you tell anyone who would listen about your encounter and how it changed your life? I doubt very seriously those two grown women tell the story of Santa in their house anymore. It makes me wonder how many of us who have met Jesus have stopped telling our story. Have we lost the luster of a Savior born in a manger who came to die for our sins? Jesus was born for you! He was born so that all who believe in Him "should not perish but have everlasting life." Maybe you have grown up and decided that maybe Jesus isn't real like some believe Santa Claus is not real. Maybe you have decided that there is no real magic in finding peace in Jesus Christ. Maybe you have forgotten what it was like to be lost in your sin without any hope.

Christmas is a time to be reminded that Jesus is real. We celebrate not to have a happy holiday, but to have a Merry Christmas. Without Christ there is no real Christmas. I know the world has tried to steal away the real meaning by gifts and fanfare and all types of festivities. Yet without the story of Jesus, we wouldn't even have a holiday. We wouldn't even know to give gifts. We wouldn't even know that there can be "Peace on earth and good will to all mankind."

So, I guess I will end this Christmas story with a very famous saying from Joshua, the man who led Israel into the Promised Land. I will borrow it from him and make it relevant to today. "Choose you today whom you will serve. Will it be the people who run the nation? Will it be the Hollywood crowd who runs our lives from a television? Will it be the social media crowd who knows our every wish? Choose, but for me and my house we will celebrate and worship the King born in a manger, died on a cross, and rose again and lives in our hearts by the Holy Spirit!"

Merry Christmas!!

## "Saying Yes to Jesus"
Acts 16:31

Let me tell you about one of the best Christmas presents I ever received. One Christmas Eve as we were sitting around waiting on the Christmas Eve service, I received a Facetime call from my oldest son, Joshua. He said Foster had something to say to me and Pearl (what he calls Peggy).

So, I got Pearl and Foster came on the phone with the biggest smile and said, "Papa, I got saved tonight." Well, needless to say, I was overjoyed. Tears of joy filled my eyes and Peggy and I just started telling Foster how proud we were of him and his decision to follow Jesus. We told him it was the best Christmas present ever.

As Foster moved away from the phone, Joshua explained to us how he began asking questions again tonight during the service and afterwards. He had asked a little bit last year, but this year he wouldn't let up. Joshua said he got the little book that I had used almost 30 years ago when I led him to the Lord and let Foster guide himself through the plan of salvation. At the end Foster was ready to invite Jesus into his heart.

Now, the next best thing to come out of this call was what Foster told me before he moved away from the phone. He said, "And Papa, I want you to baptize me." Well, that was a double Christmas present for me. I told him I would be honored to do it.

So, on Sunday, Jan. 12 of the next year, I went to Canton to baptize my oldest grandchild. I remember the day I baptized Joshua. I had to submerge a large pot for him to stand on so that he would be tall enough to see over the edge of the baptistery. Joshua was 7.

Now, this wonderful news of Foster getting saved has got me to Just Thinking! God never stops using the message of Jesus to change lives and recreate new lives. Foster is a very smart little boy. If you don't take my word for it, hang around him a little while and question him about things and you will find out how smart he is.

He had been listening and learning about God and his son, Jesus. He was contemplating these things in his brain and when the time was right, he told his dad he was ready to ask Jesus into his heart.

Foster was 8 when this happened. He will learn and grow a great deal in his love for and devotion to Jesus. He will need good teachers and leaders to help him and come along beside him to help him mature into a fine Christian young man.

I cannot wait to see what God is going to do in this young man's life. I am so glad that Jesus is still in the life-changing business. I am glad that He doesn't stop with one generation or skip a generation. I can now look at my family and see four generations where the grace of Jesus has moved into a life and made a difference. I am proud of my son and the foundation he is building with his children. I can't wait until I get the call for Corbin, Reid and James. I just believe with the parents setting the example that it will not be long before these children see their need for someone to save them from their sins.

And it can be true with every family. It only takes one person to finally give in to the urging of the Holy Spirit and then you can watch what God can do in your family. When Paul and Silas encountered the Philippian jailer, he was getting ready to kill himself. After the urging of Paul, he hesitated and asked about how to be saved. The Bible records Paul's words, "Believe in the Lord Jesus, and you will be saved – you and your household."

Paul knew that if Jesus got hold of one person in the house, then Jesus had a better chance of getting the rest of them. When people see the change that Jesus makes in your life, then they want the same thing.

## "Are You Excited with Anticipation?"
Acts 1:11; John 14:3; Titus 2:13

I can't remember if it was delivered to the house or we picked one up at the store, but when I was young every year around Thanksgiving, I couldn't wait to get my hands on the Sears &

Roebuck Christmas catalog. Every year, I would sit down and begin perusing the toy section of the huge book. I would also have to mark two NFL team sweatshirts that Mom bought me every year.

Hardly a page went by where there wasn't something that I marked that I would be glad to have at Christmas. The pages of that catalog were dog-eared and ready for Dad and Mom to show Santa so that he would make all the right choices for Christmas Day.

There wasn't just one look at that catalog. I would pick it up just about every day between Thanksgiving and Christmas. Sometimes, things were added to my list - but nothing ever got subtracted. I knew I wouldn't get all I wanted, but I would put a special star on those things that I felt like I couldn't live without.

The anticipation of those Christmas Days was so much fun. There were many fun toys that came my way on those days. I remember the fun of opening up the hall door and, as a family, going into the family room to discover all that Santa had left.

I remember the GI Joes that he brought one Christmas. One of my favorite Christmases was the time he brought my bicycle. I still remember it was red. I got walkie talkies one Christmas. There was a football, a Hot Wheel drag race set and many more wonderful gifts. Santa was definitely better to me than I probably was at being a good boy all year long.

As a child, I remember everyone telling me that Santa came on the evening of Dec. 24. I would go to sleep early that night hoping that I might awaken and catch him at his craft one night. I never did. I slept right through it every Christmas Eve. Yet, every Christmas I woke up Santa had left my gifts around the Christmas tree for me to see and enjoy. I never once woke up to find he didn't come or that he had been delayed. Every year it was the same: Santa's coming. And he did!

Now, reminiscing about Christmas as a little boy has got me to Just Thinking about another promise. The angels said to the disciples as Jesus was being taken into heaven, "Men of Galilee," they said, "why do you stand there looking into the sky? This same Jesus, who has been taken from you into heaven, will come back in the same way you have seen him go into heaven." There it is, a promise.

And didn't Jesus also say, "I go to prepare a place for you. If I go and prepare a place for you, I will come again to receive you. So that where I am you may be also."? A promise!

And Paul remarked to Titus, "while we wait for the blessed hope — the appearing of the glory of our great God and Savior, Jesus Christ..." There it is again, another promise.

So, the question comes to mind: Am I anticipating the return of Jesus like I did the coming of Santa each year? Do I look forward to His return with great anticipation knowing that when I open that door, I will receive more than I have ever received here on earth? Am I as excited about all the possibilities of seeing my Savior face to face?

I want to be as excited to see Jesus as I was when I tried to stay awake to see Santa. I want to look Him straight in the face and throw my arms around Him and celebrate the very fact that He is my Savior, my all in all. I want to show Him my gratitude with the joy in my heart and the smile on my face. I don't ever want to quit anticipating the return of Jesus. It is a promise and I know it will happen!

## "The Very First Christmas"
### Isaiah 9:6

I was trying to remember my first Christmas. Well, it wasn't actually my first Christmas, but it was the first one I could remember. I'm sure if someone like my mom jogged my memory, I probably could remember others, but the one I remember the most is the one where I got a new bicycle. It was red and had a white seat. It wasn't fancy like the ones you see today. It was just a plain bicycle.

Of course, one of the things I remember about that year was that unlike most Christmases in South Georgia, this one was especially cold. Mom and Dad weren't really keen about the idea of going outside and riding, but after much begging and bundling up, they finally allowed me to ride around the block a couple of times. I had some great times on that bike and remember vividly the morning I saw it. I had it for many years and it served me well.

Those memories got me to Just Thinking! Every year we remember the very first Christmas. We retell the story of the greatest gift of all. It wasn't a bicycle, a dolly, or a wagon. It wasn't a new car, a diamond ring, or a new set of golf clubs. It was a person. The Bible calls Him, "Wonderful Counselor, Almighty God, Everlasting Father, Prince of Peace, Emmanuel, Jesus, Christ the Lord, Savior is His name."

It is no wonder that we remember every detail: Angels, Star, Shepherds, Wise Men, Manger, Animals, Swaddling Clothes, Stable, Mary & Joseph. It is the greatest story ever told. How could we ever forget? Don't forget! "Go Tell It On the Mountain!" The greatest Christmas of ALL!

## "No Conveniences"
### Luke 2:14; 20

One Christmas season I was considering all of the convenient ways Christmas has changed. If you don't know what to buy as a gift for someone, just buy them a gift card or gift certificate. If you don't want to wrap things, just put them in a bag and put tissue paper over it. If you don't want to purchase a tree or put on the lights, just buy an artificial tree that is pre-lit. If you really just don't want to do anything, you can now hire people who will come into your house and decorate for you. If you don't want to cook, just order your Christmas dinner from any grocer's deli. They will have it ready for you to pick up, and all you have to do is heat it up. If you don't want to be hassled with shopping traffic and crowded stores, just sit down at your computer and do all of your shopping online. They will deliver all of your gifts right to your door. Don't want to have to worry about how to decorate the outside? That's OK. Now you can just buy inflatable decorations that will make your yard come alive. So much for work and hassle and time spent being creative.

All of this convenience stuff got me to Just Thinking! I am so glad that God didn't take any shortcuts in sending Jesus. Maybe we just need to read the Christmas story really slowly. Take time to see each detail and every action that had to be planned down to the moment. Joseph didn't take any shortcuts after Gabriel spoke to him. Mary asked Gabriel a question about the conception, but after it was explained, she sang a song to God's greatness. You and I might have gotten really frustrated with "no room in the inn," but Joseph just took what was offered and God just orchestrated a beautiful "Silent Night." There was no convenience in shepherds leaving their flock after being scared to death by a bunch of angels singing "Glory to God in the highest and Peace on earth to all mankind." And upon finding the child just as the angels said, "They told everyone and all were amazed." Of course, with the birth of Jesus, Mary "just pondered all of these things in her heart."

There was no convenience in wise men making a trek across the desert to follow a star to find the "Christ" child. I am so glad that God took every action to bring His son to us on Christmas. Every action and every movement was done "just so" we could one day "worship the King." And, just remember that convenience was never an option for Jesus to leave heaven and come to earth to bring salvation to all of us. I hope that you will not find a shortcut when celebrating Christmas.

## CHAPTER FOUR
# JUST THINKING... ABOUT THE WEATHER!

### "Are You Protected in the Storm?"
Matthew 8:27

When my youngest son was small, he didn't like thunderstorms. He was really afraid of thunder and loud noises. Late one evening in the early spring, when thunderstorms happen, we had a really severe one about bedtime. Peggy and I were in bed watching television when the thunder and lightning began. It was no time before Caleb and Joshua were in our bedroom hopping up in the bed with us. Every time the thunder would rumble, Caleb would squish down into the covers and pull the blanket over his head.

Being a good and protective father, I pulled Caleb up into my arms and reassured him that there was nothing to worry about and everything was going to be OK. Well, I had no sooner gotten those words out of my mouth when a large crack of thunder and a bolt of lightning struck. It was so close that our TV sparked and went black, the lights went out and we all jumped at the sound.

About that time, I looked for Caleb and I couldn't find him. He had just been in my arms and now I didn't see him. After a few seconds I realized that he had jumped from my arms, dug down into the covers and was now huddled into the bottom of the bed. He was shaking and terribly afraid. It took me a minute to convince him everything was OK and he could come out from hiding. Needless to say, I was not convinced he believed me, but we were no worse for wear.

Now that storm and Caleb's reaction has got me to Just Thinking! Can you imagine what it was like for the disciples out on the sea when the storm came up and Jesus was in the boat asleep? The Bible says the wind and the waves were tossing the ship and they were all afraid they were going to die. They were in panic - and these were experienced fishermen!

Yet, when they woke Jesus up, He was not alarmed. He just went up on deck and calmed the storms with a few words. The disciples were amazed. They recognized that there was something special about Jesus. They even remarked among themselves what kind of man could calm the wind and the seas.

Well, if you know Jesus, you know that He can calm the storms in your life. You know that He holds the power to soften the blow, no matter how hard the wind blows. He can calm the seas and bring us peace even in the midst of the storm. As a pastor, I have seen Jesus calm many storms. I have watched him do it for others and seen him do it in my own life. Sometimes it is immediate, sometimes it takes some time, but He always provides the peace to make it through any storm.

I do not know what kind of storm you are in, but I want to encourage you to call on the one who can calm the storm in your life. Seek out Jesus and let Him bring you peace.

## "Is the Wind Blowing in Your Life?"
### John 3:8

Have you ever seen the wind? One evening we experienced a violent windstorm. By the way, I hope your quick answer to my first question wasn't yes. None of us can see the wind. We can see the effects of the wind. Our lights blinked a time or two and once we heard a loud crash.

I went outside to see if anything bad had happened and found out that a door that we had purchased for our back porch and not put up yet had blown over. My dog came outside with me and, while we were out, the wind made an awful sound and the dog responded by running for cover. It is pretty scary to see what the wind can do. As I got up the next morning and drove around town, I once again saw tree limbs downed and signs knocked over. I even talked to a few people who lost electricity for a few hours.

The wind came out of nowhere. I wasn't watching the weather or a local channel at the time and wasn't aware that a storm was brewing. After the first episode of the lights blinking, we turned to a local channel and saw the warnings of high winds, but no tornadoes likely. Well, that was good news but you couldn't prove it by the way the wind was whipping and blowing at our house. Yet, in just a short time, the threat was over and things calmed down considerably. We all went to bed and slept peacefully until the next morning.

All of that wind got me to Just Thinking. Do you remember what Jesus said about the wind? Here are His words as he was speaking to Nicodemus, "The wind blows wherever it pleases. You hear its sound, but you cannot tell where it comes from or where it is going. So it is with everyone born of the Spirit."

Now, if that is true about everyone born of the Spirit, why is it that we Christians have become so predictable? Go to most churches and we are about the same. We do about the same things in our worship services. Oh, there will be minor differences, but for most we sing, pray, take up an offering and listen to the preacher. We then have a time of invitation. That is a time when we are all asked to respond to something that God may be placing on our hearts and minds. Yet, I would dare say that most of us are not blown like the wind. Most of us are stuck to our pews. We don't respond because we are afraid of what others will think or say. We don't respond because, in truth, we have not prepared to meet God today and so we would not know how to act if we did respond.

In fact, we may be just the opposite of what Jesus wanted us to be. We may be stuck in a religious rut. I would love to see a group of Spirit-led wind-blown Christians who are moved by the love and compassion of Jesus Christ, who are not afraid of what others think or say. I will tell you one thing: if that breaks out in any community it would get people's attention just like a strong wind. I pray it won't go away as quickly.

## "Are You Content?"
### 1 Thessalonians 5:16-18

I love summertime when we are in for some warm weather. I love the 80's and 90's. I would rather have the temperature in the 100's than the teens and 20's. Now, I know we are all different. I talk to people about the weather all the time and you find some who like it hot, some who like it cold and some who are never satisfied no matter the temperature. Every now and then, I find someone who likes all kinds of weather. They think the change of seasons is good for us and they don't mind whatever the weather. For me though, give me warm sunshine and long days.

Now, all of this summertime talk has got me to Just Thinking! Have you ever noticed how much people are not satisfied with their circumstances? We are always complaining. Whether it is about the weather or our job or our family situation or our church, we never seem to be satisfied. We are always looking for better weather, more pay for our work, more peace in our family, or a better preacher, better music, better Sunday school teacher, better facilities, etc., etc. We never seem to be satisfied.

I believe the people who live longer and live with less stress are those who are content in whatever their situation. We look at people like this with a turn of our head and a suspicious expression. We wonder how anyone could be content with all situations. We probably think that they are either hiding something or just are not in touch with reality. Yet, God's word tells us that to be content in every situation is God's desire for us. Listen to the words of Paul as he encourages the church at Thessalonica, "Be joyful always; pray continually; give thanks in all circumstances, for this is God's will for you in Christ Jesus." No matter our circumstances we are to give thanks.

I have always believed that we are happier when we give thanks for all that God has given to us. I have always believed that if I just look around, I can find someone else worse off than I am. A few years ago, I tried to go a full 45 days without complaining. I did pretty well, but to be honest, it was very hard. I do believe, though, I was happier when I just accepted the circumstances and realized that no matter the outcome, no matter the weather, no matter the problems, God is always in control. I pray that you will know satisfaction in all of your life.

## "In or Out?"
### Hebrews 12:28-29

I was riding down the road the other day listening to the radio. There was a weather broadcast that went something like this. "It will be mostly cloudy today with a high around 50 degrees. There is a slight chance of rain in the forecast with a greater chance of rain tomorrow and the next day. The temperature will stay in the low 50's or the high 40's. By the way, if you don't like cold, wet, damp weather you can take a trip to Sydney, Australia, where today's high is 111." I thought seriously about flying to Sydney.

You see, I don't care much for cold, wet, damp weather. I don't mind the wet and damp sometimes, but I definitely do not like the cold. I like the warm, hot climate. I was so glad to hear the other day that winter had finally arrived. Now, I know it won't be much longer before spring gets here.

Let's face it, if I'm given the choice of wrapping up in a throw blanket, sipping on hot chocolate, listening to the heater run while it's set on 80 and still being cold versus sitting in the air conditioning in my shorts, stretched out in my recliner watching a ball game, drinking a tall glass of ice-cold lemonade; which do you think I will choose? No comparison.

The forecast got me to Just Thinking! There is no comparison to being hot or cold for Jesus. In the religious community there are many people who think being a member of a church is wrapping up in their pew, sipping on communion juice and listening to the preacher run on for 30 minutes once a week. That does not constitute being on fire for Jesus. There is nothing like getting into the game. We need to unwrap, loosen up and participate in the activities of all that God has for us. He has provided us with all we need to live an abundant life.

My prayer for all of us is that we will get into the game. Let's not be on and off like the weather. Remember the words of the writer of Hebrews, "Therefore, since we are receiving a kingdom that cannot be shaken, let us be thankful, and so worship God acceptably with reverence and awe, for our 'God is a consuming fire.'"

## "Light or Dark?"
### John 1:4

The summer solstice is either June 20, 21, Or 22. On that day, the sun is at its furthest point north, right above the Tropic of Cancer. Astronomers tell us that day provides approximately 15 hours of daylight. If you are a person like me who enjoys the daylight hours, there is good news and bad news in that fact. The good news is that you have plenty of time to bask in the daylight. The bad news is that after that the days will begin to get shorter for the next six months.

Let me share with you two views of light and dark. I know someone who took a trip to Iceland. They told me that for a

24-hour period it never got dark. It was light the whole day. They said it never even got twilight.

One summer, the family and I went up in the mountains for a few days. We visited one of the caverns. When we got way back up under the mountain, our guide turned off all the lights and we were in total darkness. I mean, I literally could not see my hand in front of my face.

The light and dark have got me to Just Thinking! In spiritual terms, that must be what it is like to be a child of God compared to not being a child of God. As a child of God, we are children of Light. When we are not His children we walk in darkness. Being a child of God is living where the light never goes out. Refusing to be a child of God is living in darkness never having seen the light. If you are living in darkness, let the Holy Spirit be your guide to turn on the Light of Jesus in your life. "In Him was life; and the life was the light of men."

## "How Do You React to the Storm?"
### Matthew 5:45

One day a group of us from the church went to Georgetown and took a boat ride down the river. On the way back in we got caught in the middle of a thunderstorm. With about 30 of us on an open pontoon boat with a captain and one other worker, we all gathered in the middle of the boat and hoped for a safe return to the dock.

As the lightning and thunder and rain pelted us on the river, one man hid in the bathroom. Many crouched down in the middle of the boat and were protected by others. Some huddled up with their spouse and did their best to protect. All joked about praying and giving an invitation and getting volunteers for church service.

As I look back on the event, it came to my attention that although all of us were affected in one way or another by the storm, not all of us were affected the same way. Some got off the boat and looked as if nothing had happened. Some got off and their hair was windblown and they were slightly wet. Some got off the boat quickly. Others waited their turn. Some of the US got off soaking wet.

The results of the storm got me to Just Thinking! How often do we get caught in the storms of life and see differing results? The storm of cancer hits our family and we lose a family member to death. The storm of cancer hits another family and that member is cured. An automobile accident takes the life of an innocent individual who was not at fault. An automobile accident is caused by a reckless driver and the driver is spared. The hurricane rips open my home and destroys my property while my neighbor's home and property are spared. The thief comes in and steals and ransacks my neighbor's home, but leaves my property untouched. My family is besieged by the evils of alcohol and drugs, while my neighbor's family is left unscathed from the world.

Yet, the scriptures say, "This is what God does. He gives His best - the sun to warm and the rain to nourish - to everyone, regardless: the good and bad, the nice and nasty." (Matthew 5:45, The Message)

What you do with what God gives to you is up to you! In the storms of your life, I pray that you will not panic, but pray; do not fear, but have faith; do not give up, but find grace; do not turn away, but trust. Allow the God who created you to keep you and give you peace.

### "God's Got You!"
Matthew 6:26

"Rain, rain, go away, come again another day." Ever had a time when you felt you had too much rain? Like you think it will never stop raining. When I was sitting at my computer terminal and typing this article, guess what it was doing outside? You've got it: RAINING.

Now, don't misunderstand me. I know we need rain. I know God has given us just what we need for our everyday living, but to be honest during times like this I think we've had enough rain. The rain has got me to Just Thinking. Isn't that the way it is in our lives? We are never satisfied with what God has for us. We are always telling Him what we think we need. I mean, it's like we have a better handle on our life than He does. Let's face it. Wasn't it Jesus who said, "Look at the birds of the air; they do not sow or reap or store away in barns, and yet your heavenly Father feeds them. Are you not much more valuable than they?"

The answer is YES! We are more valuable to Him than the birds or the air. I hope you will think about how important you are to God. Your heavenly Father loves you and wants to care for you. So let Him. "OK, Lord let it RAIN!"

## "Cleaning Up Our Trash!"
### Hebrews 10:25

Have you ever experienced a hurricane? Having lived near the coast for a good part of my life, we have had the displeasure of experiencing a few. We have been blessed because we have not been in the direct path, but were close enough to see wind and storm damage. After the storm the yard is literally strewn with limbs and debris that have to be cleaned up. After one storm, I know personally I made numerous trips to the county dump station to throw away limbs and straw.

Now, every time I would go to the dump, I would bump into people I knew. I even remarked to Peggy that we could have had church with all the people I saw.

Seeing so many people from our church got me to Just Thinking! Why did so many people make a trip to the trash dump? Why was I bumping into so many people I knew? The trash dump is not a very attractive place to go and meet people. Why was I having such a great day meeting and visiting with these people? I think I know why. You see, we all saw the necessity of cleaning up our yards and getting rid of the trash.

People don't go to the dump to meet people. They don't go to socialize or visit. They go out of necessity to get rid of their trash. This thought got me thinking. Why isn't the church thought of in the same way? What if we saw a necessity to attend church? What if we saw the need to dump our trash and clean up our lives? Shouldn't church be a place where we go out of necessity? Shouldn't church be a place where we can dump the trash (sin) of our lives and clean up our hearts?

I hope you will take heart in the words of the writer of Hebrews, "Do not forsake the assembling of yourselves together..." When the storms of life leave your yard cluttered, bring your debris to the Lord. He knows how to get rid of the trash!

## "How White are You?"
### Isaiah 1:18

Let me let you in on a fact about me: I am not a fan of snow. I am not a cold weather fan and I sure do not like snow. It just seems to be an inconvenience and causes more trouble than it's worth. I will have to say that it is pretty when it is falling.

I guess I would like it better if it only fell on the ground and stayed off of the road. The beauty of the snow is the purity of the white flakes as they pile up and blanket the ground. The white makes everything look so clean and pure.

Now, I know many of you reading this probably love snow. If you live in the South, you might wish you got more snow so you could enjoy the beauty of the white covered fields. I will admit that after a snowfall there is much to say about a fresh covering of the white flakes.

Now, as I write about snow it has got me to Just Thinking!

Are you not amazed as I am about why God created snow white? Think how odd it would have been if when the snow fell it was a different color. What if it was blue? Or what if it was yellow? Blue and yellow are pretty colors, but they just wouldn't convey the same message. Can you imagine anything whiter than snow? The prophet Isaiah said that when God cleanses us from our sins that we would be washed, "whiter than snow!"

I am Just Thinking about what a wonderful fresh start there is to a life that gets a cleansing from a wonderful forgiving God. When God cleanses you of your sins it is as though a fresh blanket of snow has fallen on your life. I hope that the forgiveness of God has washed you whiter than snow. That is one type of snow that I will never get enough of!!

## "Who Is Right?"
### Acts 1:7

Have you ever noticed the inconsistency of weather forecasters? Let me share with you a story of the forecast once when we lived in the upstate of South Carolina. They said that the mountains would not get any snow until after it hit the upstate of South Carolina. That was on Monday. On Tuesday, my son Joshua called from the North Carolina mountains and said they had dismissed school at 10 am and that he had about 3 1/2 inches of snow on the ground.

The whole time the weather people were telling us that we would maybe get up to 12 inches of snow and the storm would be one of the worst we had seen since 2005's ice storm.

Well, I wasn't in the upstate in 2005, but we had snow about three years ago. We got more than eight inches and were in the house for several days and it seemed worse than the storm I mentioned above. I kept hearing them tell me when the snow would start. It never did start when they said it would; it was always later. Then, to really seal the deal for me, the forecaster said after we had already received five inches on Wednesday that the worst was yet to come. We never got any more snow after the initial snow. Go figure!

People got frantic. The bread and milk were gone. There was no ice melt, so people sought recipes on how to make your own ice melt. On Tuesday the snow didn't stick on the roads, but on Wednesday the roads were covered. There was constant extended news coverage on the weather. But guess what: things got back to normal and the temperature was supposed to be 70.

If I ever change professions, I want to be a weatherman. You don't have to be right about anything; just guess. And the great news is if you are wrong, you can always blame it on the computer model.

All of these prophetic weather reports got me to Just Thinking! The Bible is full of prophecy. There is an Old Testament prophecy that predicts the fall of the Jewish nation and the exile of its people. There is an Old Testament prophecy about the coming of the Messiah. There is prophecy about the birth of babies, the destruction of property, and miracles. The New Testament is full of prophecy, also. It tells that one day Jesus will return.

Now, there are a great deal of people who research the Bible, read the text and ponder its meaning. They are searching for the secret of the unknown. They make prophecies about the impending doom of the world and Jesus's return. Some of them give us dates to look for and times to get ready. So far, no one who has set a date has been correct.

Now, there is nothing wrong with asking "When will Jesus return?" The Apostles asked, "Lord, will you now restore the Kingdom?" The problem seems to be with Jesus's answer: "It is not for you to know the time or dates the Father has set by His own authority."

Some just don't want to accept the fact that the Father isn't going to tell anyone until it is time. Now, does that mean we need to forget about it? Absolutely not! We need to remind everyone that no one knows the time or day, but the diligent servant will always be ready. And the diligent servant will also do their best to make sure others are ready.

Are you ready? The scriptures say that Jesus will return when we least expect it. I believe that the one who made this prognostication knows what He's talking about.

### "Are You Growing?"
1 Peter 2:2-3

I love it when the weatherman says the high will be in the 70's. I love it when he says there will be plenty of sunshine for the next few days and we will be getting a taste of spring. I don't know about you, but I love the taste of spring. I want a full course meal.

Spring can't get here any too soon for me. I am not a cold weather person. The cold and wind and rain and snow — that is for the birds. I am ready to go out of the house in the morning without a coat. I am ready to sit outside in the evenings and enjoy the night air. I am ready to start working in my flower garden and see the roses bloom. (I am not ready to cut grass, but thankfully someone does that for me.) I am ready for the days to get longer and the sun to shine brighter. I am ready to sweat.

One of the things that I really love about spring is the new growth. I am anticipating my weeping willow trees to take off again this year. Last year, my saplings went from a three-foot stick to a tree more than five feet tall with many branches. I wait as I watch for my roses that we transplanted to start budding, and I get to wear a real rose some Sundays. I will help Dad with a garden at his house this year, and I can't wait for the fresh vegetables and vine-ripe tomatoes. When the trees, flowers, and vegetables grow, it just reminds me that there is something out there that is greater than I.

The warm weather and sunshine have got me to Just Thinking! When is the spring of your spiritual life? When can others begin to see new growth in your Christian life? I do not want my life to be a reflection of the same old things. We remember singing "Give me that ol' time religion," but that "ol' time religion" changed people into a newness of life.

What areas of your life are the same today as they were last year? Is there not something in your life that you can work on to reflect the Spirit's work within you? Maybe you need an attitude adjustment. Maybe you need to clean up your speech. Maybe you need to clean up your thoughts. Maybe you need to work on your relationships. I don't know where you need work, but I do know where I need work.

It is time we quit just accepting our faults as something we have to live with and that we begin to clean them up. Peter wrote to the early Christians, "Like newborn babies, crave pure spiritual milk, so that by it you may grow up in your salvation, now that you have tasted that the Lord is good."

I pray that all of us will put on some new growth this season as we GROW in the Lord. I promise you will like the taste.

## "He Has Done Great Things!"
### Psalm 126:2-3

Have you noticed that when the weather begins to warm up people get in a better mood? There is something about warm and sunny weather that brings out the best in people. Maybe it is the fact that we don't rush from building to car, or home to car, or car to work. We stroll out to the car and leisurely get in and go on our way.

But that fact is not true for everyone. One day I was at a window getting help with some business and the lady on the other side of the window was busy working away for me. I mentioned that I felt sorry for her having to be all shut up in that office all day when it was such a beautiful day outside. She quickly told me that she didn't care to be outside because the pollen was terrible and she just couldn't stand it. It is amazing how we are just never satisfied. Or if we are satisfied a little, there is always a black cloud hanging over us that reminds us that the day is not perfect.

This encounter has got me to Just Thinking. I wonder if we could live perfectly. I wonder if our lives could sustain everything being just right. I wonder how it would be if every situation in our lives always turned out great and we never had a setback or disappointment.

It just seems to me that we have gotten used to the worst and so now we expect it. We expect the doctor to give us bad news. We expect the police officer to stop us for speeding when several others got away with it. We expect to get in the line where there is a price check and we get delayed. We expect it to rain if we are planning an outside activity. I think you get the picture. I believe as people of God we need to start having a more positive outlook on things in general. I know we face disappointment and frustration, but when we face them, we are not alone and we have someone to stand alongside us. We not only have the Spirit of God, but we have each other.

I wish it could be said of us what the Psalmist said after being returned from exile, "Our mouths were filled with laughter, our tongues with songs of joy. Then it was said among the nations, 'The LORD has done great things for them.' The LORD has done great things for us, and we are filled with joy. "Now that is a great attitude of life. No matter what the situation or problem, "the Lord has done great things for us."

So, I hope that whatever your situation is today you will recognize that the Lord has done great things for you!!! Don't look at the negative things in life. Search for the positive. Don't try to find the errors in life. Find the corrections. God is on your side. He hopes for you and loves you and wants your life to be good. So, hold your head up. Don't worry about the pollen or the rain or the heat. Just lift up your heads and rejoice for "The Lord Has Done Great Things!!!"

## "What is Your Temperature?"
Hebrews 12:28-29

Summer can be really hot. Sometimes it can be hotter than we like. Speaking of temperature, how would you rate your spiritual temperature? How would you rate the temperature of your church? I have been thinking a great deal about how we measure up on the hot and cold scale. Would you say that as a church you are on fire? Maybe you wouldn't rate it as cold as ice, but just simmering.

When I cook and put something on simmer, I have reached a certain temperature and I want it to maintain that degree of heat for an extended time. I'm keeping it warm, but not overcooking it.

I suspect that we are too comfortable with our church and spiritual life on simmer. We get hot once in a while, but mostly we are just simmering. We are maintaining a constant temperature and we are satisfied.

But the scriptures call us to action. Maybe we need a little (and I do mean little) science lesson. What makes something elevate in temperature is that the heat gets to motivate the molecules in the liquid or solid and they begin to jump around (so to speak). The movement of the molecules produces energy, which in a fancy equation equals heat. Now, we don't think of that at any time when we put something on the stove or in the oven to heat. We just expect the food to get hot.

Now, talking about heating something up has got me to Just Thinking! I believe it can be true of the church and our spiritual condition. Sometimes, we need something to motivate our spiritual molecules. We need to get moving. We need to produce some energy. We need action to produce excitement, which in turn elevates the spiritual fervor of our lives. We too often just want peace and contentment, but maybe we need a jolt of energy. What can produce such energy? What can elevate our spiritual temperature? Have you and I taken our spiritual temperature and found out where we are? What do you think "spurs" us on to a life of abundant living?

As I am writing this my mind is racing to the passage of scripture in Hebrews. The writer has cited the saints of old and is calling the church to action. In the final verses of chapter 12 he warns the reader that God will not sit by and allow us to abuse His good name. Finally, he says, "Therefore, since we are receiving a kingdom that cannot be shaken, let us be thankful, and so worship God acceptably with reverence and awe, for our "God is a consuming fire."

Is God consuming your life with the fire of a "kingdom not shaken?" Or are you just on simmer? I want to encourage you to get moving and generate some heat in your spiritual life so that you may be pleasing to God.

## "Have You Put on Your Armor?"
### Ephesians 6:11

I came out of my house with a cold 41 degrees on the thermometer. I even grabbed a coat and put it on. If you know me very well, you know I do not enjoy wearing coats or having them with me. Hopefully, the sun will shine bright and warm things up a bit and I can leave it in the truck.

Now, grabbing a coat on a cold morning has got me to Just Thinking! It made me wonder how many of us prepare for the spiritual battles we have every day. Some of us face small - and sometimes we may even think insignificant - battles along the way. We may not even pay attention to a small temptation whether we get away from it or give in to it. We may wake up every morning with a spiritual struggle and battle it all day long.

Yet, how are we preparing for those battles? We pray!! That is good, and asking God to guide us and provide us with wisdom and direction sure is a great way to get started. What about during the day in the middle of the battle? Maybe it is a co-worker who is tearing us down. Maybe in school we are struggling with doing the right thing. Maybe we are fighting to overcome an urge. Maybe we are dealing with family issues that are sometimes too much to bear.

How do we get through the tough times? Just as I put on a coat to "bear" up against the weather elements, the Bible speaks of ways to "bear" up against the spiritual battles that we face. Listen to Paul as he encourages the church at Ephesus, "Put on the full armor of God so that you can take your stand against the devil's schemes."

Be assured that the devil is scheming to keep you from being all that God wants you to be. So, take charge and be prepared. Here is the list of what to put on: The Belt of Truth; Breastplate of Righteousness; Shoes of the Gospel of Peace; Shield of Faith; Helmet of Salvation; Sword of the Spirit, which is the Word of God.

When we go into battle with our armor on, we can be assured of God's presence and we can be assured of victory. God does not leave us or forsake us. So, let's begin putting on that needed armor just like we would put on a coat in the winter. Don't leave it behind; it will always come in handy.

## "Have You Been Cleaned Lately?"
Luke 5:12-13

It was the first day of spring. I am glad that things are beginning to warm up and we have more warm days than we do cold ones. Spring reminded me of an event in my life a few years ago.

Peggy and I had escaped down to the beach for a nice meal and just an evening out. We were sitting in the restaurant when two families came in and were seated close to our table. They ordered and then the adults grouped together and the three children grouped together at separate tables. The waiter quickly returned with the tea for the adults and the soft drinks for the children. The children began to act like children; playing with their straws, rolling up their napkins, drinking most - if not all - of their soft drinks. After a few moments and the table looking a mess, the children (all at the same time) raced off to the restrooms and left the table empty.

The busboy happened by, saw the general mess of the table and must have assumed that the persons eating at the table had finished and left. Like someone who was spring cleaning, he began to clean up the mess. He cleared the table in just a moment. The adults noticed and stopped him but it was too late. He had cleaned up a mess before the children had finished. We all had a chuckle about the incident and the children returned and there was no harm done.

All of the spring cleaning and messing up got me to Just Thinking! What in our lives needs cleaning up? Most of us are just the opposite of the busboy. We are slow at cleaning up the messes in our lives. We put off the necessary cleaning that needs to be done. Do you need to clean up a damaged relationship? Do you need to clean up a problem at work? Have you avoided someone because you are afraid of the mess you will make? Do you need to clean up your heart and make it right with God? What needs cleaning up in your life?

It was interesting to me that the busboy apologized and quickly returned with fresh soft drinks and silverware. He did his best to re-supply the children and make things better than they were.

We need to clean up some things in our life and make them better than they are. All we have to do is ask of Jesus and he will clean us up. He will make us better and give us a new start.

Listen to the story of Jesus' encounter with a leper. "A man with leprosy came to him and begged him on his knees, 'If you are willing, you can make me clean.' Filled with compassion, Jesus reached out his hand and touched the man. 'I am willing,' he said. 'Be clean!'"

Why don't we all make a springtime vow to ask Jesus for the cleansing power of His touch?

## "Have You Got It When You Need It?"
### Psalm 119:105

Well, this week has been a rainy week. We have had rain almost every day. As a precaution I have worn my raincoat to work every day. My raincoat is a protective garment that helps to keep the rain off of my clothes and keeps me from getting wet. It has a hood that I am able to put up over my head and keep my head dry. Now the raincoat works really well in keeping me dry. That is when I remember to wear it.

The other day I wore it to work when it looked like it was going to rain. I wore it back home for lunch, but when I came back from lunch it wasn't raining and I forgot it and left it at home. You can guess what happened. When I got ready to head home for the day it was raining and my raincoat was at home. It was doing me no good. I had to go out in the rain with no protection. I got wet.

A raincoat is good when you have it when it is raining. It does you no good even if you own one if you don't have it when it is raining. So on days like we have had this past week I have tried to keep it handy and available. It is a smart move.

Now using my raincoat has got me to Just Thinking! Most every one of us has a Bible. Matter of fact, I would guess that most of us have multiple Bibles. They are very good at helping us discern all that God has said to us about living a Godly life. They help us understand what is expected of us as Christians and followers of Jesus. There are times in our lives when we dive into the Bible, read it and seek to understand what it is saying to us. Yet, what about those times when we leave it on the shelf? What about those times when we abandon the reading of God's word and just go out into the world all alone? The Bible is there, but it is doing us no good unless we read it.

The Psalmist said, "Thy word is a lamp unto my feet, a light unto my path." The word of God illuminates the way for us to travel. It gives us direction and help in our earthly journey.

Yet, as good as it is in helping us live, it will do us no good to own a Bible and not read it and study it. It can be compared to a raincoat. It is good to own, but it does us no good if we don't have it when it's raining.

## "It was the Right Decision!"
### John 8:16

When you have to make a decision that impacts a great deal of people it is not always easy. Peggy called to the back on Saturday night and said, "It's snowing outside, pretty hard."

I had watched and listened to the weather reports that weekend. Everyone seemed pretty sure we would have a little dusting of snow and it would all be gone by Sunday morning because the rain would wash it away. And, along with the rain, the temperature was to get into the 50's with sunshine. I went to bed not worried about Sunday services. Roger Davidson, our chairman of deacons at Reedy River Baptist Church, and I did touch base, but I told him what my plan was. I expected it all to be gone by morning.

At 5 a.m. I got up like normal and went into the kitchen to take my nutrition. As I looked outside, I was amazed that I saw several inches of snow stacked up on the ground. Now what? I thought.

(Let me pause here and tell you I absolutely hate calling off church. The two months during the pandemic were very difficult for me.)

I finished taking in my nutrition and watched the weather for a few minutes. The weatherman assured me that the roads would be passable by 10 a.m. because the sun was coming out and the snow would melt.

I laid back down for a few minutes. At about 6:45 a.m. I looked once again at the outside. Not much sun yet, but a hint of it in the sky. Again, the weatherman assured me things were going to improve quickly. The cars were traveling at normal speed in front of the house where at 5 a.m. they were slowly moving. The road condition had improved.

Now, let me say again that making this decision is not easy. I know that many people are waiting to find out what we have decided. I really didn't want to cancel and then conditions be all right to have church. That has happened to me and it never feels good.

I also know that no matter what decision I make someone is going to think I made the wrong decision. After a great deal of consideration, I decided to call off Sunday School and give the parking lot a little more time to melt off. I notified the TV stations and then sent out an email and text messages to publicize the decision.

In the end, I was glad with the call I made, but I know some people stayed home because of the snow and that is OK. I just wish it would snow on Monday morning and be gone by the weekend. Since we have lived in Greenville for the past 13 years it seems like it always snows on the weekend.

Now, making the decision about church has got me to Just Thinking! Our heavenly Father made a decision that affected the whole world. He chose to send His son, Jesus, to teach us how to live and show us the Kingdom of Heaven on Earth. He sent Jesus to die for our sin and to claim victory over death, sin, and hell.

It wasn't an easy decision. If you remember the first time the Earth went bad, God just sent a devastating flood. He rescued four families and all the species of animals. We have now repopulated the earth and again we have gone bad. Sin is growing every day and the world is more concerned about itself than the God who made it.

That first decision to send Jesus must have been excruciating. I can't imagine the pain and thought process it took to give all you have for the good of others. And even though He did it there were some who were not happy about it. They rejected Jesus and even put Him to death. There were others who embraced Jesus and Jesus gave them the keys to the Kingdom.

Today, people are still unsure how to live the Kingdom life. Even religions argue about what is right and what is wrong. We all seem to want it our way. Yet, there is one thing for certain. In the end it will be God's way. You can claim not to believe, and God gives you that option. Yet, for those who believe and receive Jesus, God calls them His children. And the Bible is plain that He will not cast you out if you are His.

I am grateful that God made the decision to send Jesus. I am grateful that many have received Him and are called His children. I am sad that the world cannot be more caring and giving and less selfish. I am sad that many will fail to receive what Jesus so freely gives.

Let's be sure of one other fact. God is making one more important decision that will affect us all. One day, He will send Jesus to gather His children. There are a great many debates about what happens next, but the final say will be with God. He will win the victory and that is what matters.

## "Are You Ready?"
### 1 Thessalonians 5:2

As Hurricane Dorian pressures the coast of South & North Carolina it takes me back to those days when we lived close to the coast. Many preparations were made when they forecasted a storm coming inland and the possibility that we might see winds up to 60 or 70 miles per hour.

I specifically remember one year when the boys were younger when a hurricane was coming in and Peggy and I and some volunteers were sent to the high school to cook for those using the school as a shelter. We cooked supper for about 1,000 people and were ready to cook breakfast the next morning.

We were told the storm would come in and settle right over us and cause us to probably have to stay in the school for several days. The Red Cross was coordinating the whole thing and promised us that they would make sure we have food to prepare and a generator to run the stoves to feed those that were in the shelter.

After we cleaned up the stuff from supper, we settled down on our air mattresses to begin to get ready for sleep. Not long after supper was over the electricity went out. We went about with flashlights. Peggy, Joshua, Caleb and I were tucked in a corner with other volunteers around us. Every now and then I would get up and look outside. The wind was blowing pretty hard and it was raining.

After not getting much sleep and being awake in the wee hours of the morning, the Red Cross worker came to me and said that the storm fizzled out and people were being allowed to go back to their homes if they wanted. Before we ever started with breakfast, the place was deserted. We gathered all our belongings and headed about a half mile home.

That was an interesting night, but we took it all in stride. As always happens during those types of scenarios, something funny happened. About 3 a.m., one of the Red Cross workers came into the kitchen where the volunteers were sleeping. His flashlight woke most of us up. He came over to me and pretty loudly asked if I knew if we had a doctor in the house.

There was a pregnant lady who looked like she was going into labor. As I was going to say no, my nine-year-old son Caleb stood and said, "Well I'm not a doctor, but I did sleep at a Holiday Inn last night." Everyone awake burst out in laughter.

They were able to get the lady to the hospital, but she did not have the baby then. After a few minutes, we all went back to sleep.

As Hurricane Dorian gets ready to make some lives very uncomfortable on the coast, I sit here many miles away not in the least bit concerned that I will have to make preparations for the storm. I have not once wondered if I needed to make provisions. I have not once wondered if we need to move to a different location or tie something down so it doesn't blow away. I have relatives on the Georgia and North Carolina coasts and I am concerned about their safety, but I'm not the least bit concerned for mine.

Now, reliving some hurricane stuff and thinking about my limited concern over Dorian has got me to Just Thinking! As a pastor I often wonder about those who do not give a second thought to their life after death. They think that this life is it or that it really doesn't matter how they live, that God is going to take care of all of us. They seem very much at ease when it comes to making preparations for the afterlife.

They have heard the talk about Jesus and heaven and hell, but they don't see where it impacts their life very much - kind of like I'm not allowing all the news about Dorian to impact mine. They don't think it will matter because they don't believe it affects them and their lives.

It doesn't matter that it is being talked about and debated and is described to death. They are not paying any attention to what is being said. It is like me not paying attention to what is being said about Dorian. If I was living where I lived before, we moved to Greenville. I would be listening to everything that was being said about Dorian.

I wish I had a magical way to help those who think about their decision about the afterlife. I wish I could get those who are non-attentive to the message of the gospel to pay attention. I wish I could implore them to consider the importance of making the decision to follow Christ as their Savior so that when their life ended, they would have a promise of everlasting life with him. All I can do is hope and pray for them that they would take the time to listen to the truth.

When it comes to hurricane forecasting, it is all a guess. I remember when Hugo came through and we were living near the coast. The forecasters said it was going to come inland and settle over where we lived. The next day it didn't and then they told us that right before it came ashore that it made a 3-degree wiggle and that is why it didn't. You see, forecasting is a guessing game.

The people who do not believe and will not listen believe that the afterlife is a guessing game. They believe that it may or may not be true. It may have everything to do with Jesus and then it may not.

Oh, how I wish I could help them to see the truth in Jesus. Oh, how I wish I could teach them about faith and how, when you have it, it makes a world of difference in your whole attitude. Oh, how I wish I could help them. All I can do is keep trying and pray that one day they will see the truth of the gospel and say yes to Jesus. Jesus has power that Dorian or any other hurricane will never have. One destroys; one puts lives back together. Your choice!!

## "Have You Made Plans?"
### John 14:3

Are you ready? They say we are going to experience Hurricane Florence in some way. The prognosticators are trying their best to let us know just where they think it is going to go and how it may or may not affect us in the long run. They say there is a chance that we could be hit really hard or maybe not much at all.

There are some who live in certain areas who have already made preparations and left their homes and headed for higher ground. There are some who say they will ride it out and see what happens.

On the other hand, we who are further inland wait with anticipation as to just how bad the storm will affect us. Will we get high winds? Will we get torrential rainstorms? Will we be at a high alert for tornados? Will we lose power? We don't know, but everyone is warning us to be ready.

Everyone is telling us we could get some bad, bad weather.

# JUST THINKING!

They say this storm is one of the largest since Hugo. They say the wind bands reach out 200 miles from the center of the storm. They say that we could experience a category 1 hurricane as far inland as Columbia before it turns into a tropical storm and begins to die out.

On the other hand, they say it could turn and go north or south of us and we won't see any real problems. We could take our chances, not make any preparations and be OK. The storm seems to be weakening as I write this article this morning, but who knows. One sentence I read said they will not know until later if we are going to be mildly or directly affected. So, it is up to you. Do you make preparations or just take a chance?

Now, listening to all of the prognosticators of just what might happen and all of the warnings and urging to get ready has got me to Just Thinking! Do we as a nation give much credence to the warnings in the Bible about getting ready for Jesus to return? All through the New Testament, it tells us to be ready! Stand guard! Keep watching! There is a parable that Jesus tells of the servant who is ready when the master comes and the one who is not ready. The servant who is watching and ready gets rewarded. The servant who is slack and not prepared is beaten and punished.

Do we really believe that Jesus will punish those who are not ready? If we do, what are we doing to reach out and tell those who need to get ready? Are we as persistent as the weather people and all the others who are telling us to be prepared for a storm?

Well, if you think Hurricane Florence is a storm, just wait and see the kind of storm that comes in when Jesus returns. If you and I are not ready, we will be shaken off our foundations and blown away. (I hope you understand the pun in relation to the upcoming storm.)

Jesus is returning one day and there will be those who have made preparations by receiving Him and accepting the forgiveness that He offers. There will be those who have rejected what He has offered and will be caught in the storm. Where are you in your preparations? Are you ready to meet Jesus face to face? The fact that you may not believe doesn't mean that it will not happen.

There are some people who are waiting for the coming storm and not leaving their home. They are betting that it will not affect them too much and they will survive. Is that the chance you want to take with Jesus?

I encourage you to seek repentance and find peace in Jesus. Make your preparations today so that whenever He returns you will be ready and be rewarded. Don't be one of those who are found to be without Jesus in your life.

## "It Never Changes!"
1 Peter 1:3-4

The back deck of the house we are in this week faces Mount Mitchell. Once the day warms up a little, we will sit out on the back deck. The first couple of days we were here it was partly cloudy and we had some rain showers in the afternoon.

As we would sit on the deck the sun would appear from behind the clouds and it would get so hot you could hardly stand it. Then, the sun would go behind a cloud and the breeze would blow and it would get chilly. This would go on for hours.

Some days the clouds would be all around us. It would be misting rain one minute, then it would be so hot you would feel you needed to move to the shade. Then, the clouds would come back and it would be chilly. It was weird how quickly it would change.

I went out on Monday when the ladies were gone and sat down beside Dad. It started to mist rain. I said, "Dad it is raining." He said, "Yeah, give it a minute it will be so hot you can't hardly stand it." Sure enough, it wasn't but a few minutes until the rain stopped and the sun dried up everything.

## JUST THINKING!

I have heard people say things like, "If you don't like the weather where we live, wait a minute and it will change." Well, that was never truer than the first few days we stayed on the mountain. The latter part of the week has been beautiful and sunny. But, during the first part of the week it has been up and down and everywhere in between.

Now the quick change of the weather has got me to Just Thinking! Do you know one thing that never changes? Change is something we deal with every day of our lives, whether we like it or not. Each day we wake up we have changed. We have at least become one day older. Yet, the majority of us do not like change. We want things in our life to stay the same. We often talk about how things have changed and wish they would have stayed the same.

Well, I want to remind you that if you have repented of your sins and given your life to Jesus, there is one thing that will never change. It will always be the same. The scriptures say, "Praise be to the God and Father of our Lord Jesus Christ! In his great mercy he has given us new birth into a living hope through the resurrection of Jesus Christ from the dead, and into an inheritance that can never perish, spoil, or fade. This inheritance is kept in heaven for you ..."

It never changes and will not go away. My prayer for you today is that if you know Jesus, you will remember this promise, and if you do not know Jesus that you will make it a priority to meet him and secure your inheritance today.

## CHAPTER FIVE

# JUST THINKING... ABOUT SECIAL PEOPLE!

### "My Best Friend!"
Mark 13:45

I met her in 1980 in a Religious Education class. She used to hang around with a group of guys talking to the professor about college football. We began walking back across campus together after class.

The first time we were ever together I told her I was going to be a pastor and she got up and left me sitting on a bench in the middle of the college campus. Thankfully, God changed her mind.

We married on July 17, 1982. It was the second-best day of my life. (Receiving Jesus as my savior was the best day of my life.) She has been the best wife, companion, supporter, caregiver, mother of our children and friend a man could ever ask for.

Early on in our relationship, I began calling her "Pearl." Her name is Peggy and it means "precious stone." I gave her a string of pearls the night before we got married. I have given her a new string about every 10 years. She is my precious "Pearl." She loves the name so much she taught our grandchildren to call her Pearl and that is what our children call her now.

She has been my rock through all of my cancer journey and

continues to seek the best care and recovery for my life. She has never left my side and has always been more than enough. I am the most blessed individual because Peggy Joyce Taylor agreed to marry me and be my wife. As of this printing we have been married 41 years and I look forward to many more years together.

Now, talking about my best friend and wife has got me to Just Thinking. Jesus told a short parable about the Kingdom of Heaven. He said it was like a man who was looking for fine pearls. When he found one, he went and sold everything he had and bought it. I was fortunate enough to find my pearl and make her mine. Jesus was referring to the relationship we have with Him.

As I said earlier, Peggy is the second-best thing that ever happened to me. Jesus is the best thing that ever happened to me. As much as I adore and cherish my wife, I adore and cherish Jesus even more. He has given me more and sacrificed more for me than anyone else. He is the one who gave me Peggy. There is never anything I can do to repay Him for His generosity to me.

As I think of what a great gift, He is to me, I can't help wanting you to have the same gift. Jesus is ready and willing to offer you the same thing He has given me. He offers the wonderful gift of life to all willing to accept it.

When Peggy and I married, I said "I do." It bound us for life. That is all you have to say to Jesus. "I do accept you." If you do that it will bind you to Him for life and you will never regret it.

Let me finish by saying "I love you, Peggy." And "I Love you, Jesus."

## "What Can I Do for You Today?"
### James 4:2b

It was the first Monday after I began as pastor of Calvary Baptist Church in Lake City, S.C. I was sitting in my office and a gentleman stood in the doorway and knocked on the door frame.

He said, "Rev. Simmons." I looked up and quickly corrected him and said, "I'm David."

He then said "well, I'm Bert. What can I do for you today?" That began a relationship that I will forever cherish. Marion Bert Godwin was about 20 years older than me, but he became my best friend. He came into the church every Monday morning to sign checks for the week. Every Monday after signing checks he would walk to my office and ask me what he could do for me today.

Bert was retired from the Army and had owned and operated a convenience store and oil company. He had a very lucrative business, but was retired when I met him. He was always available when I needed him. He was a great cook. He loaned me his van many times to transport youth to special events. He taught Sunday School and later became a deacon and served twice as chairman of deacons.

He loved to ride motorcycles and was instrumental in me getting my first Harley-Davidson motorcycle. He loved to raise a garden every year and I was fortunate enough to reap many benefits from that garden.

One day when we were talking about the church, I mentioned to him the need to pray more in our deacons' meetings. The very next meeting before we adjourned, he said to the deacons, "Guys, I'm getting down on my knees and praying for God's leadership in our church and I invite you to join me."

From then on, we spent more time praying for our church than discussing situations. It changed the life of our church and it changed Bert. I officiated at Bert's funeral in 2007 after he lost his battle with cancer. I was with him when he died. I drove his Harley to the grave side where we buried him. I still think of him often today.

Now, remembering Bert has got me to Just Thinking. The life of our church made a turnaround after he suggested we begin to pray more. The fellowship was better and the Spirit of God was very evident within our midst. The people in Bert's Sunday

School class told me how his lessons were transformed and got better and better after we started making prayer more important.

I am afraid that prayer does not get a prominent place within our lives and our churches. It is almost like we do it as an afterthought. We seem to do it as a filler and not a vital part of our worship. It is a sad day in a church's worship service where we do not take time for communication with an almighty God. I watched and participated in the life changing power of prayer. I experienced it then and I continue to experience it now.

James the brother of Jesus said in his epistle, "You do not have because you do not ask God?"

I want to encourage you to pray more. Spend time with the one who sees all and knows all. Take the time to invest your life with Him and watch things change. It will not be time wasted, but time invested. Thanks, Bert, for always being available and thank you for praying.

## "New Life"
### Romans 6:4

I met her in 1981. She was Peggy's mother. Her name was Mary Taylor. She was married to a Baptist minister. She was the mother of 4 - three girls and a boy. Peggy was her youngest child.

I liked her from the first moment I met her. Through the years I came to know her as Mamaw. She enjoyed her life and lived each and every day to the fullest. She was the example of a Godly woman. Her dedication to God, her husband, her family and her church was incomparable.

She loved many things in this life. She loved to sing and had a beautiful voice. She loved seafood and I always enjoyed cooking a low country boil for her. She loved reading and there is no telling how many books she read in her lifetime. She loved to laugh and it was always a joy to see her get really tickled at something. She loved to crochet and was very good at it. She taught a great many people to crochet, me being one of them. I still crochet today.

One of her favorite things in the world was butterflies. When she died, her girls got together and counted that she had more than 100 butterfly pins. She wore one every time she went somewhere. She was an inspiration to everyone who knew her. I was blessed to have known her for over 30 years and still miss her today.

Now, remembering Mamaw has got me to Just Thinking! Mamaw's love of butterflies got me thinking about new life. A butterfly is the expression of something dying and coming back to life in a more beautiful way. The caterpillar eats until one day it builds a cocoon and goes into a dormant state. The butterfly will then be released from the cocoon sometimes within the next week to three weeks. When it emerges it is totally different from the caterpillar that went into the cocoon. In most cases it is more beautiful and can do much more, most notably fly.

This is a great expression of what happens to the person who dies in Christ. We see this in the example of Jesus, Himself. He died and was wrapped up and laid in a tomb. Yet, just three days later he emerged and lived again, this time with a glorified body.

This very thing that happened to Jesus is available to everyone who believes in Him and what He did for us on the cross at Calvary. In Jesus we find new life. We find new life here on Earth and we are promised a new life after death.

Paul expressed this idea in these words, "We are therefore buried with Him through baptism into death in order that, just as Christ was raised from the dead through the glory of the Father, we too may live a new life."

Mamaw, thank you for reminding us all about this important fact about our lives. Thank you for showing in the way you lived the value of a new life in Jesus. Thank you for investing time and energy in living that life to the very best of your ability. Your example is still alive and living today as you experience new life with Jesus.

## "Are You Thankful?"
### Psalms 21:5-6

I was privileged to know and be the pastor of Mr. Fred Perry. Mr. Fred was my friend and companion for several years. I was his caregiver for about the last four years of his life. Mr. Fred lived to be 95. He was always proud of his age and his condition. I was privileged to spend a good bit of time with Mr. Fred. I had the opportunity to share with him as he saw life and lived it in new and exciting ways. I learned a great deal from him, the most important lesson being about patience and not worrying.

I cannot help but to remember one of the most important things he said to me on a regular basis. His words were simple and true. We would begin to talk about his life and he would say, "I am blessed. I know I am blessed and I thank God every time I think about it."

His attitudes about his blessing have got me to Just Thinking! How often do I thank God for my blessings? I know that during Thanksgiving we are reminded to thank God for our blessings but is that the only time I, do it? I know that when something extraordinary happens in our lives we thank God for seeing us through, but is that the only time we thank him? I don't know about you, but I want to thank God every time I think about how great my life is. I know I have a great life. I may not be rich according to the world's standards, but I am richer than all the world because of the great things that I have in my life. I have a good family, a good church, and good friends. I know people who don't feel as blessed, and maybe they complain, but I just want to be somebody who recognizes my blessings and thanks God for them.

As I remember Mr. Fred words, let me offer all of you this simple word from the Psalms, "Surely God has granted him eternal blessings and made him glad with the joy of your presence."

I am grateful to have known and spent life with Mr. Fred. I thank him for reminding me to be thankful all the time.

## "Are You Friendly?"
Ecclesiastes 4:10

I was the pastor of Albert M. Hill (everyone who knew him called him Bert and if you really knew him well you called him Check) when he died. Bert was sick and waiting on a transplant that never came.

He went to be with Jesus and finally received a transplant. His transplant was not of an earthly or organ donor, but of a spiritual donation. He was transplanted from this life to the next. His faith was strong, and although his life in this realm was short, his future life will be eternal.

I don't know of anyone who met Bert Hill who did not fall almost instantly in love with him. Bert loved everyone, from the stranger who he happened to meet on the street or in the restaurant or in the hall of a hospital to an old friend who he hadn't seen in years.

His interest caused him to be an instant success with children, youth and adults. Even through some tough times of bad feelings and bad news, Bert continued to keep a smile and a caring tone for others. Even as his life was slipping away, he was concerned about others who had lost loved ones and needed comforting. Bert went out of his way to make others around him feel important and almost never sought his own needs without first looking to the needs of those around him. He was one of the most unselfish people I knew. I was privileged to be his friend.

Now, the fact that Bert was a friend to almost everyone he met has got me to Just Thinking! You know it is difficult in this world to have true friends; those people who would go out of their way to do anything and everything they could for you. I was told as a young ministerial student - and have even said today - that when you die, if you have really five good friends, you are most blessed.

But I must admit that Bert Hill had many friends. The reason he had so many friends is that he, himself, knew how to be a friend. He knew how to show friendship and let others know what a friend is supposed to be. I was always amazed at how he wanted all of his friends to meet his other friends. He always wanted to share friends because he knew we would all be better knowing each other.

I wish for you today that you would covet the friends you have. Maybe today you need to call a friend and thank them for their friendship. Maybe you need to cultivate more friendships in your life and be willing to share yourself with those around you. Maybe you need to recognize just how blessed you are with the friends that you have.

I want to say to any of you who don't have many friends that maybe you need to be friendlier. My friend Bert went to a better place where he will see his best friend face to face.

He reminds me of what the writer of Ecclesiastes said many years ago. "If one falls down, his friend can help him up. But pity the man who falls and has no one to help him up!"

Thanks, Bert, for all the times you helped me up. Thanks for all the people you helped. Thanks for being a friend and teaching us all more about friendship.

## "How Well Do You Trust?"
### 2 Timothy 4:18

I want to introduce you to a friend of mine named Larry Crowe. Larry was a driver for Sunway Charter Bus Company out of Myrtle Beach. I have known Larry for many years. I have never been to Larry's home or met his wife. I did meet his son once, but I have never met his daughter. I know Larry likes to fly and is a good Christian man. He is involved with his church and has a son who is a youth minister. His daughter was considering going into the mission field after she graduated college.

Now, I am introducing you to Larry because, even though I don't know everything about Larry, I know enough to trust him explicitly. Larry was a driver for a charter bus company. He has taken me and groups that I have been in charge of to many places. He took me to two World Changer trips: one to Mississippi and now to Illinois. He took our church and me to Carowinds and has taken the senior adult group to many different places, like the shows at the beach and to Pennsylvania to Amish country.

I trust Larry when he is driving and behind the wheel of that big bus. I trust him so much that I will sometimes slip into one of the seats and take a nap. I know he knows how to handle the bus and take us to where we are going and get us back safely. He never minds helping out and taking us to other places when we need to get ice for the coolers or make a Walmart run because someone forgot something at home. He will accommodate us and he does his very best to make sure our trip goes off without a hitch.

I am glad to call Larry my friend, and he knows that if I plan on taking a trip anywhere far away with a group from our church, I am going to call on him.

Now the trust I have in Larry got me to Just Thinking! How much trust do I put in God to get me through every situation of Life? Do I trust God enough to get me to and from the places I need to go? Do I trust God that even when traffic is tight and I have never been to a certain place in life and be able to see my way clear that I can slip away and take a nap because I know God knows where he is going?

There is an interesting thing that happens when Larry is driving us in that bus of his. Time seems to go by faster and the long trip doesn't seem as long. I believe that is true also when we put our trust in God. Time moves along faster and we are not as tired at the end of the day because we have our trust in God.

Paul admonishes his friend Timothy in many ways, but as he

cautions him about the evils of life, he tells him about his trust. He says, "The Lord will rescue me from every evil attack and will bring me safely to his heavenly kingdom. To him be glory for ever and ever. Amen."

Just as I am sure that Larry will bring me safely back home every time we leave, I am just as sure that God will bring me safely to His heavenly kingdom when my trip on this earth is over. I pray that you have the same assurance.

## "Have You Shared Your Faith?"
Philemon 1:5

I spent a week preaching at a summer camp. I want to tell you about one young lady named Mallory. I met Mallory early in the week and remembered her name every time I saw her. We spoke about every night and she was very complimentary of the worship services. On our off day most of us went to the beach where one of the young people was baptized in the ocean.

On Thursday, Mallory told me this story. "At the beach Wednesday a young girl came up to me and said hello. I thought she was with World Changers and I asked her how she liked it. She told me she wasn't with World Changers and was from Virginia and was down with her family at the beach for vacation. I began to ask her if she went to church. She told me no and that her parents weren't very religious. We talked for a while and then I turned to go.

"As I walked away, I knew that God had given me an opportunity to share His love and I failed. I was angry with Satan and I knew that he was winning. After we ate, I went out looking for my new friend. I found her by herself playing in the sand. I sat down with her and we began to talk. I asked her if she had witnessed the baptism. She said that she saw it but didn't know what it meant. I told her about Jesus and his love for all people that if she would give her heart to Jesus, she too could experience the love of Christ. She told me she wasn't sure but she appreciated me sharing with her. Before I got up to leave, I asked if I could pray with her. She told me yes. I grabbed her hand and just asked Jesus to bless her and help her to find His love. When I said Amen, she didn't look up or release my hands. She just kept holding on. I saw her moving her lips and then began to hear her pray. She told God thank you for sending me to her and that she wanted to experience love like I had shared with her. As she continued praying, I began to cry because it was so meaningful to me. "When she said Amen, she looked up and saw me crying. She apologized because she thought she had hurt my feelings. I told her no that I was just happy for her. She told me that she had never felt the feeling at any time in her life that she was feeling right now. I went and met her parents and we exchanged addresses. As we said goodbye and I walked away, I realized that Satan hadn't won the victory after all that Jesus had. That was the first time I had ever shared my faith with anyone."

That was Mallory's story and it got me to Just Thinking! I wonder if you who are listening to me have ever shared your story. That was the story of a 15-year-old girl who I believe is out to change her world with the message of Jesus Christ. Camp can be about impacting the life of young people who will not allow Satan to win the victory, but will share their story with all they come in contact with. I pray that youth who are given the opportunity to share their faith will do it and our world will really change.

Listen to the words of Paul to Philemon, "I pray that your partnership with us in the faith may be effective in deepening your understanding of every good thing we share for the sake of Christ." It is my prayer for all of us.

## "What's In a Name?"
### Philippians 2:8b-11

As a camp pastor, I tried to memorize everyone's name. I worked really hard and would make many mistakes. I broke the names down by crews, would learn them and continue to say their names over and over to them. As I would see them at the school and at mealtime, I would say their name. Sometimes, I would get them wrong or would have to let them tell me the first letter of their name, but most of the time I could guess it.

Some of the adults asked me how I did it. I couldn't give them an easy answer. It was just hard work. I would make mistakes sometimes and call someone by the wrong name. It would make me try harder to learn their name.

There were some names that came easy and there were some names that were hard. I met a great many Ashleys and Joshes and sometimes when in doubt I would just say one of those names. I met some girls especially who looked like other girls and I would inevitably get their names turned around.

Finally, during the Friday night worship, I was talking about being Jesus' friend and told them how special it was that Jesus knew each of their names. I asked them all to stand and I called each one of their names. I missed a couple, but after a small hint I was able to name them also. Everyone thought it was such a treat to have his or her name remembered.

Now, all of the names and remembering them got me to Just Thinking! What do you think the most important name I remembered all week was? I had some unique names to remember. One young man was just J.W. There was a girl named Magdalene. One girl's nickname was Elmo. I just knew her name was Elizabeth, but it was Lauren. I met Ashleys with a y and an ee. I met one Jordan with a y instead of an a or o. I met male and female Jordans and Erins. Everybody's name was special and important to that person.

But the best name we spoke all week long was the name of Jesus. When we would tell others about Him and how much He loved them was the best of all times. We proclaimed the name of Jesus to all who would listen and take just a moment out of their day to hear.

I can't wait until we all hear the name of Jesus and recognize Him for who He is. The words of Paul are so important, "Therefore God exalted him to the highest place and gave him the name that is above every name, that at the name of Jesus every knee should bow, in heaven and on earth and under the earth, and every tongue confess that Jesus Christ is Lord, to the glory of God the Father."

Now that is a name worth remembering and saying over and over.

## "Have You Thanked Him?"
### Psalm 150:6

I want to introduce you to Cathie. Cathie and I were in high school together and were friends. Cathie suffered a severe stroke that paralyzed her whole body at the age of 29. She is no longer with us, having passed away after living an invalid for many years.

I visited with Cathie several times. The first time, she was in a nursing home and could only move her eyes. She would blink them if her answer was yes and shake them side to side if the answer was no. It was really sad.

She finally moved to a trailer that was equipped for her condition. Modern technology allowed her to be in some control over her life. She now had a computer that she could use to communicate her thoughts and feelings. The last time I visited her in her trailer, I asked if she remembered me. She quickly began typing on her computer. It took her anywhere between 3 and 5 minutes to complete a sentence. Her first one to me was, "You look the same." I laughed and told her that was impossible. We talked about her dog, "Rusty Wallace," and her love for NASCAR. We talked about mutual friends and she also wanted to know about my family. After a few more minutes, I asked her if I could have prayer. She turned off the TV and said, "Yes."

I prayed for her, that God would bless her and provide for her needs, that she would have peace in her life. I hugged her and watched her as tears flowed down her cheeks, even though she couldn't cry. The last message she gave me was "Thank You very much for coming."

Now, spending those few times with Cathie has got me to Just Thinking! The final words of Cathie rang in my head as I left. I wonder if I have ever said that to Jesus. I wonder if I just told him "Thank you for coming."

As Christians, we call on Jesus for many things in our lives. We depend on Him and ask Him to answer prayers. Have we ever just thanked Him for coming? Do we praise God for sending Jesus? We take many things for granted in this world. I do not want to take for granted the fact that God sent Jesus into the world for me. I want to praise and thank God for that and many other things.

So, I am reminded of the Psalmist words, "Let everything that has breath, Praise the Lord. Praise the Lord." When you talk to the Lord and ask Him for the things in your life, make sure before you finish you don't forget to say, "Thank You very much for coming!"

## "Are You Part of the Family?"
### Psalm 52:8

My grandmother passed away in 2000. Her name was Julia Vashti Simmons. She was a wonderful woman who bore 13 children and had many grandchildren and great-grandchildren.

She has left a remarkable legacy for all of us. When I think of her, I think of many things:

- Cornbread - she made the best I ever remember eating.
- Crabapple jelly - until a hurricane blew down her trees back in the late 60's, she made the best and only I've ever eaten.
- Handmade quilts - she used to hand them out to the herd of grandsons who slept on the living room floor when we were all there at the same time.
- Eggs - I used to go with her and gather them up when she had her hens. She would always warn me to be careful not to let another one peck me, because then I would have two belly buttons.
- Sewing tobacco on a stick - she was the fastest I've ever seen.
- Raw oysters - she loved them as much as anyone I know. I used to love to share a meal with her at her favorite restaurant.
- Laughter - many people thought she didn't laugh much, but if you ever got her tickled, she could not stop.
- Love - she helped teach me how to love God and love others. She never took people for granted. She loved you for who you were and not for who she wanted you to be.
- Family - she had a big one and I am very proud to be a part of it.

Remembering Granny has got me to Just Thinking! Do you belong to a family where you can sit back and speak of all the wonderful things that you have observed and participated in? Do you belong to the Family of God that testifies about the wonderful things that God has done for you? Is it hard for you to think about something good to say about your relationship to God's family?

I believe in family! I am proud to be a part of the Simmons

family! My praise for Granny is because of who she was and what she meant to me. Yet, most of all, I am proud to be a part of God's family!

For as the Psalmist said, "I am like an olive tree flourishing in the house of God (family); I trust in God's unfailing love for ever and ever. I will praise (him) forever for what (he) has done; in (his) name I will hope, for (his) name is good. I will praise (him) in the presence of (his) saints."

Earthly family is important. It is nice to belong to a loving and caring family. Yet, there is nothing like being a part of the family of God. If you are not a part of God's family, I pray that you will call on His name and let Him adopt you into His family. It is not hard and He is ready and willing. My hope for you is to be a proud family member too!

### "Serve Well!"
1 Peter 4:10

Do you know the definition of stress? Let me give you one: Broken down on the side of the road in a church bus with 15 seventh- and eighth-graders who are hot, anxious to get home and need to go to the bathroom.

That was the condition on June 9 as we were coming back home from church camp. I will admit that as I saw the thermostat that recorded the overheating of the bus that I said a silent prayer, "Lord, keep us safe, keep us happy, and get us home as soon as possible."

It wasn't long before we were befriended by State Highway Patrol Officer Christmas. He had been working since 6 a.m. that morning, but was not too busy to give us a hand. I will never forget the words he uttered, "I am here to help you in any way I need to."

He did. He transported several of the young ladies to a service station to use the restroom. He bought, out of his own pocket, bottled water for the group. As he left, he let me know that if I had any other needs before our help arrived, that I was not to hesitate to call. He had informed the main dispatch that we were here and that they were to respond immediately if needed.

Now Officer Christmas's kind act has got me to Just Thinking! Christmas is a time when a special gift was given by God to the people of the world. Well, on the day the bus broke down, Officer Christmas was given as a gift by God to a group of 19 stranded youth and adults.

All too often we complain about our law enforcement officers and say they are sneaky, unforgiving, harsh and just out for themselves. Yet, that is not the truth. Officer Christmas showed the true meaning of "to protect and to serve."

Isn't that what Jesus calls us all to do: serve our fellow man? Are we not to be on the lookout for those who need a helping hand, a kind word and listening ear?

Jesus was the perfect example of a servant. He said that is why He came to be a servant.

Peter says, "Each one should use whatever gift you have received to serve others, as faithful stewards of God's grace in its various forms."

I am thankful that Officer Christmas didn't just think of himself on that Saturday. He had every reason to pass us by and let us fend for ourselves. I'm sure after a long day he was tired and ready to go home. Yet, he thought of his fellow man. What a Godly thing to do. My prayer to God is that all of us would do likewise.

## "Remember to Laugh"
### Matthew 25:21

When I first moved to Lake City, one of the first persons to greet me was a Catholic deacon named Joe 'Conner. Joe was the administrator of the St. Philip's Church and the Johnsonville mission.

He and I became great friends. We tried to play golf once a week and we were each other's confidants. We shared our joys and hurts with one another. We also shared our successes and frustrations.

One day, I visited Joe and Kathy in their home and saw a picture of "Jesus Laughing" hanging on his wall. I was amazed at the artist's rendition of Jesus, having never seen anything like it before. I was overwhelmed by the drawing and inquired where Joe had purchased it. He beat around the bush, saying he was not sure where they had purchased it.

A few months later during the Christmas season, Joe and Kathy gave me a framed picture of "Jesus Laughing." He confessed that he did know where he purchased it, but didn't want to tell me because he decided right then to purchase it and give it to me as a gift.

My good friend Joe died after a long and hard battle with cancer. He was 59 years old.

Remembering Joe has got me to Just Thinking. Knowing Joe and the way he lived and enjoyed life - for Jesus - makes me believe that Jesus met him in Heaven with a grin on His face.

Joe's funeral was a celebration of his life and growth. Not only did he grow, but he helped me to grow. He taught me about life and how not to take it so seriously, but to enjoy the benefits of it in relationship to God.

I know Joe heard Jesus say, "Well done thy good and faithful servant, enter into the place that I have prepared for you."

I will miss you Joe, but I know you will share some of those great stories with our Lord and He will rear His head back and give you a great big laugh. Lord, help me to help others to grow in knowledge of you. Help me to be a friend to the friendless. Help me to help others to laugh.

## "Respect is Due!"
### Psalm 96:7-10

I am sure many of you have visited Washington, D.C. When I have been, I am always overwhelmed at the sights and sounds of that city. I am very much astonished at the memorials to the war veterans. All of these memorials are spectacular to see and amazing to look at.

As we visited the Smithsonian Institution's National Museum of American History, we were directed to a new exhibit about the Vietnam Memorial. National Park Service workers collect the items that people leave at the memorial in honor of and to remember their fallen loved ones and comrades. I was fascinated at the objects people left. We saw a high school block letter left by a friend. We saw some Army boots and a note from a sister. We saw a Congressional Medal of Honor returned with a letter condemning the United States' involvement in Southeast Asia. We saw a rifle magazine with a bullet hole and a note we could not read.

I was overwhelmed with the respect and gratitude that was paid to these men and women who sacrificed their lives for our freedom.

Now, looking at all of these mementos has got me to Just Thinking! How much respect and gratitude do we give to Jesus for His sacrifice for us? He gave up so much so that we might have freedom. He gave up so much so that we might have abundant life. He gave up so much so that we might have hope and peace for our future.

Do we worship Christ like we do the men and women who sacrificed for our earthly freedom? Upon his recognition of the Ark of the Covenant, King David coined these words, "Ascribe to the Lord, O families of nations, ascribe to the Lord glory and honor and strength, ascribe to the Lord the glory due His name. Bring an offering and come before Him; Worship the Lord in the splendor of His holiness. Tremble before Him, all the earth! The

JUST THINKING!

world is firmly established; it cannot be moved. Let the heavens rejoice, let the earth be glad; let them say among the nations, 'The Lord reigns!'"

We owe a great deal of respect to those men and women who paid the ultimate price for our freedom. I will forever be grateful for their sacrifice and the sacrifice of their families.

Yet, Jesus paid the ultimate price for my sin. He deserves my ultimate praise. Let us not forget to pay Him the respect He deserves. I pray that you will respect and honor the one who gave all for you.

### "Do You Believe in Miracles?"
### Ephesians 3:20-21

What is your favorite miracle in the Bible? Is it Jesus raising Lazarus from the dead? How about the parting of the Red Sea? Many people like the story of the healing of the 10 lepers. Children love the story about the walls of Jericho falling down.

I believe in miracles, but I don't believe that I ever really witnessed one until one day in a hospital room. I prayed for a miracle. I prayed that God would heal a lady who was a member of the church I was pastoring, Mrs. Nervina Lackey. The doctors told us that she had suffered a major brain stroke and might never regain consciousness.

Her son and I prayed for her on Tuesday night. I directly asked God for a miracle, that she would sit up in bed and tell her son that she loved him. Two days later on Thursday, Mrs. Lackey spoke at 2 a.m. By 1:00 p.m. she was sitting up in bed carrying on a conversation with me, her son, and her niece. She completed the miracle by telling her son that she loved him.

The doctors told us that they must have misread the CAT scan. I believe that God did a miracle in Mrs. Lackey's life. I wish the story had a happier ending. Because of a unforeseen accident while in the hospital, Mrs. Lackey's blood pressure dropped and damaged her liver and she didn't fully recover. I officiated at her funeral the day after Easter.

Now, witnessing this miracle has got me to Just Thinking. We just do not know what God will do if we pray and believe. I have made that statement many times, but now truly believe it. I have seen God do a miracle. I know many people will doubt and say if he did a miracle in her life why not in other lives? I do not have the answer to that question, but I know that God can. To me that is the most important thing. GOD CAN!!

I believe it has something to do with our faith, our humbleness, and the way we approach Him. I believe it has everything to do with GOD.

I have read it and quoted it many times, but now I truly believe it, "Now to Him who is able to do immeasurably more than all we ask or imagine, according to His power that is at work with us, to Him be glory in the church and in Christ Jesus throughout all generations, for ever and ever. AMEN."

## "What Do You Need?"
### Philippians 4:19

It had been a long and frustrating week. I was tired and mentally exhausted. I needed a boost. About that time, I received a call at about five o'clock in the afternoon. The voice on the other end of the phone said, "I know you won't recognize my voice, but this is a voice from the past."

When she told me who she was, I was thrilled. Some good friends of ours from when we played ball in Walterboro were in Lake City for a high school baseball game. We quickly got ready and went to see these friends who we had not seen in some six years.

It was fun to be reacquainted with these friends and see how their two boys had grown up into fine young men. I was very touched when Robbie, my friend, came off of the ball field to greet me. He opened his arms and we embraced as though nothing had ever been lost over those six years. We spent some fun times together. We had shared some good days in conversation about our families, God's provisions, and, of course, baseball.

Now, God sending those friends at just the right time has got me to Just Thinking. God never lets us down. It seems as though when we go through tough times and need a lift, God is always there to provide what we need. He promises never to leave us or forsake us.

I am grateful to God for lifting me up when I am down. I am grateful for the McClures for providing that lift that I needed. I am excited about the renewed friendship and the possibilities ahead.

I am reminded once again of the faithfulness of God and of what Paul wrote to the Philippians, "You can be sure that God will take care of everything you need..." (The Message) If you are down and out, look to God. He will take care of you.

## "Take a Chance"
### 1 Timothy 1:18

I was reading the obituaries of the local newspaper where I experienced my first pastorate. In it I noticed that A. L. Meacham had died at 83 years of age. Well, to you that doesn't mean anything, but to me I was saddened. You see, A. L. Meacham was the Director of Missions for the Henry County (Ky.) Baptist Association. Early in January, 1983, Brother Meacham called me and asked me if I would be interested in preaching at a small country church in Defoe, Ky. I was a seminary student at the time in Louisville.

The name of the church was Union Baptist. I thanked Bro. Meacham for the opportunity and instantly agreed to preach. Before he hung up the phone he said, "By the way, David, the church is in need of a pastor. Is it OK if I tell them they can consider you as a candidate?"

Excited, I told him yes. What a break for a young seminary student! I was only a first-year student and was going to get a chance to possibly pastor a church. Well, to make a long story short, the church called me and I spent a little over four years there - all because Bro. A. L. Meacham was willing to take a chance on me.

Now, getting that chance has got me to Just Thinking. How often do we give opportunities to those around us to do good for the Lord? How often do we give people an opportunity to be responsible and learn responsibility?

I thank God for people like A. L. Meacham. He was willing to give me a chance. Isn't that what Jesus did for people like Peter, James, and John? What about the other disciples? What about other outcasts like Zacchaeus and the woman caught in adultery? Jesus saw good in everybody.

Paul befriended a young man named Timothy. He poured his life into him and set him to do the work of the Lord. Paul admonishes Timothy in two letters that we have record of in the Bible. I wonder where Timothy would have been without Paul's wisdom and instruction.

In one of the letters Paul says, "Timothy, my son, I am giving you this command in keeping with the prophecies once made about you, so that by recalling them you may fight the battle well."

As I am reminded of these words, I am reminded that we all should be willing to give others a chance. We never know what God might do with that person and what glory God might receive. Go ahead; take a chance!

## "Learning to Trust"
### Ephesians 1:18

Let me introduce you to Robert (Bob) A. Carter. Bob lived to be 100 years old. He is a Pearl Harbor and Battle of Midway survivor. He is my hero and should be an American Hero.

JUST THINKING!

Bob was on the destroyer USS Hammann, when it was sunk during the Battle of Midway. He got on a raft with about 15 other men. Nineteen hours later when Bob was rescued, the three men on top of the raft were dead and there were only four men hanging on to the rope on the side. When I asked Bob years ago what happened to the other eight men that were hanging on to the rope he said, "They would just lose hope that we would ever be rescued and they would turn loose of the rope and drift off from the raft and drown."

None of them had had time to put on a life vest when the Hammann was torpedoed. The battleship sank in a record time. I remember asking Bob when he told me this story why he hung on. He told me because he knew he would not die. I asked him how. This was his story as best as I can remember:

"David, when I was 19 years old, I was on the USS Tennessee when the bombing of Pearl Harbor began. I watched my best friend lose his life. I watched the admiral of the (battleship) USS West Virginia vaporize before my eyes. I watched many good, brave men die fighting for freedom. Weeks later, after I had recovered from shrapnel wounds to my legs and the USS Tennessee was back in the states for repair, God spoke to me and told me that I would not die in this war.

"I believe what God told me, and not long after that they were looking for volunteers to go back to Pearl Harbor to help with the cleanup. I went. While there, they asked for volunteers to go on night maneuvers on the USS Yorktown and I volunteered. That was the ship I was on in the Battle of Midway. It was torpedoed, and that is why we were on the USS Hammann when it sank. I never hesitated volunteering because I believed in God, so I not only had hope we would be rescued; I knew we would."

Wow! That is the only word that comes to mind. Bob Carter was a a dying breed in the US today. There were not too many Pearl Harbor survivors still living when he told me all of this. Before long, they will all be gone.

I visited Bob in Dallas for the last time in 2018. Although he hasn't seen me since I have had cancer, he knew me right away. I asked him if someone had told him I was coming because I told his son. He said no, but he pointed to our church newsletter which I sent him and said, "I knew that when I read that David Simmons was getting a three-month sabbatical, I knew he was coming to see me. I not only hoped he would - I knew he would."

We embraced for several minutes and then we spent 3 ½ hours catching up and remembering. I took him pictures of my family. He has always cherished pictures. I never saw Bob again in person, but, as I told him before I left, I know that I will see him in heaven. It was funny that he introduced Peggy and I to many people and he introduced me as his pastor. I was honored.

Now, my time with Mr. Bob has got me to Just Thinking! Bob listened to the voice of God and believed. He wasn't afraid because not only did he hear and believe, but he had hope. Do we practice that type of hope in our lives? We seem to lose hope whenever we hear bad news. We panic when we are not sure how we will handle it or what we will do. Yet, God promises us that He will always take care of us. He will always be there. There is nothing on earth that can steal our hope, yet we allow so many things to do it. Any circumstance that interrupts our nice life causes us to lose hope.

Well, I don't know about you, but when God says it, I believe it and have hope. Hope from God is not a wish or guess. Hope from God is a sure thing.

Paul wrote, "I pray that the eyes of your heart may be enlightened in order that you may know the hope to which he has called you, the riches of his glorious inheritance in his holy people." God's hope is real.

I am reminded of the quote from the movie "The Shawshank Redemption." The quote is in a letter from Andy Dufresne, the escaped convict, to his best friend that is a recent parolee, Ellis Boyd Redding. Red finds the letter which was hidden many years earlier and ends with this quote, "Hope is a good thing, maybe the best thing, and no good thing ever dies."

God's hope never dies! When God gives you something to hope for then you should never fret, just believe. It worked for Robert (Bob) A. Carter. It can work for you!

## "Making the Move!"
### Luke 15:20

Have you ever taken a trip down memory lane? I spent a few days with my college roommates. It was a very interesting two days to say the least. One of my roommates I had not seen in many years. The other, I had spent a brief time with, but not really quality time to find out what had been happening in his life.

Well, it didn't take long for the three of us to find out a very important lesson. No matter how long we had been separated, it was like we picked up where we had left off years ago. Everything seemed the same. We were right back in the same groove. We were out walking on Monday night and Darin (Bubba as we call him) said, "We should have gotten together long ago. It is like nothing has changed between us."

This short reunion has got me to Just Thinking. Maybe you are reading this article and you are thinking about people you have lost touch with. Maybe you are thinking about the church you have lost touch with. Maybe you are thinking about God, who you have lost touch with.

It doesn't really matter why or how you lost touch with them. What matters is that you seek to reclaim those lost relationships. God is ready to receive you back into a relationship. We do not have to have reasons or excuses why we fell out of relationship with Him. We just need to make a commitment to recover that feeling of security.

The church is a place of acceptance. We need to recommit our lives to the work of the Savior. In the story of the prodigal son, the father was watching and waiting for the son to return. God is waiting for you. He wants to renew that relationship.

Luke records these words of Jesus, "But while he was still a long way off, his father saw him, he ran to his son, threw his arms around him and kissed him."

Don't stay away. God is waiting for you. Our long-lost friends are probably willing to reunite as much as we are, but someone has to make the first move. Don't be afraid to go back and make amends for time lost.

## "If that isn't Love!"
### John 3:16; Romans 5:8; 1 John 4:7

In 1997, my great-uncle Dave passed away. He was 97 years old. My father and mother named me after him. David Kelly was my grandmother's brother.

He taught me a great deal about life. He taught me not so much in what he said, but in how he lived. For instance, Uncle Dave was a bachelor for 78 years. Yet, he loved and finally married his sweetheart. Edna was the love of his life. He worshiped the ground she walked on, but because of some circumstances they never married until late in life.

Uncle Dave promised to wait until she was ready. Never did anyone believe that he could wait so long. Finally, after Dave built a house to her specifications and did everything possible to let her know he loved her, Edna gave in. At the age of 78, Uncle Dave finally saw the fruit of his labor come to a happy ending. Edna and Dave were married. He was 78; she was 76. I was fortunate to have supper with them on the night they were married. I have never seen Uncle Dave so happy. What he had waited for all of his life was now his.

Remembering my Uncle Dave has got me to Just Thinking. How much does Uncle Dave's love and patience mimic the love and patience of God? Many times, in our lives we put God off.

We have excuses and good reasons why we can't give our lives to God. We find the things of this world more pleasing to us than what God can offer.

God has created His world to our specifications. He has done everything possible to continue to let us know He loves us. Even sending His own son, Jesus, to die on a cross for our sins was an unselfish act to prove His love to us.

Jesus said it to John, "For God so loved the world He gave..." It is the ultimate act of love. Jesus's love is portrayed by Paul when he said, "Even while we were yet sinners, Christ died for us."

That is the epitome of love. Yet, many times we still refuse to give our lives to him. And God is patient. He loves us and wants us to know the joy, peace and happiness of a life surrendered to Him.

I have always wondered how much Aunt Edna missed out on by not marrying Uncle Dave earlier. I understand that Uncle Dave was always with her, but surely, she missed out on the intimacy of the relationship by not becoming his bride sooner. We too can sit back and wait, but we will miss out on the intimacy of a great relationship with God.

David means "Beloved." Uncle Dave took seriously what John said, "Beloved, let us love one another, for love comes from God." Don't miss out on the love of God. Don't wait too late to discover the relationship you can have with Him.

## "A Servant's Heart"
### Galatians 5:13

Betty Snyder was an amazing woman. She asked me one Sunday if I would accompany her to visit one of our homebound members. I agreed and we set a time and date. When we arrived at the home she got out and retrieved several magazines: Home Life, Open Windows and the latest Sunday School quarterly. She also pulled out a half of a pound cake. She looked at me and said, "I love bringing them gifts." We went into a broken-down trailer and visited.

As we drove home that day, she told me she would like to take me to visit several more of the homebound that she ministered to. I told her I would be glad to go anytime. As I exited the car when we got back to the church, I thanked her for her service and the wonderful time spent together.

That was the beginning of a wonderful relationship between Mrs. Betty and I. We went and visited many other homebound in the 13 years I was her pastor. Every time she would bring magazines and some type of baked goods. She seemed to never age. As she got older, she was visiting homebound people that were younger than she was, but she kept right on going.

Mrs. Betty went home to be with Jesus. She quietly went home and she is forever in the presence of the Lord that she served so faithfully.

Reminiscing about Mrs. Betty has got me to Just Thinking! Whose life are you impacting for the Kingdom of God? Whose life are you investing in so that they may see Jesus in your ways and actions?

Mrs. Betty touched so many people in so many ways. Her kindness and gentleness are just two practical ways in which she showed the love of Jesus. Mrs. Betty, although up in years, never got old. She stayed young by serving and doing all she could for the cause of Jesus. What a servant heart she portrayed in her dealings with people wherever she encountered them.

God has called each of us to make a difference in someone's life. He hopes to instill in each of us a servant heart so that we may make a difference in others' lives. Are we too busy worrying about our own life that we do not see the ones around us who need us? Are we so wrapped up in our own lives that we miss opportunities to do good to those around us.

Paul wrote, "You, my brothers and sisters, were called to be free. But do not use our freedom to indulge the flesh; rather serve one another humbly in love."

The life Mrs. Betty lived reminds me that we have a responsibility to "serve one another." We have a responsibility to smile and show Jesus in everything we do. My prayer is that we will all see fit to make a difference in the world in which we live, that we will seek to share our lives with someone we know that we may show them Jesus. Every life we touch with the Spirit of Jesus will be better because of His influence in our lives. There is no telling how many people were touched and inspired by Mrs. Betty. And she did it because she Loved God and Loved People!!

CHAPTER SIX

# JUST THINKING... ABOUT THE CHURCH!

## "What's On the Inside?"
Matthew 23:27; Mark 7:15

World Changers was a youth camp that gave a unique opportunity to show the love of Jesus in a practical way. Each church group that attended was divided up into crews that go to different area homes and perform certain tasks. There is roofing, painting and various other home improvement jobs completed to make the resident's house a nicer place to live.

One year, I was placed on a crew with a 24-year-old crew chief named Bryan. We had three adults and eight youths on our crew. We were named the Bone Crushers. Our task for the week was to paint a tin roof with Kool Seal aluminum coating and to put vinyl siding on this large two-story house.

As we gazed at the house the first day, we saw a red rusty roof and a house with nothing but felt paper wrapped around it. The sponsoring church had already removed the asbestos shingles the previous weekend, but the task was enormous for a group of inexperienced amateurs.

We dove in on Monday painting the roof. We completed most of this task with rollers, but had to touch up the high spots with mops. We began siding on Tuesday, and by Friday we had completed most of the work except the very highest ends where we were still waiting on the metal to be placed on the soffit.

Although we didn't complete our task, we were pleased about the amount of work we completed and it was refreshing to know that the men of the church planned on finishing the job on Saturday morning. What we once had seen as a run-down old house now had a bright, new shine to it.

Now, the condition of the house from start to finish got me to Just Thinking! Because we changed the look of the house, did the house really change? The outside looks different, but has the inside of the house changed?

I can tell you that having worked on the house, it is still leaning. I know, because we followed the studs in the house as we nailed the siding on. The studs were at an angle; they were not straight up and down. I can tell you that there were hundreds - if not thousands - of dirt dauber nests that we covered up with the vinyl siding. We would rake those we saw on the surface off, but we saw many of the insects go into cracks and behind the black felt.

Although the aluminum coating that we painted the roof with made it look better, we were not able to cover all of the holes and creases evenly because of the steep roof and our inability to stand on the roof. We did the best we could with our homemade extensions, but we still left some areas uncovered.

My point is that it is not what a house looks like on the outside that makes it a home. It is what is on the inside. We can whitewash the outside all we want, but if the inside of our home is filled with strife and abuse and ridicule, we are still in need of repair.

Jesus made two statements about the inside of our lives that I would like to quote to you. He said to the Pharisees, "Woe to you, teachers of the law and Pharisees, you hypocrites! You are like whitewashed tombs, which look beautiful on the outside, but on the inside are full of dead men's bones and everything unclean."

Then He said, "Nothing outside a man can make him 'unclean' by going into him. Rather, it is what comes out of a man that makes him 'unclean.'"

Jesus emphasized that what is on the inside is what is important. I am glad that we gave the house a new look. Now, I believe the church house should look good. I believe we should do everything possible to make God's house a pleasing sight to all who come. But, we must not just focus on aesthetics. We need to focus on the inside. How do we look spiritually? How are we growing the Kingdom of God on the inside? As people, we need to work on the inside so the outside is just not fluff, but has a quality that God can be proud of. Don't forget God looks on the inside.

## "Every Day is a Good Day!"
### 1 Peter 2:2-3

For several years we held a children's camp called Camp Sonbeam at Lynches River County Park. We had many children ages five through 12 participate. It was a great time of singing, learning and doing fun activities.

We have three groups represented at our camp. They are called the Fireflies, the Shooting Stars, and the Lightning Bolts. They go about together in their groups and stay together all day. It is remarkable to see all that they accomplish. On the first day they have to come up with a cheer about their group and all they are about at Camp Sonbeam. It was fun to see them sing about "having fun in the 'Son'" and "learning about the Son" and cheering on each other for their accomplishments.

Children are definitely a joy to be around and watching them enjoy life is one of my most favorite times of the year. Every day before we went home, I would ask them their favorite thing they did that day. One would say swimming and another would say shooting the BB guns. One would say lunch, or recreation, or games. Each day, one or two would smile a big smile and say everything.

The experience of Camp Sonbeam and the good things got me to Just Thinking! Surely, God has made everything good in His time. We are blessed to be able to enjoy the good things of life and enjoy all that God has given to us. Yet, so often when we enjoy what is good, we sit back, relax and get lazy. We enjoy it for a while and then only talk about what a good time we had.

We forget that when we live for God, every day is good. We forget that, "This is the day the Lord has made and we should rejoice and be glad in it."

I hope that no matter what you're doing - if it is helping children find the joy of Jesus or slaving away at work - that you will find that God is good all the time.

It is the same with the church. We need to enjoy every opportunity we get to come together as a body of believers. We need to experience the goodness of God, whether it is in a worship service, Sunday School class or a fellowship time. We don't need to miss out on the goodness of God.

Listen to the words of Paul as he talks about learning more about God. He says, "Like newborn babies, crave pure spiritual milk, so that by it you may grow up in your salvation, now that you have tasted that the Lord is good."

Once you taste how good God is, you just want more. I pray you will enjoy each and every day. I also pray the church will bring out the best in all of us.

## "Change Can Be Good"
### 1 Corinthians 9:22b

Do you remember when video projection systems began to be installed in church sanctuaries? Now, I know there are some who did not like it. It was a change, but I believe that it enhanced our opportunities to worship and do things that we hadn't been able to do in the past.

I understand that most of us do not like change. Yet, even though we resist change, we all do it every day. I remember when my dad put the first window air conditioner in our house. It was a small unit placed in my parents' bedroom. Before that, all we had were open screened doors and electric fans. Some of you probably remember when there weren't even electric fans.

I remember when Dad bought the air conditioner for the living room. It was a great day for all of us. Now, if you look at a house to buy and it doesn't have central air, you won't even consider buying it.

You see, change can be good, although at first, we do not want to accept it. I knew some people who thought air conditioners wouldn't last. Well, I guess we have all accepted the change.

Now, all of this change has got me to Just Thinking! I believe that change for change's sake is not always a good idea, but change that enhances our opportunities to reach people for Jesus Christ and enhance the work of the church is always good. There are times when we resist change just because we have become so entrenched in our ways that nothing can move us.

I, for one, believe that Paul was entrenched in his belief in who Jesus was and what Jesus offered, but even Paul said that he was willing to change to reach people. Listen to his words to the Corinthian church, "I have become all things to all men so that by all possible means I might save some."

Did you hear the words, "by all possible means?" I believe that Paul never compromised the gospel, but he looked for ways to make the gospel become alive to whatever group he was around. He showed us that when he visited Athens, Greece. He recognized their shrine to the unknown god and, instead of ridiculing them for their ignorance, he gave them a revelation of who the unknown God was.

I believe it is up to us to be ready for change if it helps us to reach people. I do not think for a moment that we need to change the Good News of Jesus Christ. It is unchangeable, but we do need fresh ideas and concepts of how we can spread the Gospel of Jesus Christ. So, if somebody says "change" at your church, don't immediately resist, but take time to assess the value in the Kingdom of God.

### "Are You Missing Out?"
Philippians 4:19

I accompanied a group of senior adults on a trip to the Outer Banks of North Carolina. We had a great time learning about the area and seeing the sights. We were met and accompanied on our stay by a young lady named Connie Clupper. Connie was our tour guide and host for the three days we were in the Outer Banks.

She helped us to experience some of the places and scenes that I might not have experienced by myself. She chose some great restaurants and a great hotel for us to stay. Truly, it was worth having a guide who knew the area and all of the worthwhile attractions. We learned some unknown facts about the area and got to experience some places we probably wouldn't have seen had we been on our own. It was great having someone who knew the area to show us around.

Now, having a tour guide for our trip has got me to Just Thinking. Do you ever wonder why we miss out on all of the wonderful blessings that God has in store for our lives? Maybe it is because we are trying too hard to be our own guide. Maybe we are depending too much on self and not enough on someone who knows all the great things to do.

Jesus said continuously to His disciples, "Follow Me!" When we follow Him, we can say what Paul said, "But my God shall supply all your needs according to His riches in glory by Christ Jesus."

When we are listening to the Holy Spirit, we can follow His

lead and discover things we never would have discovered on our own. I don't know about you, but my life is much better when I have someone to lead and guide me.

What is true for our lives is also true for the church. We need the Holy Spirit to guide us as a church. We need to pray and ask God for spiritual guidance as we seek to be a church on mission for Jesus.

Do you need to book a tour of life? Do we need to book a tour guide for our church? Do so today by contacting the greatest travel agent of all time. Call on Jesus.

## "Do You Know the Pilot?"
Matthew 8:27

On another trip with senior adults, we went out to see the dolphins in small water craft. There were two boatloads, with 12 of us on the second boat. We had moved into the channel when, all of a sudden, our boat's transmission broke. The passengers in the boat didn't know anything had happened, but the boat captain knew something was wrong. He immediately called someone on his hand-held phone.

We began to drift out further into the channel. Normally, there would have been no danger at all, but on this occasion, there was a container ship moving into the channel. Needless to say, there were a few tense moments as the ship blew its horn and the other dolphin boat raced to pull us out of the channel. We successfully made it to safety and the ship went by us without incident.

After we were tied up to the other boat and began our trip back to the dock, I asked the captain why we didn't experience a large wake from the ship. He looked at me and said, "As soon as I knew we couldn't move, I called the channel pilot. He is a friend of mine. I told him to notify the ship that there was a disabled watercraft in the channel and to slow down. When the ship passed us, it was only coasting."

Now, this incident got me to Just Thinking. When our life is in trouble and the large ships of the sea of life are bearing down on us, what do we do? Do we panic? Do we try to fix the problem ourselves? Do we call on the people around us to help out? Or do we do as the captain did? Is our first call to the channel pilot, our friend, Jesus? He can calm the seas and slow down the ships until we reach safety.

I wonder if the channel pilot would have helped out as quickly had he not been a friend of the captain. It is always good to have a friend in the right place. Do you have a friend in Jesus? He can calm the storms of your life and guide you to safety.

We also need that pilot to guide our church. When we get into rough waters or scary times, we need Jesus to answer our call and get us out of the difficulties of life. The church cannot be successful depending on itself. We need the author of the church to lead our way.

After Jesus calmed the storm the disciples said, "Who is this? Even the wind and the waves obey Him?"

Jesus is the ultimate pilot. He has experienced it all and He knows how to navigate life. It is always good to be able to call on Him when we are in distress. I hope He is your friend.

## "Are You Focusing on the Finish?"
### Hebrews 12:1-2

I'm sure you have probably visited a theme park sometime in your life. Well, if you haven't, let me tell you that you spend a great deal of time waiting in line. You walk up to a ride and your first thought is the line isn't long. Then, you begin to walk through the maze of short lines until you find yourself at the end of the line of a group of people that if you stretched this line out it would be about a half-mile long.

So, as I was standing in line to take a 60-second thrill ride, I began to notice people. I found myself amazed at what people do waiting in line. Some stand still facing straight ahead, saying nothing, waiting for the line to move. Others get involved with people around them in conversation. The children are anticipating the ride to come and are straining to catch a glimpse of the riders who are already experiencing the thrill.

Sometimes these individuals get so caught up in what is going on that they fail to see that the line has moved and there is now a huge space between them and the person in front of them. I found it particularly interesting that someone three rows away will shout out, "Hey move on ahead!" and then the line will begin to move until someone else is daydreaming or involved in conversation or is so focused on the ride that they also didn't see the line moving.

Watching all of the people and their reaction to waiting in line has got me to Just Thinking. Isn't our journey down the Christian life kind of like standing in line for a thrill ride? I mean, we all start at the end of the line and it seems as if eternity is so far away. We become distracted along the way; either with ourselves or friends or family or we even get caught up in the end versus the journey. Does someone have to tap you on the shoulder and tell you to move on? Or, are you like some who get discouraged over waiting so long and finally get out of line and decide it isn't worth it?

Although the initial interest is always high, we often fail to keep our eyes on the final destination. We are like Peter when he stepped out of the boat to walk on the water. As long as we have our eyes on Jesus, the journey is possible. Yet, as soon as we get distracted by the storm around us, we begin to sink. It is always good to keep focused on the final prize.

In the church we have many different people. Some are just standing around. Some are actively seeking to move ahead. Some are just waiting for the finish. And, there are some who are getting so distracted they have allowed a large gap to come between them and what God wants for their life.

We can get distracted with all that goes on in the world, but we need to keep our eyes on the finish line. The writer of Hebrews said it best, "Let us fix our eyes on Jesus, the author and perfecter of our faith..."

My prayer is that you will focus on the one who has done everything for us and provided a much better life for us. Just as individuals, the church needs to keep our eyes on Jesus. Every once in a while, someone needs to yell, "Hey, move on ahead!!!"

## "Keep Trying!"
Colossians 3:17

It took three tries, but it finally happened. I had a great experience at World Changers. Most of you know that the previous two years at World Changers have been somewhat difficult for me. In Savannah, although we had a great week with the youth, I had a terrible time as a crew chief. In Norfolk, the week went better but I still felt as if there was no organization and our job did not get finished.

This year in Meridian, Miss., I felt like everything finally clicked. I had a great crew. I had great adult leaders. We rebuilt a carport and roofed it. We completely re-roofed 18 square of shingles. We replaced some Masonite siding. We painted the outside trim. We put in two ceiling fans, put up a clothes line and painted and roofed the doghouse. That sounds like a great deal of work, but when you have good people and the right equipment it is easy to do.

The success of this week has got me to Just Thinking! How often do we give up on things before we have a chance to get it right? It took me three times to feel successful at World Changers. What if I had given up? What if I had never returned for that third year? What if I decided it wasn't worth it? Sometimes, I believe we give up on God in the same way. He calls us to do something and if it doesn't go our way, we just say it wasn't His will. Or, we decide that maybe He has something else in mind and we go off in another direction without giving it our best effort.

It not only happens in our individual lives, but it happens in the church. Maybe God wants you to teach Sunday School and you have had a bad experience. Maybe God wants you to volunteer your time in children's ministry and you are afraid you will not fit in. Maybe God wants you to serve on a committee and you're just waiting to see if you are asked. Maybe God wants you to give up trying so hard and let Him lead you and let Him be in control.

Don't give up! Success will come when we put our best effort forward and do it with the right frame of mind. Paul reminded us that we don't do it for any other reason than for the Lord. Listen to his words, "And whatever you do in word or deed, do all it the name of the Lord Jesus, …"

Don't give up, Keep Trying!!!

## "Where is Your Faith?"
### Hebrews 11:6

When Peter was walking on the water and began to sink, Jesus reached out His hand and said, "You of little faith, why did you doubt?"

I feel like Peter sometimes. My oldest son, Joshua, came home from two weeks of summer camp as a volunteer counselor. On that first evening back, he began to talk about the camp and his visit to a day camp put on by a church he had visited.

He was so excited and said, "Dad, I know we can do this."

I thought, "There is no way!"

I must confess to you that I didn't have much faith in the vision that God had given my son. He continued to talk about it and convinced me that we at least needed to look into it. After much prayer, I finally agreed. The church agreed to name a committee to look into the possibilities. We met, named the camp and solicited the community for participants. The registration went slowly. At one time we only had 15 campers signed up. Once again, my faith dwindled. I was considering canceling the camp. Joshua was forever confident.

Finally, the time came when we had to make a final decision. With 25 campers signed up we went ahead with the decision to have Camp Sonbeam. We enrolled 27 campers for the week and the rest is history. We could not have had a better week sharing God's love with campers and adults. I have never been a part of something that was so successful and so enjoyable.

I remember a sign that a pastor of mine had behind his desk as I was growing up. It read, "Plan something so big that unless God intervenes it is bound to fail!"

I have no doubts in my mind now that God used a 17-year-old young man to lead his old unbelieving father to experience a blessing from God.

Joshua's faith in this camp has got me to Just Thinking. If God can accomplish such a great work for His kingdom through Camp Sonbeam, just think what he could do for his church if we would only believe. I have seen Him do miraculous things in the church when people believe. I have seen ministries grow. I have seen people come. I have seen budgets grow and ministries being added to reach out to the community, the state, the nation and the world for the cause of Christ. Most of all, I have seen people come to know Christ as Lord and Savior and see the growth in God's grace to be a stronger people of God.

The church can accomplish great things for Jesus when we only believe. Faith is the most important ingredient in seeing God do things among His people.

The writer of Hebrews said, "And without faith it is impossible to please God, because anyone who comes to him must believe that he exists and that he rewards those who earnestly seek him." God will reward the church that comes to Him in faith.

## "Is Sharing Jesus Worth It?
### 2 Timothy 2:25

"Jesus Loves me this I know,
For the Bible tells me so,
Little ones to him belong,
They are weak, but He is strong.
Yes, Jesus Loves Me,
Yes, Jesus Loves Me,
Yes, Jesus Loves Me,
For the Bible tells me so."

I guess this is the first song I ever learned as a child. I have probably sung it more than any other song. I can tell you that I have taken it for granted and never knew the real significance of it until a mission trip with the young people of our church.

We were leading an outdoor Vacation Bible School for the campers at a state park. As part of our program, we always sang songs with the group. One morning we were singing "Jesus Loves Me." Two 9-year-old twin girls from New York state were participating in the school. Their names were Sarah and Jane. While singing "Jesus Loves Me," one of our adult counselors noticed that Sarah and Jane were not singing. When asked why, they told her that they had never heard the song before. Needless to say, we sang it again, just to help them learn it.

Now, the fact that these two young girls had never heard "Jesus Loves Me" has got me to Just Thinking. Can you even imagine never having learned the song, "Jesus Loves Me?"

Well, I certainly learned that I do take even the simplest things for granted as far as God is concerned. Sometimes, I wonder whether anyone is really getting anything out of all the time and effort put into doing Bible schools and talking to children and youth. I can honestly tell you now that if nothing else took place at that state park during that week, there were two little girls who left their knowing the song "Jesus Loves Me."

It got me thinking how often we take for granted the people who come into our church. We just assume that since they have come, they must know something about God and are there to enrich their lives. I don't want to miss out on the opportunity of sharing the love of Jesus with someone just because I assume they know. The church always needs to be ready to share the basics of what it means to experience God in community. We need to make sure that we take every opportunity to teach everyone that Jesus loves them.

Paul instructed Timothy about those who do not know the truth. He said, "Opponents must be gently instructed, in the hope that God will grant them repentance leading them to acknowledge of the truth."

We must always be willing to see the need and meet the need to help those who do not know to see the reality of Jesus. After that week on mission and meeting those two precious little girls, I will never wonder again if all the effort is worth it.

## "How Do You Respond?"
Matthew 16:18

I was at a large rally of young people and adults. Someone had brought a beach ball and everyone was knocking the ball up in the air. I noticed some interesting things about the way the ball was punched into the air. Some individuals would lightly tap the brightly colored ball and send it spinning into the air. Some would use their fist and attack the ball and bat it far away from them. Others would grab the ball with both hands and then systematically serve the ball into orbit above them.

There were also other responses to the ball. Some would duck their heads as to not come in contact with the ball. Some would leap at the floating ball and miss it. Others would try to pay attention to the stage and act as if the ball wasn't there at all.

Now, everyone's reaction to the ball has got me to Just

Thinking! Are we not like this when it comes to the life of the church? Some of us go all in and give it everything we've got. We manhandle it and struggle to get all we can out of it. Some of us lightly tap at it and hope it continues on its merry way. Some of us have it mapped out systematically and force it on. Others watch it go by, while others seem to miss it completely. Then, there are those who act as if it isn't happening at all.

Where are you on the road of life inside of your church? Are you missing out on one of the most precious gifts that God has given to us? In a great many ways, life in the church is like that beach ball. It has many highs and lows, ups and downs. Sometimes it moves great distances and sometimes it hardly moves at all.

Yet, God has a purpose and plan for the church. He wants us to live abundantly inside of His church. Jesus said, "... and on this rock I will build my church and the gates of Hades will not prevail against it."

Jesus founded the church to succeed - not to fail. We each have a part to play and we each need to be active in seeing the church grow for the sake of the Kingdom of God. My prayer is that we will all become a part of the church to see it move in a mighty way in our communities. I implore you not to just sit idly and watch the ball, but get up and help it to move and make a difference in the lives of the people around you.

## "Are You Facing the Impossible?"
### Mark 10:27

Have you ever faced a task that you thought was impossible? The first youth World Changers trip I ever participated in was in Savannah, Ga. We slept on school room floors, ate school food, showered in gym locker rooms and shared all of this with 340 others.

During the day we volunteered our labor to paint, roof and

# JUST THINKING!

do various other jobs around homes in the Savannah area. I was given the task of being crew chief of 14 high school youth with one other adult. Our job was to roof a home. The task seemed impossible as we looked at it for the first time. Before we left, we held hands and prayed for safety, courage, and strength to complete our job. As we began to work on Monday, the task seemed even more difficult than we imagined. Yet, we continued on. Each morning we prayed. Some days it seemed we made no progress.

Finally, on Friday afternoon at or about 1:30, the last shingle was trimmed from the roof. As the ladder was being taken down, I spoke to Mrs. Lola Washington, the homeowner. "Mrs. Washington, you now have a new roof."

Standing under her porch she proclaimed, "Thank you, Lord. Now let it rain."

AND IT DID!!!

The drops started slowly and then we had a downpour. As we drove away, the water was rolling down the newly placed shingles and running onto the ground. I could not hold back the tears in my eyes.

Now, completing that impossible task has got me to Just Thinking! How often do we face impossible tasks in our churches, but look to God to pull us through? And how often do we stick to the task and God answers our prayers?

God truly answered my prayer that week. Not one of those young people fell off of the roof. Other than small cuts, no one was seriously hurt. And, although we didn't do all I would have liked to accomplish, we did roof the house.

That night I prayed and thanked God for answering my prayers. I am sure that sometimes we feel overwhelmed with the task at hand in our churches. I am sure we feel that some things we are called to do are impossible. I want to remind us that with prayer and hard work, God can and will see us through.

The disciples questioned God about impossibilities. I am reminded of what Jesus said to the apostles. "Jesus looked at them and said, with man it is impossible, but not with God; for all things are possible with God."

Don't ever forget that all things are possible with God. Allow Him to show you how to overcome the impossibilities in your life and in your church.

## "Are You Listening?"
### Matthew 11:15

Does God ever speak to you? I have talked to people who told me that God spoke to them in an audible voice. I have talked to people who said that God spoke to them in a vision or dream. I have talked to people who said that God speaks to them all day long.

Well, I can tell you that God spoke to me. I have never heard him in an audible voice, but I did know when he spoke. I had a really neat experience happen one Sunday in church that I would like to share with you.

My music ministers pick out our hymns three months in advance. Yesterday was the end of the quarter so we were singing songs that were planned well ahead of time. My message yesterday was on who makes plans for our church. I talked about the fact that the preacher doesn't make the plans for the church and the people don't make the plans. The most powerful people don't make the plans and neither do the prideful people. My point was that the preeminent God, supremely in charge of the church should be the one making the plans for the church and that we need to have a love relationship with Him so that He can reveal His plans for the church.

After the sermon I gave an invitation and asked the congregation to stand and sing the invitation hymn No. 318. The title of the hymn was "The Nail-Scarred Hand." As the musicians began to play everyone joined in the singing of the first verse. Here are the words, "Have you failed in your plans of your stormed-tossed life?"

I stopped singing and began to smile. God had spoken. God was validating the very fact that we have failed in our plans and the only way to truly know what His plans are for our life is to place our lives in His hands. I stopped the music immediately after the singing of that first verse and pointed out my realization of God speaking to us. I don't know if anyone else noticed the connection, but I sure did. God spoke and I wasn't about to miss His message.

Now, all this talk about God speaking got me to Just Thinking! How many times do we miss out on God speaking to us because we are not tuned in to Him? It would be very easy to say what happened on Sunday was just a coincidence and that it wasn't really God speaking.

Well, you can believe that if you would like, but to tell you the truth, I know God was trying to say something to the church. I don't think there are any coincidences when it comes to following God. He is ready to speak to us through our prayers, Bible study, circumstances and any other venue that He can use.

Yet, so many times in our lives we have selective hearing. We only hear what we want to hear. We only want to hear what is convenient and pleasing to our ears. We do not want to be made uncomfortable with new truths. I guess this is why God would periodically say, "Let him who has ears hear what the spirit says."

I don't ever want to miss out on what God has to say to me. I hope that we will all listen and then respond to God when He speaks.

## "I'm Glad He Volunteered!"
### Romans 8:32

The definition of volunteer is a person who performs or gives his services of his own free will. I love volunteers. I don't know what the church would do without volunteers. We need volunteers to keep the nursery. We need volunteers to take up the offering. We need volunteers to teach Sunday school. We need volunteers to serve on teams and committees. We need volunteers to serve in all areas of our church.

If the church didn't have volunteers, then we would not be operating at all. One time our church honored our volunteers. We gave them a banquet and said thank you in a very special way. We treated them as royalty and gave them a red-carpet welcome. I know that they were not expecting anything for their service, but the leadership of the church felt that we wanted to do something special to say thanks. Well, the night went off better than expected. We had a good turnout, a wonderful meal and an inspirational challenge to continue our efforts to reach a community for Christ.

Now, all of the volunteer emphasis got me to Just Thinking! As was pointed out to us by our speaker, can you imagine the discussion as someone was needed to be a sacrifice for the whole world? Can you see the looks as it was decided that someone from heaven would have to be an atoning sacrifice for all the worlds' sins? Can you imagine the hush that fell over the conversation as it was explained that the only way to atone for the sins of the world was the shedding of blood? Can you imagine the shock as all the angels in heaven stood in opposition to the Son of God as he volunteered to be that sacrifice?

I can only tell you that I am eternally grateful for the volunteer service of Jesus the Christ. I will never be able to say thank you enough for His free gift that He gave to all of humanity. I will never understand why He was so willing to take my place and die for my sins. Yet, I will always be in awe of His ability to volunteer for me.

As I think about His sacrifice and volunteer service, I am reminded of what that provides for me. God through His unconditional love for us freely gave all so that we might have life. The scripture says, "He who did not spare his own Son, but gave him up for us all - how will he not also, along with him, graciously give us all things?"

If Jesus can volunteer for me, then I hope His example

continues to inspire me to volunteer for others. Never believe that your service is in vain, but know that all you do for God doesn't go unnoticed.

## "Are You Fishing?"
### Matthew 4:19, Luke 15:7a

We took some children from our church on a fishing trip. We were very blessed to have some of the men of our church go along with us and enjoy the fun and excitement of children catching fish. We drove over to Lee's State Park and fished in the pond. Do you know how much fun it is to watch children catch fish?

Well, I have fished on and off for many years. I wouldn't say I was an accomplished fisherman, or even know what it takes to always catch them. Matter of fact, Peggy always jokes with someone who invites me to go. She tells them if they take me, they are setting themselves up for no fish at all. I have fished enough to know that you must cast out into the unknown and just wait for the fish to come along and take your bait.

Well, that is what I used to believe until this day. We have a young boy who went fishing with us. He was standing close to me next to the pond and was casting his line out into the water. All of a sudden, he cried, "There is a fish right there swimming next to the bank. I'm going to catch him."

Well, I kind of laughed, because I have never seen anyone just see a fish next to the bank and catch the fish they were looking at. Of course, I didn't discourage him as he frantically reeled in his line. As soon as he got his line reeled in, he carefully placed his hook with the cricket in front of the fish. I just knew at any moment the fish would quickly swim away from the bank, but guess what happened? You guessed it, the fish took the bait and the young boy had caught the first fish of the day.

He was so excited. He jumped up and down and cried out to everyone that he had caught a fish. All of the other children came running and the trip had now been a success because someone caught a fish. I just never would have believed that you could see a fish and then catch the fish that easy.

Now, all of the seeing and catching got me to Just Thinking! Jesus called out to the fisherman at the seashore. He said, "Come and follow me and I will make you fishers of men."

Centuries have gone by and Jesus is still calling men and women, boys and girls, to put down their nets and become fishers of men. Today, the church has every tool imaginable to reach out to our neighbors and tell them about the wonderful love of Jesus. We have seminars, books and sermons on how we should all be witnesses to the wonderful sacrifice of Jesus and the eternal life He promises to all who believe.

We sometimes feel guilty and even feel good when the pastor preaches on our lack of soul winning and say we are going to do better. But, the truth of the matter is that most of us feel inadequate in sharing our faith. I think maybe that we need to quit trying so hard to be perfect in casting out our line into the depths of the unknown and need to learn from a little boy with a fishing rod.

Maybe we just need to look around us and find someone who needs to know about the love of Jesus. Maybe instead of trying to do it all perfectly, we just need to dangle the bait before the one who needs Jesus and ask them if they would like to accept Him as their Lord and Savior. Maybe we need to just believe that if we are faithful in placing Jesus in front of the one in need, they will jump at the chance to find love and acceptance. Maybe we need to learn from a little child that the only way to catch a fish is to place the bait in front of its mouth.

Remember these words of Jesus, "I tell you, there is rejoicing in the presence of the angels of God over one sinner who repents." It only takes one and then you are hooked for life as a fisher of men.

## "Are You Thirsty?"
### John 4:10,13

Lee State Park is the home to 17 natural springs. We were able to observe a couple of them as they were consistently gushing out from the ground. I have visited the spring that is set up for people to actually drink from. I have even got a drink from the ever-flowing stream of water.

The water was fresh, clean and cool. It was a refreshing change from seeing the dingy water of the pond. You can also notice the pool of water that sits beneath the spring. Although there is a dirt floor below the pool of water, the water is crystal clear. It is amazing to watch as the water seems to just replenish itself from below with no help from a pump. The water flows free and clear eternally.

Now, the fresh, clear, and inviting pure water got me to Just Thinking! You remember the story of Jesus and the woman at the well? Jesus asked her for a drink and they began talking about the reasons why a Samaritan woman shouldn't be talking to a male Jew.

Then, all of a sudden without any warning, Jesus tells the woman, "If you knew the gift of God and who it is that asks you for a drink, you would have asked him and he would have given you living water."

The water that I saw gushing out of the ground made me think about that water Jesus offers to all who will accept. You know it takes a sacrifice to get people to serve in the church. Sometimes, you have to beg and plead to get volunteers to teach children in Sunday School or to keep the nursery. I am glad when you have plenty that want to help and see the church flourish. You know if just one person can experience the refreshing water of Jesus, every moment spent serving God will be worth it.

After the discussion with the woman at the well Jesus said, "Everyone who drinks this water will be thirsty again, but whoever drinks the water I give him will never thirst. Indeed, the water I give him will become in him a spring of water welling up to eternal life."

What a joy it will be to know that the spring of water is living in each and every person; not the fresh, pure, spring water of the ground, but the eternal water of Jesus that makes it so we never thirst again. The church should be a place where people can experience the fresh clear water of Jesus. The church should be a place where the water never runs dry. My prayer is that if you are thirsty, you will try Jesus for an eternal thirst quencher.

## "Are You Following an Expert?"
### 1 Corinthians 3:10-11

On a summer work project with the youth of the church we found out we would be putting on vinyl siding. I asked our crew chief if he had ever put on siding before. He said no. He asked me, knowing this was my sixth project, if I ever had put vinyl siding on before and I said no. We asked our crew of one other adult woman and the eight youth had they ever put on vinyl siding before and they all said no. Well, you can imagine our stress as we spent Monday painting the roof and wondering how we would ever get started putting on siding if we had never done it before.

On Monday afternoon, one of the men from the church came by and told us about Dave. Dave was a man whose wife attended the church that was sponsoring this project. The man told us that Dave would be here on Tuesday to help us with the siding. We all gave a great big sigh of relief.

On Tuesday morning Dave showed up. Dave was 66-years old and was a retired union carpenter. When Dave showed up, everything got into gear. We began putting up siding and getting the youth involved with the project. Dave taught me a great deal about putting on siding. Matter of fact, I said that had I been to this project before I sided my own house, I could have done it myself. It is amazing how much you can accomplish if you have someone around who knows what has to be done and how to do it.

Now, Dave's expertise got me to Just Thinking! Who is the

expert when it comes to getting life right? Who is the expert when it comes to growing as a Christian? Who is the expert when it comes to growing and sustaining a church? I believe I know the answer, and the answer is Jesus.

Jesus is the one who can teach us and has shown us how to live life and do it abundantly. Jesus is the one who showed us how we should treat our brothers and sisters and live each day as a servant. Jesus is the one who said that if we were to build a church, we would have to build the church on His principles and examples. Jesus is the one who said if we want to be His disciple, we must love each other.

It is good to have an expert on the project when you are doing something that you are not familiar with. When Paul spoke to the church at Corinth, he spoke about building something that would last. Listen to his words: "By the grace God has given me, I laid a foundation as a wise builder, and someone else is building on it. But each one should build with care. For no one can lay any foundation other than the one already laid, which is Jesus Christ."

We can learn and grow from others around us, but we had better make sure that all our teaching and growing comes from the one who laid the foundation. Jesus is the expert and we need to be the students. The more we learn from Him, the more we will be like Him. What a mess we would have made of that house had it not been for Dave. What a mess we make of life and the church without Jesus.

## "How Much are You Giving?"
### Romans 12:1

One day, we prepared two different meals for two different groups at our church. We had the privilege of cooking for and feeding the Salkehatchie Summer service group which was in the city to work on some homes in our area. We served them our famous fried chicken with all of the trimmings. We fed about 80 and we had plenty for them to eat. They are always a very gracious group and appreciate what you do for them.

Then, after we finished cleaning up from that lunch, we had a quick turnaround to begin a fish fry. The men's ministry of our church got together and fried fish for the church. We invited the whole church to come out and enjoy the fish. We had the fish donated from some of the fishermen in our church.

We gathered our frying pans, made some coleslaw and fried some French fries. Now, as we were preparing the fish, someone asked me if I knew how many to prepare for. I said no. But we decided that we didn't want to fry too many fish and have a good many left over. So, we put some of them back into the freezer and went with our decision not to fry them all.

Well, for the first time in my life I think we fried just enough; not too many and not too few. Matter of fact, as I went back to the serving line, I saw one fish left on the plate. I tried to give it to someone and they couldn't eat it, but someone else came along and gobbled it up.

I was amazed to see all of the fish eaten or prepared to take a plate to someone who was unable to attend. Now, I must admit to you that most of the time that I am in charge of cooking anything I always fix too much, but this time it was just enough.

The fact that it worked out to be just enough got me to Just Thinking! How often have we given too little in the service of God in our church? How often do we give too much? I would contend that we most often give too little and then feel guilty about how little we give. We beat ourselves up because we don't do enough. Yet, God is always ready and willing to accept our gifts in whatever capacity we give it. God calls us to give our best.

The words of Paul ring true: "Therefore, I urge you, brothers, in view of God's mercy, to offer your bodies as living sacrifices, holy and pleasing to God - this is your spiritual act of worship."

Whatever you give to God is pleasing to Him. It is not pleasing if you give it reluctantly or begrudgingly. God wants what you give to be a desire from your heart. If you do service to God out of your heart, you will always be giving to him the best you have. That is all He asks of us.

## "Is There Film in Your Camera?"
### Psalm 126:2

At the church's day camp, we take a great many pictures of the children having fun. On Monday we always take a picture of each group and then we print every participant a copy of their group.

My son, Caleb, was in charge of taking the pictures. He took all of the pictures on Monday and carried the camera around to all of the groups participating in different activities. He continued to take photos and watched as the camera snapped the shots and the flash went off.

He continued to take these photos until Wednesday morning when he got curious about the fact that it said he was taking his 46thh photo on the same roll of film. He had heard of high exposure film, but he was a little suspect. He began investigating and discovered that there was no film in the camera. Everyone began to laugh at him. He was laughing the loudest.

He called me on the phone as I was returning to the church to pick up some supplies. I answered the phone and he said, "Dad, I know you will probably get mad, but to tell you the truth I think this is very funny. I've been taking pictures with no film in the camera."

At first, I was frustrated because we had lost some good pictures, but to tell you the truth it was hard to be mad because Caleb was laughing so hard on the other end of the line. We laughed about that incident and we were able to get film in the camera and get our pictures taken in plenty of time to provide each participant with their picture.

Now, the fact that Caleb took all those pictures without film in the camera got me to Just Thinking! There are times in our life where we are doing good things and performing well for others to see, but there is nothing on the inside. The church can look good on the outside, but inwardly we are struggling with relationship issues, financial issues, or leadership issues. We paint a good picture on the outside, but on the inside, we are sad or stressed or just downright miserable.

We sometimes need to look at things in a different light. We need to take life with a slightly less-serious tone and look at things from a different perspective. I could have gotten really mad at my son and really raked him over the coals for not doing his job and getting the pictures he was supposed to get, but to tell you the truth, all that would have done is made us all feel worse.

Instead, we just regrouped and took a different perspective on the matter, laughed about it and got the job done. I do believe that laughter is one way that we can get through some tough times in our life. I believe that if inside our heart where the difference really matters, we have the love and acceptance of Jesus we can get through any circumstance.

When the captives were returned from exile the Psalmist wrote, "Our mouths were filled with laughter, our tongues with songs of joy. Then it was said among the nations, 'The LORD has done great things for them.' The LORD has done great things for us, and we are filled with joy."

God makes the bad things good. I invite you if you have been drawing a picture without God to put him in the camera of your life and start to enjoy life in living color.

## "How High Have You Climbed?
Matthew 5:48, Philippians 2:12-14

One of the highlights of the church day camp is when we take the children to the climbing wall. Now the climbing wall is 35 feet high. From the ground, it is very scary looking when all you have to hold on to a few fake rocks placed on a flat-boarded surface.

# JUST THINKING!

I am always amazed at the children who quickly jump to the front of the line to climb and also those who slink away from the chance to make their way up the steep incline. The ones that amazed me the most were the little girls. They would strap on the harness and put on that red helmet and up the side of the wall they would go. They weren't inhibited in the least.

I want to tell you about one young girl named Ally. She was one of the first to climb up the wall. I didn't watch her the first time, but she didn't get very far before she came down. She then began to bug me about when she could climb again. I told her that if we had time she could climb again. Every few minutes she would ask me if she could have another turn. Finally, after everyone who had wanted to had climbed, I allowed Ally to harness up again. While she was waiting, her older sister climbed to the top of the wall.

It finally became Ally's turn again. She was hooked up to the rope and up she started. I watched her this time as she quickly went up about 10 feet. Then, she came to her obstacle: her arms were not long enough to reach the next rock. She struggled and strained to be able to go up another step, but finally, after several minutes, she descended the wall.

I praised her for her efforts, but it was to no avail. She began to cry because she was unsuccessful in climbing to the top of the wall. We all consoled her and told her that next year she will be grown and be able to climb to the top. Nothing really seemed to matter to her except that she was not able to climb to the top.

Now, the fact that this 5-year-old little girl was upset about not accomplishing her goal got me to Just Thinking! How many of us are satisfied with just trying? How many of us are comfortable just getting on the wall without trying to get to the top? How many of us have gotten to a place in our spiritual lives where we have quit striving to go any higher?

Do we feel the same way about the church? Are we complacent with where we are and really not looking to go any higher? We can use the excuse that at least we try, but to tell you the truth,

God wants us to strive to be the best we can be. Didn't Jesus say, "Be perfect, therefore, as your heavenly Father is perfect"? We have accepted mediocrity way too long. We have been satisfied with just sitting on the wall instead of setting our goal to get to the top of the wall. I only wish that as Christians we would set our goal to get to the top of the spiritual platform. I wish the church would always be willing to move to a different level. I only wish that we would show as much disappointment in our own lives when we fail to become all God wants us to be as Ally did when she didn't complete her goal.

Let us remember what Paul said about striving., "Not that I have already obtained all this, or have already arrived at my goal, but I press on to take hold of that for which Christ Jesus took hold of me. Brothers and sisters, I do not consider myself yet to have taken hold of it. But one thing I do: Forgetting what is behind and straining toward what is ahead, I press on toward the goal to win the prize for which God has called me heavenward in Christ Jesus."

I don't think it is a coincidence that Ally was climbing heavenward. I only hope that we and the church will get off the ground spiritually and not quit until we have reached the goal that God calls us to.

## "Are You Working?"
### Matthew 9:37-38

During the COVID epidemic, Peggy and I took my mom and dad and drove to Savannah to be with my brother and his family for the funeral of his wife. We arrived in Savannah around 8 p.m. and started toward the hotel.

Before we got to the hotel, we began to look for a fast-food establishment so everyone could get a bite to eat.

As we drove around, we found that all of the fast-food establishments we drove by were already closed at 8:30 p.m.

This was highly unusual for a Sunday night. We could find no food establishments open. They ended up eating crackers and drinking drinks from a vending machine at the hotel.

You have probably noticed, like I have, that most of these establishments have signs outside saying "hiring." Many of these establishments are offering incentives for people to come and work. There are many opportunities for employment, yet it seems like no one wants to go to work. I even read a news report the other day that grocery stores are having to close earlier because they cannot get people to work so that they can stay open later. Businesses are having to adjust and so are the consumers. There is a need, yet the need is not being filled.

As I recognized this dilemma, it got me to Just Thinking! There is a shortage of workers in the church today, also. Matter of fact, this shortage is something that hasn't just started, but been going on for many years. Jesus even pointed it out to His disciples when He said, "The harvest is plentiful, but the workers are few. Ask the Lord of the harvest, therefore, to send out workers into his harvest field."

There is a world of needy people and God needs workers to work the field. Each of us who call ourselves Christian has a responsibility to share the message of Jesus with others. It is our job to let others know what Jesus has done for us and that He can do the same for others. We need to pray that Jesus will send us to those who need to hear the message of Jesus. We need to pray that God will place us in the right situation so that we can share His love with others.

I would hate to think that one day the church will have to close because it cannot get enough workers to serve. It would be a tragedy for someone to come to the church and find a sign that said, "Not open for lack of workers."

Remember, someone told you about Jesus and His love. So, we have the duty to tell others. We cannot hoard this wonderful news. Let's take it upon ourselves to keep the church open so that others will hear the word and come to a saving knowledge of Jesus.

If we don't tell, how will they hear? You and I have a job to do so let's go about doing it.

# CHAPTER SEVEN
# JUST THINKING... ABOUT HEALTH!

### "How Is Your Vision?"
### John 20:28-29

I see the eye doctor at least once a year now. For about 40 years I was very blessed with good vision. I can tell you that over the past few years my eyesight has diminished. I can't see as well as I once could. I especially have trouble reading and seeing up close.

I began remedying the situation with some cheap reading glasses that I kept close at hand. They helped to begin with, and I also noticed that I read better where there was a great deal of light.

The first doctor I saw told me that I am a little nearsighted. He said that in reality that has helped my ability to see up close. He said that is why it has taken this long for my close sight to get so bad. He said my nearsightedness is overcompensating for my vision up close.

Over the years the eyesight continued to get worse. At later appointments the doctors told me that my eyesight was continuing to diminish. After several visits, I was finally fitted for bifocals. In recent visits, I have had to have my prescription changed as my eyesight continues to worsen. I am glad to have these professionals to help me get a handle on my eyesight.

Now, having my eyes checked has got me to Just Thinking! Have you had your spiritual sight checked lately? Have you had a self-examination to find out how you are seeing the things of God? Many times, we get lazy and decide that we don't need to refocus. But in reality, we need to make sure we are seeing things as God sees them. We have our own opinion and our own ideas and sometimes we have decided that they must be OK with God.

I remember what happened when Thomas doubted that Jesus had risen from the grave. He would not believe until he saw the nail prints and the place where the spear had pierced Jesus' side.

There are times when we are like Thomas and don't believe unless we see. Our eyesight has to be readjusted to see things as God sees them. He will show us things if we only ask.

Thomas asked, and Jesus appeared and told him to see the nail prints. Thomas's confession was that he fell on his face and proclaimed Jesus as "My Lord and My God." Do you remember what Jesus said? This was His response to Thomas: "Because you have seen me, you have believed; blessed are those who have not seen and yet have believed."

Our eyesight needs to be the eyesight of faith. We need to see as God sees through the eyes of faith. We need the Light of the World to illuminate our way so that we can see. Jesus is the Light of the World, and if we put our faith in Him, we will always see perfectly the ways of God.

## "Talk About Inconveniences!"
### Luke 2:11

You've heard the saying "Been There, Done That!"

Well, I feel like that a little since I spent a day in the hospital. I had a little bout with a kidney stone. I won the war, but it sure took its toll in the battle. It had been many years since I had been

# JUST THINKING!

in the hospital as a patient. Now, I go to the hospital a great deal. Matter of fact, when they were admitting me and would ask me if I had ever been in their hospital before, I would always answer, "Not as a patient."

I realized something that subconsciously I really already knew. I like being the visitor instead of the visited. Visitors can come and go as they please. There is no one trying to stick you with a needle, take your temp, or read your blood pressure. Visitors can go out and eat real food for their meals - not brown water that they let a chicken look at. Visitors can go home and sleep in their own beds without a nurse coming in at 2 a.m., turning on the light, waking you up and asking if you need anything.

Yet, where would we be without doctors, nurses, and hospitals? I am sure glad I had them, even if for only one day. It was a gift from God to know I had a place to go to take care of my problem. Sure, it was an inconvenience, but I do not know what I would have done without them.

Now, the visit to the hospital has got me to Just Thinking. Talk about inconveniences, how about what God did for us at Christmas? Inconvenience of a virgin birth; the acceptance of Mary by Joseph; having to travel to Bethlehem to pay taxes; no rooms; a stable to have a baby (I bet Mary wished she could have had the inconveniences of a modern-day hospital); the giving up of one's own son for the salvation of the world.

Now, there is real inconvenience. Yet, we take it for granted and Christmases come and go. Do we really ever appreciate all that God went through to bring Jesus to Earth? Do we ever consider all that Mary and Joseph had to deal with in bringing Jesus to life? We get so comfortable with our lives I think sometimes we fail to recognize all that was done so that you and I might receive salvation.

Remember what the angel said: "Today in the town of David a Savior has been born to you, he is the Messiah, the Lord." The baby born in Bethlehem was "Jesus, Christ the Lord." Each year at Christmas we may think, "Been There, Done That." But we must realize that each year we celebrate the true Gift from God; Jesus. I'm glad it wasn't an inconvenience.

### "Cancer Can't Win!"
### 1 Corinthians 15:40

Well, it happened. I guess we all are aware of the possibilities, but when it happens to you it is still a shock. My father had surgery to remove cancer from his prostate.

Cancer is a word that sends all of us (no generality here) wondering about life, its quality and how we have lived it.

And there that word hangs its ugly head - not just with a church member or acquaintance, but now it hangs its head over my Dad. During my ministry, I have watched many people face cancer. I have seen many of them die. Yet, I have also seen many of them LIVE. The dreaded word from any doctor to their patient is, "You have cancer."

Dealing with cancer with my Dad has got me to Just Thinking! When something invades your personal life like this has mine, it makes you sit down and take notice of it. A very dear friend of mine gave me a poem a few months back. It was written by Dan Richardson. Dan was a believer in Christ, but he lost the battle with cancer. This poem was distributed at his funeral.

"Cancer is so limited...
It cannot cripple love,
It cannot cripple hope,
It cannot corrode faith,
It cannot eat away peace,
It cannot destroy confidence,
It cannot kill friendship,
It cannot shut out memories,
It cannot silence courage,

It cannot invade the soul,
It cannot reduce eternal life,
It cannot quench the Spirit,
It cannot lessen the power of the resurrection."

Truer words have not been spoken. Cancer is an earthly disease. It cannot destroy us unless we allow it to. Paul wrote, "There are also heavenly bodies and there are earthly bodies; but the splendor of the heavenly bodies is one kind, and the splendor of earthly bodies is another."

Let us never forget that our greatest enemy is not disease, but despair. Whatever comes your way, have faith and trust and don't despair, but Believe!!!

## "Are You a Child of the King?"
Romans 8:16-17

In January, 1994 my father was diagnosed with prostate cancer. That ugly word "cancer" had reared its head in my family and all of us were scared.

Now, January has come and gone. My dad recuperated from surgery and the doctor says is gone. Dad will live a normal life without the threat of cancer of the prostate. What comes to mind? Relief! Gratefulness! Thankfulness! All of these words help to create in me a feeling of joy and excitement.

At Duke University Hospital they treated my father like a king. We could not have asked for better treatment from doctors, nurses and the whole hospital staff. Everything they did was first class. We had a great big room. Mom had a bed to sleep in as she stayed with Dad. There was a small refrigerator in the room that they kept stocked with drinks and water. There was a menu so Dad and Mom could order at meal times. It was all unbelievable.

All of this royal treatment got me Just Thinking. Paul records in the Bible these words, "The Spirit Himself bears witness with our spirits that we are God's children; and if children, then also heirs, heirs of God and fellow-heirs with Christ - if in reality we share His sufferings, so that we may share His Glory too."

Now why do I (I can't speak for all of you) get so surprised when God has me treated like a king? Why am I so surprised when I see prayers answered? I have realized in my own life through this experience with my dad that I need to believe in who I am. Who I am is "A Child of The King."

I am not just a citizen of this world; my citizenship is in another world. It is a world unlike anything I could ever imagine. My prayer is that I hope you are a child of the King. I pray that you know who you are and what God can do for you. We must realize that we may have to suffer some, but we all will share in His Glory.

I am grateful for all of the care that my dad and mom were given during his hospital stay, but I shouldn't be surprised. When you are part of God's family, you should expect nothing but the best.

As my dad said after the surgery, "God's done it again!"

## "Praising God in the Tough Times!"
### 2 Corinthians 12:9

I have been fortunate to spend time in hospitals as a volunteer chaplain. One afternoon, I went into a room and met the Pates. Mrs. Lura Pate was the patient, having had surgery a few days earlier for cancer. Mr. Earl Pate graciously rose to greet me and welcome me into the room. I asked Mrs. Pate how she was doing and her response was, "Better today, thank the Lord."

As I began to explore Mrs. Pate's life, I found out that she has had numerous types of cancer over the past 40 years and many surgeries to correct and help her win the battle with cancer. Despite having been in and out of the hospital, having heard numerous doctors tell her of her plight, having been confined at home with an open wound for nine months, Mr. and Mrs. Pate still praised God for His loving and merciful care and concern for her life.

Matter of fact, as I related to them, I was supposed to be the one to bring a little sunshine into their lives and they had, in turn, given me a greater sense of hope and peace having met them. After listening to their story and being told time and time again of how good God had been to them, I left that room with a greater sense of what it means to "Rejoice in the Lord always." The Pates sure did.

Now, the conversation with the Pates has got me to Just Thinking! How many times do we complain about the little inconveniences of life? How often do we gripe about small hardships and little problems? Upon leaving Mrs. Pate's room that morning, I realized just how much I have to be thankful for in life. After leaving Mrs. Pate's room I came to a realization: I promised myself to be more grateful for what God has given me and complain less.

Mr. and Mrs. Pate helped me to see more clearly what Paul wrote: "My grace is sufficient for you, for power is perfected in weakness."

The Pates had had their share of problems. They had their share of heartaches. They could have griped and complained about all they had gone through. Yet, they still praised God for His goodness to them. What a testimony of God's goodness!

Thank you, Mr. and Mrs. Pate, for helping me to start trusting more in the Power of God and His Sufficient Grace.

## "He Has Overcome the World!"
### John 16:33

I arrived at the hospital just a few minutes late. They had already taken the patient down to have a heart catheterization. I walked in and spoke to his wife. She greeted me with a smile and we began to talk. We talked about all sorts of things.

Finally, after about 40 minutes, the doctor walked in. The wife, in a very relaxed mood, stood and spoke to the doctor.

She even asked how his vacation had been the week before. He walked over and sat her down. He sat across from her on the bed and looked at her very seriously. "I'm sorry," he said. "We will have to take your husband to surgery. There was a complication with the procedure and we need to do open-heart surgery immediately."

The wife went from calm and reserved to hysterical. She began to scream and cry, "WHY? WHAT HAPPENED? IS HE OK???" The doctor tried to reassure her. Then, finally, she yelled, "YES! GO AHEAD! DO THE SURGERY! GO TAKE CARE OF MY HUSBAND!!!"

The doctor told her there would be some papers to sign. She signed them and they were off. She became a nervous wreck. Finally, I was able to calm her. We prayed together. She went and called her son and daughter. Her husband had successful open-heart surgery and fully recovered.

Now, this frantic display of uncertainty has got me to Just Thinking! Sometimes in our life when we think we have everything under control, something or someone comes by and slaps us right in the face. We go from soft, calm and controlled to frantic, without hope and uncontrollable. It's as if time stands still and we have to try and overcome the shock of the moment.

Life can be so cruel, especially when we feel we've lost control. This wife had expected a doctor to walk in and tell her that everything went well with the procedure and that her husband would be back in the room in a few minutes. In a matter of seconds this expectation was destroyed. She went from being totally in control of her emotions to uncontrollable.

It happens to all of us at one time or another. Yet, In steps Jesus. When we are a believer, these situations are never a surprise to Jesus. He knows everything about us and is there with us during these times.

It is why he spoke these comforting words: "In this world you will have trouble. But be of good cheer I have overcome the world."

If you are struggling with the uncertainties of life, I recommend that you go to the one who has overcome all that life can throw at you. I recommend Jesus to you.

## "The Pictures of Life!"
Psalm 139:1-3

I officiated at a funeral for a friend who passed away after his battle with cancer. I met him as part of my cancer support group. He was 56 years old and had battled cancer for 16 years.

As Peggy and I stood in line to speak to his wife and children there was a series of pictures chronicling his life showing on a video screen. The pictures began when he was a young boy and continued up through adulthood. There were pictures of him enjoying life. In every picture, he was smiling and seemed to be enjoying everything he was participating in. There was a picture of a hunting expedition where he had bagged a big deer. There was a picture of him sitting in a lounge chair, just taking it easy. There was a picture of him and his wife dancing at their wedding. Every picture showed a man who was happy and carefree. Every picture painted life as good.

As I watched these pictures it got me to Just Thinking! Have you ever noticed that pictures do not always tell the whole story? There are not too many pictures of the hard times of life. There are not too many pictures where we are experiencing pain. There are not too many pictures of us dealing with life's difficult times. The pictures we take show us with smiles on our faces with family and friends sharing life. Yet, all of us know life is not just full of smiles.

Life is full of uncertainty. We take pictures to remind us of the events in life that make us happy. We seldom take pictures of events we want to forget. Yet, it is often those tough times in our lives that help to shape our lives. We often get stronger and more adept at living life through the hard times.

As I reflect on the whole of life, I am glad for the good times with family and friends. I am glad to take pictures with my family to remember fun outings and vacations. I am happy to share those memories and be reminded of those times. I know that God has blessed me with those times and I cherish every one of them.

When the hard times come, I am also thankful. I am thankful that I do not face hard times alone. I am thankful that that same family who smiles with me in the picture is standing beside me during the tough times. I am glad that God is with me in the tough times as well as the good times.

The Psalmist said, "You have searched me, LORD, and you know me. You know when I sit and when I rise; you perceive my thoughts from afar. You discern my going out and my lying down; you are familiar with all my ways."

God sees every picture of my life. He is with me in every situation. He doesn't just show up for the smiles, He shows up for the difficult times also.

When you look back on your life, I hope you find God in all the pictures. I hope you will know that He was there. I hope you will allow Him to give you joy and comfort you in the uncertainties of life. God is for us and with us. Hopefully, that will make you smile.

## "His Ways are not My Ways!"
### Isaiah 55:8-9

My cancer journey began on a Friday night. We had finished the annual cruise-in at church that evening and Peggy and I went home. Somewhere around midnight, she woke me up and ended up calling 911. The ambulance transported me to Bon Secours St. Francis hospital. Through a doctor there, an ear, nose and throat specialist was called in and they began working to diagnose my problem.

After several trips to the hospital in the next few weeks, they finally told me the diagnosis. It was cancer. I remember hearing that word for the first time and not asking "why me?," but "why not me?"

My life changed drastically, to say the least. I have had to make many major adjustments with my body. When the cancer returned in my right knee, again life had to be adjusted. As the results of the radiation continued to wreak havoc on my throat, more adjustments had to be made. Needless to say, my life has not taken the course I would have hoped it would. There are things I hoped to be doing today that I am unable to do.

Now, I do not know why these things have taken place in my life. I have really never had a pity party where I asked why, but I have wondered about the circumstances that have placed me where I am today. Yet, let me say this unequivocally: I trust God no matter the circumstances.

Like Isaiah recorded God as saying, "'For my thoughts are not your thoughts, neither are your ways my ways,' declares the Lord. 'As the heavens are higher than the earth, so are my ways higher than your ways and my thoughts than your thoughts.'"

I have come to understand that His ways are not my ways. So, I take what He has given me and try to do my best with the results. I have not complained, but I still seek to see what He has in store for my life. I will live it to the best of my abilities until the day He calls me home.

The results of cancer in my life have got me to Just Thinking! Why is it so hard to trust God? We deal with life's troubles and cower in the unknown. Yet, if we are children of God, we should always know that He cares for us and our situations. Yes, we may have to endure some hardships, but we never endure them alone. We as His children, of all people, should know that He is on our side.

Yet, I deal with so many Christians who worry and fear the things that they have no control over. Many years ago, I helped take care of a 90+-year-old man. He used to tell me, "I do what I can and then I throw it over my shoulder and keep going."

That is not a bad attitude. It is using what God has given us to do our best and then trusting Him with the rest. The more we trust, the less we worry. The less we worry, the more joy and peace we feel in our everyday lives.

I want to encourage you to trust God more. Don't allow the worries of this world to get you down and destroy your lives. Allow the peace of God to fill you with courage to face whatever comes your way, knowing that you never face it alone. God will always be by your side to help you and lead you through. You can always depend on Him. Trust God! He will not let you down.

## "Listen More!"
### James 1:19

For most of my life my voice was my strong point. I have always had a very robust, strong voice. I was often told when I was a boy to calm down and not speak so loudly. I could talk with anyone and about everything. I loved conversation. In school, I was often told to quit talking. I always seemed to have something to say.

Life has changed for me since my cancer journey. Talking has become more of a challenge. Words used to come so easily; now they are sometimes a struggle. I am slower to just jump into a conversation because my words are not so easily understood anymore. I used to be able to command a crowd with my voice; now it no longer has the strength to stand alone. I am grateful for the ability to continue talking, but I now realize what a privilege it is to speak.

When they put the tracheostomy tube in my throat, I was afraid my talking had come to an end. Yet, they entered the room one day to give me a valve that allows me to speak while wearing it. I am grateful. Yet, without the valve words do not come unless I block the tube. Life has changed, and I am adjusting.

The fact that words come a little harder has got me to Just Thinking! For most of my life I always had an opinion on whatever topic was being discussed. I would jump in with both feet and wade deep into the conversation. I am now learning to listen more and talk less.

I am reminded of what James says in his book, "My dear brothers and sisters, take note of this: Everyone should be quick to listen, slow to speak and slow to become angry, ..." These are wise words spoken to all of us. We need to learn to listen more and speak less.

God's Word is the great teacher. We would do well to listen to it more and implement those words into our lives. As we learn to listen more, we may have more to say that is worth listening to. So, I am learning to listen more. I am learning to pay more attention to what others are saying and not be so quick to talk.

I am grateful to be able to speak, but I want my words to reflect what God is saying and not my own opinion. My prayer is that God would help me to focus my words on His way and that I would reflect His intentions. May God help us all to listen more and talk less.

## "God is Working!"
### John 5:17

I only know what I have been told. On a Sunday morning, I did not wake up and Peggy called EMS. I was in cardiac arrest and had to be shocked back to normal. I was rushed to Prisma Health's trauma unit and was put on a respirator. They were not sure how badly I had been affected.

Sometime during the morning, with Peggy by my side, I woke up. Peggy said one of the nurses called it a Jesus thing. I was able to communicate with sign language and writing in her hand to find out what was going on. Both of my boys were there. It was a pretty scary time for all of them.

The main reason for the problem was the lack of oxygen getting into my system. Without significant oxygen the body begins to shut down, and mine did that morning. The doctors were able to resuscitate me and provide me with adequate oxygen for my body to begin to function again. I am grateful for all of those who helped me while I was in distress, starting with the Duncan Chapel Fire Department, the EMS team, and the doctors and nurses at Prisma's trauma unit. I was grateful to have my family close at hand during the fight and was glad to be able to come back to them and live another day.

I am now learning to live with a tracheotomy. My breathing is better and my oxygen levels are holding steady. The valve that they gave me to help me talk was a surprise and a blessing. I believe I am here because God saw fit to restore me. He listened to the prayers of many people and answered those prayers. I am blessed beyond measure and give God all the glory for what He has done in my life.

Now, this new experience has got me to Just Thinking! Even when we are not aware of it, God is working in our lives. Jesus made this very clear when He said, "My Father is always at work to this very day, and I too am working."

I do not remember anything that took place early that Sunday morning. I only know what I was told. I believe that God has His hand in my life and my recovery. He was at work.

How often do we rely on God in the unknown? We worry about the unknown, but do not put our total confidence in Him about it. We must learn to trust completely and without reservation. I know prayer works, because I felt it once I knew what was going on. I knew that my family and friends were praying for me and my healing. It made a difference.

I want to encourage you to trust in the unknown. I want to assure you that the God who sees you in the daytime is also there when you are asleep and unaware. He is a God who wants the best for you because He loves you and cares deeply for you. We must never give up on God because we have hard times or struggles. Sometimes, God uses those struggles and hard times to make us more like Him. He helps to shape us into His image.

So, I want to thank God for saving my life. He saw me through a difficult time and gave me the ability to continue on with a new normal. I pray that whatever you are going through today in your life, you will allow God to work in your life and that you will trust Him even in the unknown.

## "Encouragement Makes a Difference"
1 Thessalonians 5:11

I have had many PET (positron emission tomography) scans throughout my cancer journey. I remember when the doctor told me we could start just having one a year since I had been in remission for several years.

We were elated. Yet, it was sad because I would not be able to say thanks to some very important people who had guided me along the way in my cancer journey. Well, I reached out to a very dear friend who works at the Cancer Center. Her name is Jennifer Huggins. Jennifer works as a nurse practitioner in the Palliative Care department. I told her my good news and expressed my regret about not being able to tell two people thanks for all they had done for and meant to me during these last four years. I asked her to please relate to these two people my gratitude.

Well Jennifer was elated with my news and promised she would relay the message the next day. I had done all I could at the time. I was not able to go and say thanks myself, because they will not allow you in the building unless you have an appointment. So, I just trusted my friend to relay the message. The next afternoon, I received a call from Dr. Dyar's office. I saw on my phone that the call was coming from his office. I wondered what this was about. Well as I answered the phone one of those very special people, Katie, was on the other end.

"Mr. Simmons, it's Katie. I just got your good news and wanted to call and tell you how happy I am for you. I appreciate you letting me know and the kind words you sent." I was elated. Katie and I talked for about five minutes as I again related to her how thankful I was for her friendship and that I would never forget her kindness to me. We talked about family for a minute and then said goodbye.

That call made my day. She didn't have to call, but she thought enough of me to speak to me at least one more time. It does make a difference when people acknowledge their gratitude and thanksgiving for what other people do. Katie will always be special to me and I hope that in some small way I have touched her life in a positive way.

This call from Katie has got me to Just Thinking! Who do you need to call and just express thanks to? Who do you need to call and just let them know what an impact they have made on your life? There is something about hearing that you are making a difference in someone's life. There is something about realizing that your life matters.

Paul expressed to the Thessalonians, "Therefore encourage one another and build each other up, just as in fact you are doing."

Imagine if we went around encouraging one another and expressing our thanks to one another instead of trying to find fault with each other. We are too often settling on the negative instead of the positive.

And what about our thanksgiving to God? Are we in a constant state of thanks to God for all He has done for us? We too often complain about what we do not have, instead of all that God has done for us. We complain if it is too cold or too hot, yet how many of us thank God for heaters and air conditioners? We complain that doctors and medicines cost too much, but do we thank God that we have the resources and insurance to pay for it?

Expressing thanks and encouraging one another is an attitude of the heart. Jesus said that whatever is in the heart comes out of the mouth. My prayer for us is that our attitude will be one of appreciation and thankfulness for all that God has done and all that others have done for us.

## "Spiritual Hearing"
### Revelation 2:7

I woke up and couldn't hear out of my left ear. All of a sudden, it stopped. I figured it would clear in a couple of days.

By Wednesday it hadn't cleared and I called my ENT. He has been my ENT since 2013 and is the doctor who found my cancer. When I called for an appointment, I found out he was on vacation and that the next week was all filled up, so the earliest I could get an appointment was the following week. I went in at 9 a.m., but before I saw him, I had a hearing test.

Now, it has been a long time since I had a hearing test and although similar to the one I had before, it was different in many ways. I guess technology has caught up even with those tests. I stayed in the soundproof room for about 20 minutes hearing words and tones in my ears. I could hear almost nothing in my left ear.

We exited the room and the technician explained to me that I had profound hearing loss in my left ear. She told me this was probably from a condition that she named, but I didn't actually get it. She said Dr. Wood would explain when he came in.

After the nurses got my vitals and made sure they had my medicines up to date, Dr. Wood came in. He explained to me that I had sudden sensorineural hearing loss (SSHL). He said it comes from a virus. He explained it was like Bell's palsy, which also is caused by a virus, but the effects go away and things return to normal over time. The only problem with SSHL is that it doesn't go back to normal over time. You have a window of four-to-six weeks that you have to start treatment or it may never reverse.

Then, he said that to combat SSHL they use steroids. At that I grimaced. I can't take steroids because it counteracts the Keytruda that I take for cancer. He then told me that there was a steroid injection that they could do that could possibly help. I told him that would probably be fine.

Now, living with and learning about SSHL has got me to just thinking! Our preaching pastor has been preaching out of the book of Revelation recently. He has been preaching on the seven churches that Jesus spoke to in this book.

After Jesus addresses the church He says, "Whoever has ears, let them hear what the Spirit says to the churches." Well, we all have ears, but are we using them to hear Jesus when He speaks? I am afraid that after many years of going to church and hearing sermons, that sometimes we do not use our ears to hear the Spirit when It speaks. We hear the preacher, but when we leave the church our lives really never change. We really never apply any of the truths to our lives.

We have Spiritual Hearing Loss and it just hasn't happened. It has happened over the course of many years. We hear the good news of salvation, but then fail to hear the word to grow and mature. We listen to the things that meet our criteria, but fail to hear the things that challenge us to move closer to what God would have us to be.

I want to challenge you to hear the Spirit of God. Hear the words of the message and allow it to sink deep within you and ask God to use those words to create in you the person He wants you to be. Do not live with Spiritual Hearing Loss forever. Take the time to allow Jesus to inject in you the words of life that help you to become the person God wants you to be.

## "God is Enough"
### Lamentations 3:19-26

I remember the day my cancer treatments began. I began my new journey into a life that has changed dramatically. At the time of that first treatment, I weighed 255 pounds. I was diabetic, had high blood pressure and several other medical complications.

The next day I began the 35-day, seven-week trip of my first radiation treatment. The first few weren't so bad. Those first few weeks flew by and then I began to deal with the cumulative effect of the treatments. The chemo didn't make me sick, but I began to

lose all my energy. The radiation finally burnt my throat so badly that I began using a feeding tube in my stomach to receive all of my nourishment. At the time, that really wasn't enough to sustain me. As each day went by, the treatments began to deal me a new blow. After about the fourth week, the second chemo treatment and 20th radiation treatment, I completely lost my voice.

It was a scary time. I could barely speak over a whisper. Peggy bought me some small dry erase boards so that I could write down my communications with her. The nutritionist kept pushing fluids and nutrition, but I just didn't have the appetite or the will power to force myself to take in fluids. Slowly, my body began to deteriorate. I couldn't concentrate while reading my Bible. I was sleeping in a hospital bed at home, trying to rest at night with not much luck. My world was turned upside down.

As the treatments ended, I hoped for better days, but the days got worse. I was expecting to start feeling better and I began to feel worse. I didn't realize it, I fell into a depression. I was so fatigued that I didn't want to get out of my chair at home. I was calling out to God, yet I felt alone and afraid. I was worried about my livelihood and my ability to return to my position at church. I would go to the office, only to get there and not be able to climb the stairs. The energy just wasn't there.

Yet, the whole time God WAS there. He was in the depression and showed up in many ways. I received notes and cards every day encouraging me and telling me I was being prayed for. I had the best nurse, my wife, who continued to encourage me and tell me I could do it. God was so prevalent in my sons and their wives as they came around often to show support.

As I began to find some type of normalcy, it got me to Just Thinking! I realized that God had a new normal for me. He began to reveal Himself in new and fresher ways. He began to show me things I never would have seen before. I realized, like Elijah, that God showed up in the most unusual ways. He was in the cancer. I found Him there and I still experience Him in the midst of my struggle today. Through the dark days and in the bright sunlight of days God is there. He never leaves me, nor has He forsaken me. Although there were times I wondered where He was, He always came through and showed Himself true.

Jeremiah was known as the weeping prophet. Almost everything He did was rejected and ridiculed by those who heard him. The book of Lamentations is simply a book of poems of crying out to the Lord. The word Lamentations actually means "to cry aloud." Yet, right in the very middle of these five chapters Jeremiah speaks the truth of God.

Even in the midst of our grief and suffering we find a faithful and loving God. Here is how Jeremiah said it: "I remember my affliction and my wandering, the bitterness and the gall. I well remember them, and my soul is downcast within me. (Pay Attention) Yet, this I call to mind and therefore I have hope. Because of the Lord's great love, we are not consumed, for His compassions never fail. They are new every morning; great is your faithfulness. I say to myself, 'The Lord is my portion; therefore, I will wait for him.' The Lord is good to those whose hope is in Him, to the one who seeks Him; it is good to wait quietly for the salvation of the Lord." (Parentheses added by author.)

I can tell you that over my cancer journey I have experienced this wonderful love and faithfulness of God. He has come through better than I ever could have imagined. He has done great things for me. I do not now - or ever - want to quit serving Him and giving Him glory. He is enough! I need nothing else!

## "A Fresh Flow"
### Acts 3:19

Radiation therapy for my cancer caused my esophagus to close, so now I feed myself through a tube. As of this writing, I have been doing this for 10 years. I am very used to it and it causes me no undo stress.

When I found out this would be a permanent life change, I

was given a Mic-Key button. It is inserted into my stomach and has to be changed periodically. The bubble that holds it in place ruptures and the button is not secure. Another problem with the button is that the longer it stays in my stomach, the slower the rate of delivery of the liquid nutrition. When I put a new button in, the flow is fast and quick. It takes me a short time to deliver the nutrition - sometimes as quickly as 15 minutes. The longer the button stays in the stomach, the slower the delivery of the nutrition.

And when the button bursts and I leave it in for several weeks before I change it out, the delivery is slowest of all. Sometimes it takes as much as 40 minutes to deliver the nutrition.

By now, you have either quit reading or you are wondering what in the world David is trying to teach us in this description of his eating habits. Well, I am not trying to gross you out, but I do want you to know that experiencing and talking about all of this has got me to Just Thinking! Do you remember the freshness of experiencing God for the first time? You were finding joy and excitement in reading His word. You were taking as much time as you needed to pray and experience His presence. You were looking forward to Sunday worship and Wednesday Bible studies and prayer to see all that God had in store for you. The time just seemed to fly by and you were diving into every opportunity you could just to be closer to God.

Now, after years of reading and praying and worshiping, it seems like "old hat." You endure! You hurry through your Bible reading. You say your prayers, but don't really pray. You come and worship, but your mind is somewhere else. Well, like my button when it gets older and bursts, the flow is just not as good as it once was. Something has gotten in the way. You have allowed complacency to cloud your view. You have decided you've heard a sermon preached on that passage before. You have listened to a Sunday School lesson on that topic. You've been around so long it is just not exciting anymore.

Maybe it's time for a new vision. Maybe it's time for a new perspective. Maybe it's time for you and I to get our focus off of self and put it on Jesus and all that He has done for us. Maybe it is the sin of just plain pride that makes us think that there is nothing new for us to learn. Well, I'm for confessing that sin and looking into all that the Holy Spirit can teach me to allow the flow of God's goodness and grace to fill me to the brim.

When Peter is talking to the people in Jerusalem during that very first sermon after Jesus' resurrection he says, "Repent, then, and turn to God, so that your sins may be wiped out, that times of refreshing may come from the Lord."

We need a time of refreshing. We need a steady flow of God's love and grace. We need to want more of God and seek Him with our whole heart. There would be less complaining, less dissatisfaction, and fewer empty pews if we all wanted to come to church and find more of God.

If it's been a while since you have recommitted your life to Jesus, why not now? If it has been a while since you started reading God's word fresh and new, why not now? If it's been a while since you just set time to pray and listen to the Holy Spirit, why not now? If it has been a while since you came to worship with nowhere else to go, why not now? The church will come alive when the Holy Spirit is allowed to come alive in each of us. I'm all for a new Spiritual Flow in our lives.

## "A Spiritual Checkup"
### Colossians 1:9b-10

Every time you go and see a doctor, they take your "vital" signs. The nurse comes in and takes your blood pressure. While she is testing that, she takes an oximeter and places it on your finger to read your oxygen level and your heart rate. Then, she takes a thermometer and places it under your tongue to see your body temperature. If any of these small tests are not in a fairly normal range, the nurse alerts the doctor and they begin taking caution to do something about it.

# JUST THINKING!

If your blood pressure is high, they may give medicine for you to take to regulate it. If your oxygen levels are low, they may prescribe oxygen at home or send you to a pulmonologist who looks at your lungs. If your body temperature is high, they realize you are fighting an infection and they prescribe an antibiotic. These simple tests are vital to your general wellbeing, and if any of them are askew they will seek to get you help so that you will feel better. It is good to have these small, easy tests to let us know how our health and wellbeing are doing.

Now, the fact that the doctor can tell so much about our general health by these simple tests has got me to Just Thinking! What is the test to check your spiritual health? Is there some way to judge whether you are doing well spiritually? If you went into the pastor's office and he started asking you some easy questions, how would you fare? If I asked you such questions as how often do you talk with God more than just blessing your meals, what would be your answer? How often are you reading and studying the Bible other than at church on Sunday? How often are you speaking with a friend, neighbor or acquaintance about your faith in Jesus? When was the last time you served someone other than family or friend?

Now, I realize these may strike some of you awkwardly, but these are simple questions that help us judge how we are doing spiritually. These are simple disciplines that show us whether we are truly being disciples of Jesus or just spectators. A spectator looks at the playing field, cheers on the team and criticizes the coaches. A disciple gets in the game, works with the team and supports and encourages the coaches. Paul wrote to the church at Colossae and said, "We continually ask God to fill you with the knowledge of his will through all wisdom and understanding that the Spirit gives, so that you may live a life worthy of the Lord and please him in every way; bearing fruit in every good work, growing in the knowledge of God."

When it comes to Jesus' church what are you - a spectator or a disciple? If you had to see the pastor for a checkup, would he have to prescribe some tasks so that you could start being a disciple and not a spectator? I realize that as a disciple you and I have to do nothing for our salvation, but Jesus didn't just stop with saving the apostles. They became men of integrity who shared a message of hope and love with the world. You and I must do the same. So, let's get a spiritual checkup and start being disciples for Jesus!

### "How's Your Heart?"
### 1 Samuel 16:7

So, I was at my regular cancer checkup. The nurse took the vital signs and, after reading my pulse, said, "41." She didn't say anything, but I already knew that that wasn't right. She went on like everything was alright. Finally, Amanda, one of the physician's assistants, came in and we talked and caught up a little. Then, she listened to my heart. She listened a little longer than normal and backed away and asked me if I felt OK. I assured her that I did, all along knowing what was getting ready to come out of her mouth. "You are in A Fib (atrial fibrillation) I believe. Your heart is beating irregularly."

This has happened to me before, so I went and saw my cardiologist. They placed a 24- hour monitor on my body so we could see what was going on. The very nice nurse who placed the monitor said I was throwing PVCs (premature ventricular contractions), but she wouldn't say I was in A Fib. So, she placed several leads on my chest. These leads are attached to a small recording device. Now, when I say small, I mean small. This device is a little larger than a tube of ChapStick. She put the battery in the device and told me to take it off at 9:35 Thursday morning. I am to return the monitor and they will read the results. If, during the 24 hours, I were to feel any problem with my heart, I push a button on the device and record the time and what I was doing when I felt the problem.

# JUST THINKING!

My amazement is in this very small device that is recording my heart rhythm. This very small device is recording every beat of my heart and, after they read the results, will tell them every beat and whether it is doing what it is supposed to be doing. This very small device is recording the very essence of my life. Without a heartbeat you can't live. Yet, this small device can do nothing about fixing or healing my heart if there is something wrong with it. It can only give me the results of what my heart is doing.

Now, having been hooked up to the monitor and also being in awe of what this little device can do has got me to Just Thinking! Unless you are connected to a monitor or your doctor has ordered an EKG (electrocardiogram) of your heart, no one can just look at you and know how your heart is doing. A doctor can listen to your heart and hear whether it is acting normally or not, but until he takes these tests, he or she cannot really know what is going on. The average lay person that we come in contact with every day has no clue how your heart is doing.

Not so with God! God knows each of our hearts intimately. Matter of fact, when others come up to you, they see your outside appearance and make assumptions based on how you look and what you may say or do. Yet, when God sees you, He looks directly at the heart. He knows if it is beating properly. He knows whether it is aligned properly. He knows where your heart's allegiance falls. Although God is concerned about your health, He is more concerned about your heart's spiritual condition.

When Samuel went to anoint a new king after King Saul had failed, Samuel was sent to the family of Jesse. Jesse had seven sons pass by and every time Samuel thought he had found the right one, God told him no. Finally, the youngest son, David was sent for. When Samuel saw David, he anointed him king over Israel. God told Samuel, "The Lord does not look at the things people look at. People look at the outward appearance, but the Lord looks at the heart."

It is true for you and me, also. God does not assess us on how our day is going or are we doing everything right. God is looking at our heart and wanting to know who we believe in and who we are living for. God is checking to see if the beat of our heart is beating to serve and glorify Him. He is checking to see if our lives are imitating Jesus and the love and kindness He shared while on the earth. God is looking to see who is in control of our heart.

Along the journey of life, many people have had heart issues that they had to have a cardiologist look at and prescribe some sort of treatment to help their heart stay healthy. Some have had surgeries and procedures that have helped the heart function and provide life-saving results. Yet, with all of the advancements in heart health, people still die when their heart quits beating. There is only one remedy to fixing our hearts forever. That is the remedy that Jesus gives us when we allow Him to sit on the throne of our hearts. When we give Him our heart, then we never have to worry about losing a heartbeat. It may stop beating and end our life here on Earth, but when we have Jesus as our savior, our eternal heart continues to beat healthy and strong forever. If you have never invited Jesus into your heart, why wait? Just call on His name, confess your sins, and ask Him to save your soul and your heart will beat forever.

## "Is Your Mind Made Up?"
### Hebrews 13:8

I have had many PET scans because of my cancer. Let me tell you what happened one time as I was preparing for one of these scans. It was originally scheduled for Dec. 26. On Dec. 24 I received a call telling me that the PET had been canceled because they had failed to get proper authorization from the insurance company. So, they called me and set the scan up for Jan. 7 at 4:45 p.m. It was the first available time. The lady who scheduled me told me the next available time was Jan. 16. I sure didn't want to take that long before the test so I agreed on Jan. 7.

At about 1 p.m. Jan. 6, I received a call from a person who said she was with the scanning department and that they had a cancellation and if I wanted, I could come in around 1:30 p.m. the next day. I told her that would be great. I called a friend who was going to drive me to the center and he said earlier it would be no problem for him. Then I called Peggy to tell her the scan had been moved up.

I then settled back in and began working again. At about 3:30 p.m. the same lady called back and said, "Mr. Simmons, we can't take you at 1:30 p.m. because someone has already taken that time and I didn't know it when I scheduled you."

Well, it really frustrated me, and she tried to explain what had happened. She said I could go back to 4:45 p.m. I told her I would, but not to call me and try to change it again because I had friends helping me out to get there. She said she wouldn't.

Well, the next morning around 9:30 I had a message to call a certain number that I did not recognize. When the lady answered, she told me her name and said that there was a cancellation and I could still come in around 1:30 p.m. if I wanted to. I started laughing and told the lady that I said yesterday I wouldn't change it again. She was a little confused and then I told her the story the day before. She apologized, said 4:45 would be just fine and for me to be there by 3:45 pm. I agreed.

Now, all of this canceling, scheduling and rescheduling has got me to Just Thinking! I am so glad that Jesus doesn't change His mind like we do. I would hate to know that He all of a sudden decided to change the way we are saved or decide that only a few people deserve grace. Can you imagine Jesus promising He will return and then changing His mind and deciding that what He said while He was here on earth was no longer relevant?

Very often, we are wishy-washy people. We change our mind about a great many things. We like something and then we don't like it. We struggle with making up our mind about simple things, like where to go eat or what to watch on television or what movie to go see. And one minute we might make a decision to do one thing and then another we have changed our minds.

Jesus doesn't change His mind. His mind was made up when He came to earth. His mind was made up when He walked among His people and taught the Kingdom of God. His mind was made up when He established the church. His mind was made up when He died on the cross for our sins. His mind was made up when God raised Him from the dead to be the example of what will happen to all those who believe. The Bible says, "Jesus the same yesterday, today and forever."

I pray you have made up your mind that there is no one like Jesus, and that He not only saves you, but makes each day brighter. If you haven't made up your mind yet, what is stopping you? If you haven't trusted Jesus with your life, I pray you will change your mind!

## "Is Your Light Shining?"
### Matthew 5:14

After knee surgery, I had to take IV (intravenous) antibiotics at home. Before I left the hospital, they sent one of their representatives to make sure I knew how to stay infection-free while administering the drug and to make sure I understood everything about it. Her name was Peggy. She was an older lady and as we began to talk, we realized right away that she was a disciple of Jesus.

Before long, we had left the medical stuff and were focusing on Jesus. She told us about her church and how much she loved worshiping and serving. She said she only worked with the antibiotic company part time. She was in her 70's. She told us about her two girls and her grandchildren. She continued to say how much God had blessed her over her life and how happy she was to continue to give back to Him for all He had done to her. She was such a joy to listen to and such a sweet person to talk to.

My wife, Peggy and I really enjoyed her visit and information. Before she left, I asked her to come over to my bed. I took her hand and prayed for her and thanked God for her. I asked God to continue to bless her and provide her with the good health she had so that she could continue to bless others like she was doing. When I finished praying, she hugged my neck and thanked me. When she left the room, I realized I probably would never see Peggy again, but I was so happy I saw her that day.

Now, Mrs. Peggy has got me to Just Thinking! You are never too old to bring a little of Jesus into someone's day. To begin with, Peggy didn't talk about her faith. She told us later she has to be very careful about what she does and doesn't say because of policy. Yet, as soon as she walked into the room and introduced herself with a very bright smile, I knew she must know the Lord. As she began to tell us why she was there, she was so pleasant and there was a definite air about her that let you know that there was so much more to her than what you saw.

After a few minutes when I began asking her questions, she told us about her faith. Yet, without even saying a word, she was expressing the love of Jesus. I can't remember how many times she told us that for her and her faith it was all about loving others as God had loved her. I told her my mantra: Love God! Love People!! She loved it and said that is what it is all about. We had such a good time sharing all that God has done for us in our lives.

It makes me wonder how often we could be Peggy to people we meet? How often does our smile brighten someone's day? How often do our words come off soft and loving to entice people to ask why we are so joyful? This lady in her 70's knew that God wasn't finished with her. She knew that He had so much more and that loving others was an important part of that equation. Jesus said, "In the same way, let your light shine before others, that they may see your good deeds and glorify your Father in heaven."

My prayer for all of us is that we never get too old or tired or frustrated that we don't have a smile on our face for Jesus.

Thank you, God, for bringing ladies like Peggy into our lives. May we all seek to let our light shine so others will see our good works and glorify You.

## "God Knows!"
### Philippians 1:6

During my cancer journey I saw doctors about every three weeks. After one of my PET scans this is what took place. I saw the nurse practitioner because the doctor was out of town. That was OK, because I really like the nurse practitioner.

Normally, they are very prompt and I hardly ever wait too long for her to come into the room. This day was different. I knew I was her first patient of the day and I wondered what was taking so long. We waited. Finally, she came into the room and the first words out of her mouth were an apology for making us wait so long, but she added she wanted to talk to a doctor and get his opinion before she told us about the scan.

First and foremost, the good news is that the cancer in my lymph nodes in my leg are still in remission. No new growth; the scan showed everything the same. I asked was this bad since it was not changed? She said they considered it a win anytime cancer is not growing. We rejoice and give glory to God for remission.

The second good news was that the cancer has not spread. There were no new tumors or occurrences of disease in my body. We rejoiced and gave glory to God for this news. Finally, she said that there is a "hot spot" on the right side of my knee. She had consulted with a doctor, who said he was not sure what it was. It could be the knee mechanism that is causing the "hot spot." The only way to really tell was to get an X-ray. Everything else was good. I went and got my Keytruda infusion and we went home.

On Monday of the next week, I went for the X-ray. A few days later, I called to find out if they knew anything more from the

X-ray. I talked to a nurse who got me my doctor's nurse because he still was not back in town. His nurse told me they really were not sure from the X-ray what the "hot spot" was, but that they all agreed it was not something to worry about. In other words, "they didn't know what this is."

A few days later, one of the young ladies who checked me in for appointments called and told me my nurse practitioner wanted her to call and tell me what my cancer doctor was thinking after he got back and saw the scan and X-ray. He said that without a biopsy that there was no way to tell exactly what the "hot spot" was. He didn't see any reason to do a biopsy at this time since my lymph nodes were showing improvement. As long as the treatments seem to be working, he felt like this was something just to watch and not bother at this time. In other words, "We don't know what this is."

Now, the fact that these very knowledgeable doctors do not know all the answers has got me to Just Thinking! You would think with all of the advancements in medicine that this very expensive and inclusive scan would tell them something more than there is a "hot spot." The X-ray seemed to be a waste of time since that didn't seem to clear anything up.

Now, I am not worried. I am not fretting over the unknown. The reason is that, although these very smart doctors don't have a clue as to what we are dealing with, I have a God who does. This "hot spot" is no surprise nor it is new to God. He knows my every pain and every need. He has seen me through this far, and I believe that He will continue to see me through. I am blessed in all my limitations to be able to continue to serve Him in the role that He has called me to perform. I don't plan to stop or give up just because "we don't know." I believe that God has a plan for my life and that until He tells me differently, I will continue to follow Him and where He leads me.

Paul said this to the Philippian church: "...being confident of this, that he who began a good work in you will carry it on to completion until the day of Christ Jesus."

God is in control and you will never hear him say or have a feeling that He doesn't know what He is doing. You may not like it, or you may not agree, but the creator of the World doesn't have to ask for your opinion. I believe that my God will take care of me. Therefore, I do not fret or worry about a test that says something that no one understands or can figure out.

Do you have this assurance that God has your life under His control? I pray that if you do not that you will take a minute to call on His name and accept Him as your Savior. He promises to always care for you and never let you down.

## "It Works"
### Matthew 19:26

OK. I sure don't want to bore you, but I have to give you a quick lesson so you will understand my story. If you know anatomy, then please disregard these next few sentences.

Every one of us has a lymphatic system in our bodies. It is a highway of small vessels that transport fluids throughout our bodies. Your lymph nodes are the main points of gathering this fluid. This fluid consists of blood and other fluids that may be in your tissues. Your lymphatic system takes these fluids and properly redistributes the fluid or places it in the kidney so that it can be expelled from the body. The cancer that was active in my right leg damaged my lymph nodes and my lymphatic system. Therefore, these fluids back up in my leg and cause my right leg to swell.

Several years ago, I was introduced to a lady named Debbie Smith. She is a lymphatic system therapist. At first, I thought it was a joke. I went to see her and she massaged my leg and then had me wrap my leg from toe to hip with something that resembles an ACE bandage. It is not as stretchy as an ACE bandage and holds more pressure to the leg.

I began to wear this bandage every day. In a matter of weeks my leg looked totally different. She explained that the wrap was causing the muscles to push against the lymphatic system and forcing them to work. Well, I became a believer.

Well, at the end of last year my leg began to swell again. It was causing me some trouble, so I made an appointment with Debbie at the beginning of this year. She looked at the leg and immediately said we had to try something different. First, she told me to throw away all of my wraps because they must be worn out. She gave me new wraps and we wrapped my leg. She then told me about a new wrap that goes around my leg and attaches with Velcro. She said it will not stretch as much and hold pressure on the leg so that the muscles will cause the system to work. I ordered the new wraps and, in a week, I went back to get them. Having the new wraps from the previous week had already made an improvement with the leg. When we put the new Velcro wraps on, it provided me with a little more stability and it was quicker and easier.

I went back to see her after a few weeks to measure the leg and see how we were doing. The leg was already down to the smallest it has been and I am having fewer days of constant pain. Who would have ever believed that there was a therapist for helping the lymphatic system and that just by wearing a wrap the swelling would go down? Well, I'm a believer in lymphatic therapy.

Now all of this information about lymphatic therapy has got me to Just Thinking! How many people do you know that do not really believe in all the things that God promises us if we would just believe? The world is full of skeptics and, probably in some areas of life, I am one of them. But I can't tell you how many times people complain about things in their life and if someone mentions just give it to Jesus and let Him handle the problem, they look at you and think you have lost your mind. Jesus can't help me with my addiction, my anger, my patience, my prejudices, and on and on. Well, why can't He?

One of our problems is that we will not give Jesus a try. We fail to allow Him to come in and fix the problems in our life. I wonder how much pain and hardship I would be living with if I had gone with my gut and never had gone to a lymphatic therapist. She made a believer out of me. Well, you can take this to the bank. If you go and give your problems to the Lord, He will deliver you from them.

It saddens me when we allow things of this world to handicap us in life because we say there is nothing, we can do about them. It is really hard when I see Christians allowing "stuff" to get in their way of serving and worshiping and being all that God intends for them to be. We allow the things of this world to get us down when Jesus said, "I have overcome the world."

Please don't misunderstand me. There are things in this world we have to live with. I know. I have to live with my cancer and what it has done to my body. But I can let it take away my ability to live life or I can let Jesus handle it.

So many people have said to me, "We admire how you have handled your cancer." Well, I want to say it again. I cannot and have not handled it. I gave it to Jesus years ago and He has handled it. I don't know what that will mean for tomorrow, next week or next year. But I will not let the fact that I have cancer stop me from doing all I can do when I can do it.

How do you do it? I do it because I believe in the one who said, "Let me handle it!" Oh, how I wish the same for all of you. No matter what you are dealing with in your life, do not allow it to define you. Allow Jesus who conquered the world to give you what you need to conquer your problems. Remember, I know it sounds like it will not work, but if you try it, I believe you will see it works.

## CHAPTER EIGHT
# JUST THINKING... ABOUT MINISTRY!

### "Enduring for the Cause of Jesus"
Revelation 2:3; Matthew 28:19

I had the opportunity to travel and speak at a youth World Changers event at Fort Walton Beach. There were 18 churches and 380 participants at the project. We had 27 crews that worked on 27 houses. There were crews from Louisiana, Arkansas, Alabama, Georgia, Texas and even as far away as the state of Washington.

It was hot, the showers were not the best and the air conditioning didn't get right until Wednesday, but we were able to complete all 27 projects.

Despite all the disadvantages and hardships, the whole project came together on Friday night and everyone shouted with joy over the accomplishments. The mayor of Fort Walton Beach came by to say how grateful she was for all of the hard work. The city administration bought a shirt for every participant. The homeowners showed up to say a special thank you. We all saw what God could do if we just put the hardships behind us and pressed on with the job God had given us to do.

Along with the work on the houses, we celebrated at least

one homeowner accepting the Lord as savior, five participants who said yes to Jesus, a baptism in the Gulf of Mexico and saw the gospel of Jesus Christ spread throughout Fort Walton Beach.

With all that I saw happening that week, I was Just Thinking! Can you imagine what would happen if we all just pulled together and put all our energy into seeing the name of Jesus proclaimed in our own neighborhoods? What would happen if we just endured and kept the faith? What would happen if, instead of griping and complaining about things at church, we put all of that energy into seeing people come to know Jesus as Lord and Savior? What would happen? I'll tell you what will happen. The ones who continue to gripe and complain would have to find another place to worship because the church would become a place where things get done instead of just getting talked about.

Jesus was very complimentary to the church at Ephesus. In the book of Revelation, he says to them, "You have persevered and have endured hardships for my name, and have not grown weary."

They had plenty to complain about, but they persevered, endured and did not give up. I'm for persevering! I'm for enduring! I'm not for growing weary!

Let's put all those things behind us and do the work that God is calling us to do. Let's do what Jesus commanded, "As you go into the world, preach, teach and baptize in the name of the Father, the Son and the Holy Spirit."

If we would just do that we would stand together and shout for joy.

## "Recreation"
### Acts 22:16

I got to experience a little bit of God's beauty on a Wednesday afternoon on a World Changers Project. The crews have worked Monday, Tuesday and Wednesday morning and are given the afternoon off on Wednesday.

The Baptist association in the Fort Walton Beach area threw a cookout for all the churches who would like to take advantage of a free afternoon at the beach in Destin. It was only about a 20-minute drive, so the family and I went. The first experience I had was seeing the Emerald Coast, as the people call it.

The water had a green tint and as I splashed into the water, I immediately recognized that it was nothing like what I had been accustomed to on the East Coast. The water was crystal clear and the sand was as white as snow. I stood in the surf about chest deep and could look down and see my feet. It was really funny how you expected the water to be fresh water and then you would taste the salt on your lips. I have never seen anything like it. The second, and for me the most meaningful, creation that I saw on that Wednesday afternoon was a baptism in the surf.

We had a young girl named Jessica get saved on Monday night and she wanted to get baptized in the ocean. Her youth pastor agreed to baptize her in the ocean on Wednesday. So, after we had feasted on burgers and hot dogs given by the association, we waded into the ocean and gathered around to watch Jessica get baptized. It truly was a grand ending to a beautiful day. As she was lifted out of the surf after being baptized in the name of the Father, Son and Holy Spirit, the whole crowd cheered in admiration of the opportunity to witness God's symbolic recreation of a soul.

Now, all of the wonder of God's creation got me to Just Thinking! Do you ever just sit by and look at all that God has created? I know that I take a great deal of what God does for granted. I hurry too quickly through this world and miss out on seeing God in action. God's world is uniquely created to provide for His creation. We, His creation, messed up His beautiful world, yet God didn't get rid of us. He saw a way to provide for us again. He sent Jesus to be the complete and total sacrifice for all of us. Now, we can be recreated in His image.

Participating in ministry and seeing someone baptized is really what it is all about. We can symbolically show the world what it means to die to our sins and be buried with Christ, have the symbolic washing away of our sins and then rise again to a new lifestyle. What a beautiful picture of God's grace in action.

I hope you have shown the World who Christ is in you. Listen to Ananias as he speaks to Saul at his conversion, "And now what are you waiting for? Get up, be baptized and wash your sins away, calling on his name."

I can't think of a better way for you to experience God's recreation. If you are not one of Jesus's children, why not call on Him today?

## "Prepared for Ministry"
### Ephesians 2:19

Words can be tricky as we use them in everyday language. We really need to look at words and decide what they mean so we can get the best use out of them.

Recently, this became evident to me as I was looking at Christian ministry. The discovery is all about two words. The root word is prepare. Now, if I told you that I had prepared a cake for you what would you do? I hope that you would eat it. But, if I told you that I was preparing a cake for you, what would you do? I guess you would have to wait on it. There is a difference between something that is already prepared and something that you are preparing.

Now, the difference in this word has got me to Just Thinking! How many times have you heard someone say - or maybe you have even said it yourself - that they are preparing to be in ministry for God? You are working on yourself and trying to get ready to do something for God. Someone asked you to do something in the community or in your church and you say I'm just not prepared for that yet. You have hopes and you anticipate one day the ability to be able to accomplish the task, but you are preparing yourself for the day.

Well, I am convinced that when we accept Jesus as our Lord and Savior we are already prepared for His service. We don't need any more preparation but to say yes. We put off serving God because we say we are not ready, don't have the skills or we haven't prepared, but the truth of the matter is that God has already prepared us; we just need to do something.

The scriptures say that God has gifted everyone with a spiritual gift. He has given each of us a special task that He wants us to perform. We need to quit wasting time preparing and get to work.

God didn't say that once we become one of His that we can take time off from ministry to get all we have to do in order to make sure we have prepared ourselves for ministry. He said through His apostle Paul these words, "For we are God's handiwork, created in Christ Jesus to do good works, which God prepared in advance for us to do."

Did you get that? We are created to do good works, which have been prepared in advance for us to do. We have wasted way too much time preparing when God has already prepared us for something that He wants us to do.

The world outside our windows needs prepared people to share Jesus Christ. We need to stop preparing ourselves and just trust the God who has prepared us. I don't know about you, but I would rather eat a prepared cake than spend time preparing one. So, it is with the world. Are you preparing to do ministry or are you prepared by God?

## "A Ministering Prayer"
Matthew 5:10; John 14:18

We were sitting in a hospital's surgical waiting room. There was the normal tension of the unknown and the stress of waiting, but, all in all, the room was very subdued.

The tension got worse as a doctor, all dressed in his surgical garb and followed by his team of interns, entered the room. The doctor brought bad news about the possibility of cancer having already gone too far. The doctor left without giving much hope.

The wife of the patient lost control. She began to cry. The possibility of the loss of her husband of 52 years of marriage was too much to bear. She called out, "What can I do?! We've got to do something!"

I went to her side to console her and minister to her. Her emotions went from sadness, to control, to apology, to total despair. The hope was almost lost. She called out to God to be merciful to her and her family. After about 40 minutes of turmoil, she finally turned to me and said, "Let's pray the Lord's prayer."

I began and her words overpowered mine. I'm not sure, but I believe everyone in the room was praying. "...thy kingdom come, thy will be done, on earth as it is in heaven..."

Ministry was being done. At the end of the prayer the woman seemed to calm down. It may have been my imagination, but the emotions seemed to be more under control.

About 20 minutes later the doctor returned to tell her the good news that the possible cancer turned out to be a false alarm. The surgery could go on as scheduled. At last report the man was recovering well.

Now, this encounter has got me to Just Thinking! Prayer really does calm the soul of a believer when they place their lives in the hands of God. This lady was a believer. We had discussed her belief in God shortly before the incident took place. Yet, when all seemed lost, when her world was crashing in, the only place where real security could come from was in the words of a prayer, "...they kingdom come, thy will be done..."

God sent her the comfort that she needed for her soul. He sent that which Jesus promised, "I will not leave as orphans: I will come to you."

When your life is in a fix, when all seems lost and the world comes crashing in, do not forget that Jesus comes to all who call upon His name. He will comfort your soul. He will be there for you!

## "Let God Use Your Mess"
Luke 8:5

I read an article in Leadership magazine that has, as we say, "Made My Day." The title of the article is "There is no way to be a pastor and be neat."

My wife, Peggy, will not like the article because she is constantly trying to make me a neater person. If you ever came to my office, you would understand why. The top of my desk is a complete mess. I had a plaque on my desk that read, "A clean desk is the sign of a sick mind."

The article's writer is right: it is hard to be neat and be a pastor. I am receiving things all the time. I write notes that are important and put them on my desk to be found later. Sometimes, the ladies who clean the church come into my office and try to straighten the things on my desk so they can find a desk to dust. (Why, I don't know because no dust could actually get to the desk.) But I guess they feel responsible and I appreciate it.

After reading the article, it got me to Just Thinking! It is not only a mess in my office, it is a mess in the world. No one stands still for ministry. There are no nice, neat packages where everything's coming up roses. There are people with marital problems, health problems, family problems, business problems, money problems, etc. etc. etc.

The writer of the article reminded me that Jesus wasn't a neat person either. He is the one who told the story of the farmer who planted the seed. He didn't lay off perfectly straight furrows and plant the seed six inches apart and a half-inch deep. The Bible says, "He scattered the seed."

Some seed found on hard, rocky, weed-infested soil. Some seed fell on good soil. It was never neat, but sometimes it worked to perfection.

Too often today I believe we are trying to become perfect at ministry before we try it. We have to become perfect witnesses or perfect Sunday School teachers or perfect committee members before we will allow ourselves to be used by God. We are afraid we will make a mess of it.

Let's say yes to the ministry. So what if we are not neat? As long as we are doing our best to provide others with an opportunity to experience Jesus Christ, we can be messes if we want to. You never know when some of the clutter of your Christianity will spread out to someone and help change their life.

By the way, I never cleaned my desk.

## "Are You Making an Investment?"
### 2 Timothy 1:5

Every year our church gathered and packed shoeboxes for Operation Christmas Child. As we gathered, there were six stations all lined up and ready for the boxes to be packed. Each station was set with the appropriate number of contents for the boxes. There were just enough boxes at the end of each station to be packed and readied for the processing center.

As we gathered, I recognized just how much work went into preparing each station. There were individuals who had spent time setting up the stations and counting out the items so that each box would be filled appropriately. Much planning was spent so that each box would contain the items that were age appropriate for the children who would receive the box.

As each box was filled, I realized that each box would fill a child's heart with joy at the box's contents. Yet, the box is not just about giving goodies. The box is about giving the best gift of all. The box will also be filled with the good news of Jesus Christ.

This activity last night would not be possible if it were not for dedicated people who gave of their time and effort to see this project through. They spent countless hours preparing the display and making sure everything was ready for the work to be done. I am grateful for those who spent time doing ministry in preparation for God's work to be completed.

The project last night and all the ministry that was done it has got me to Just Thinking! As I look back on my life, I am grateful for all of those who spent countless hours helping me to grow in the grace and knowledge of Jesus. From a very early age, there were individuals who took their time to invest in my life and teach me about Jesus. They prepared before each Sunday School class and each Training Union class I attended. They invested in my life and I am a better person because of their sacrifice.

I can only imagine there are people who have invested in your life, also. There are those who spent time mentoring and discipling you as you have grown as a Christian. I cannot imagine where we would be without those who have prepared the way for us.

The question I have for all of us is are we doing for others what others have done for us? Are we preparing to make a difference in someone else's life?

Paul invested in many lives along the way. Two I can think of are Timothy and Titus. We even have letters in the Bible that Paul wrote to them.

In one of the letters Paul reminds Timothy of those who poured into his life, "I am reminded of your sincere faith, which first lived in your grandmother Lois and in your mother Eunice and, I am persuaded now lives in you, also."

Paul recognized Timothy's grandmother and mother investing in Timothy's life. Are we investing in someone so that they may grow and become more of what God intends for their life? If not, I encourage you to help make a difference. Take the time to allow God to use you to help someone along their journey. Do not keep for yourself what someone else has helped you to discover. God's kingdom will be better because you invested in someone else.

## "Using What You've Got"
### Romans 12:1-2

Every day I use six plastic bottles and one can to receive my nutrition. Several years ago, I decided that I needed to recycle these bottles and cans to help the environment. My nutrition comes in boxes, so I recycle the boxes also. You can imagine that in a week's time I have accumulated a great many bottles and cans. I place them in a recycling bin and it is picked up once a week.

When I got started on this task, I read up on recycling. They ask you to clean out the bottles so after each meal I rinse the bottles and cans and let them dry. I then store them in a small container until I get a full bag full and then place it in the recycling bin. I have to break down the boxes and get them flat enough to fit into the recycling container. It is not a great deal of work, but it does take some time and effort.

I realize it would be easier to just throw the bottles, cans and boxes away and then I wouldn't have to go through all of the trouble. Yet, I got started and now it is just a normal part of my everyday life. I hope that in some small way I am making a difference.

Now, recycling all of this stuff has got me to Just Thinking! Are we taking the everyday activities of our life and making them count for God? Ministry is an everyday occurrence. Are we throwing away valuable insight or opportunities instead of recycling them to produce something better? Are we learning from past experiences so that we can live more committed lives for Jesus?

If we continue to make the same mistakes and not learn from them, then we are not growing in the knowledge and grace that God has so richly bestowed on us. We need to take the lessons learned and get stronger in our commitment to Jesus.

Paul said, "Do not conform to the pattern of this world, but be transformed by the renewing of your mind. Then you will be able to test and approve what God's will is – his good, pleasing and perfect will." When we renew our mind, we begin to recycle the good things and put away those things that weigh us down.

It is good to look back at our life and take assessment of the things that have helped us to mature and grow. It is good to remove those things in our life that have limited us from being all that God wants us to be.

My prayer is that we will recycle those good behaviors and do away with the bad. Let's do our best to "be transformed" by the power of God and work to grow His Kingdom here on Earth as it is growing in heaven.

## "Get Involved"
### Romans 12:6a

One year during Vacation Bible School, I was fortunate enough to be able to sit in while my wife, Peggy, and her very good friend, Brenda, led the children in the music. They would teach the children the moves of the songs from a video and then they would sing the songs with the motions. Each new song had different motions and it was fun watching the children work to keep up with the music and perform the motions.

It was interesting to me that some children sought to get every move correct and did their best to keep up. Some of the children gave it a half-hearted attempt, while some just stood and didn't participate at all. I wondered what motivated them to work at it or just let it go. It looked like they were having fun and the songs were fast and upbeat, but still, some of the children didn't look very engaged.

As I watched them all week long, it got me to Just Thinking! Adults in church are the same way that those children performed with the music. The church needs volunteers to do the work of the ministry within the church building and within the community. Some adults jump right in and do their best to make a difference, while others give it a half-hearted attempt. Still others just come and sit and do nothing at all. I can't help but wonder why it is that way.

The scripture says, "We have differing gifts, according to the grace given to each of us…" We are to use them to enhance the body of Christ, His church. Why then do we not all work for the betterment of the church, together? Why is it true that 20% of the people in the church do 80% of the work?

There may be several answers to this question. Some may believe that they are not gifted enough to do certain tasks. Some may just not want to get involved because they do not think they have the time to invest. Some may not be committed to the church above what they can get out of it instead of what they can do for it. All in all, it becomes a question of what we believe God can do in us and through us. God doesn't call the qualified, He qualifies the called. We are each called to do ministry for God in some specific way. He will qualify us to do what He calls us to do. So, do not sit idly by. Get up and start moving with the music. You will be glad you did.

## "A Ministering Example"
### Luke 19:17

In 2018 I got to go to worship with Uncle Bill and Aunt Rose. We entered their small Episcopal church and she introduced me as her nephew. She always had a way of saying it that made me smile. She was proud of her church and I was happy that I got to be with them that Sunday.

Of all the things that impressed me about Aunt Rose was her dedication to getting a job done. She was diagnosed with ovarian cancer and had been through a great deal. When she was so sick with cancer treatments getting her down, she never failed to make sure that "Happy Tuesday" still took place.

"Happy Tuesday" was a senior adult gathering that she

oversaw in her church. She was committed to those senior adults and to the program of good food, good fellowship and good times. Sometimes, I think we forget about the importance of that within our churches today.

Aunt Rose, thank you for all the things you taught me growing up. Thanks for being a part of my life and loving me. Thanks for the time I visited in Jacksonville, Fla., and the time Peggy and I spent with you in 2007. You were always going out of your way to make us feel like more than family. Thank you for being a committed disciple of Jesus. You did your part and you did it well. I will be forever grateful for the time I spent with you. Thank you for instilling those same important lessons in your sons.

Talking about my Aunt Rose has got me to Just Thinking! How much are we pouring into those around us? We do our own thing today without thinking about those who are around us. And how committed are we to the jobs that God calls us to do? We often find the simplest excuses to not participate or shirk the responsibilities that God gives us because we are tired or feel under appreciated. Yet, when we are called to do something for God, we should do it with all of our might.

My Aunt Rose left a legacy. She left something behind to remind others of her life and to remind us to keep the light burning. Are we teaching our children, grandchildren and others we come in contact with the necessary lessons in life? Are we leaving a legacy for others to remember?

Ministering in the name of Jesus will never go unnoticed. Even if no one on Earth recognizes it, I can promise you that Jesus sees it. When Jesus told the parable of the talents, He spoke these words to the ones who had performed admirably, "'Well done, my good servant!' his master replied."

Aunt Rose, you performed admirably and I know that Jesus met you and said "Well done!" Thanks for your example of a minister of Jesus Christ.

## "Are You Doing Your Part?"
### Matthew 5:16

This incident took place during the COVID pandemic. I restricted my dad and mom to the house. I told them they could ride in the van, but could not get out and go in any stores. If they needed something, they were to call me and I would get it for them. They have been great and I appreciate their understanding.

Well, my mom had a craving for a hot dog. She got a coupon from a fast-food restaurant and she and Dad got in the van and drove to the drive-in. As she pulled up to the drive-thru, Mom said it was very evident that the lady taking the order was not in a good mood. She was very nonchalant about what she was doing and Mom said her voice was mopey sounding. Mom ordered her and Dad's hot dogs, fries and a drink. Mom drove up, paid and picked up their order. Instead of driving home they pulled into a parking spot and ate their hot dogs. Mom didn't say, but I guess the lady's attitude really hit her hard. Here she was working a public job, helping to feed people, and wasn't very grateful or thankful to be able to be working. Mom knew the lady needed a pick-me-up and some encouragement, so after finishing lunch, Mom pulled back into the drive-thru line. The same lady came on with her same sour attitude. "How can I help you? Would you like to try one or our…"

Mom answered, "No ma'am. We just came through and had one of your hot dog specials and it was very good. I just wanted to tell you how much we appreciate you working and feeding the public during these trying times and that we are praying for you and hope you have a great day."

Mom said she heard, "Uh, Uh, well, thank you." And from the back she heard someone shout, "Thank you, lady."

Mom drove away smiling and laughing because it stunned the lady at the drive-thru.

She also told me about a video doctor's appointment that Dad had with his gastro doctor. After the appointment was over Mom

# JUST THINKING!

told the doctor, "Well we appreciate your time and we want you to know that we are praying for all of you in the medical field."

Mom said the doctor looked at the screen and stuttered, "Well thank you so much!" Then they hung up.

Mom again chuckled at the very fact that these people seemed so stunned when people told them they were praying for them. It is almost like they don't expect it or even understand it. Mom is having a blast just lifting these people up in prayer and telling them about it.

These two incidents about my mom have got me to Just Thinking! What a difference one small little gesture can have in a person's life. Ministering in a day and time when people without Jesus have no hope and are scared, Christians have the answer to the very heart of the matter.

We are called to spread the light. We are called to share hope. We are called to be the encouragers of the world. Yet, so often when the world looks at us, they see no difference. Shame on us if we don't take advantage of this perfect scenario where we can speak encouragement to those we see and come in contact with (of course during the pandemic, from six feet away).

How many of you have driven through drive-ins and failed to share a smile or a word of encouragement? Are you telling the people thanks not only for your food, but for their willingness to work and serve the community? How many of us have told the stock person at the store we frequent thank you for doing their best at keeping the shelves stocked as best they can instead of complaining that the shelves are empty of something we need?

How many of us are just trying to survive instead of thriving in this atmosphere of fear by holding on to the unchanging hand of Jesus who will see us through?

I am so grateful for my mom. She not only taught me as a young boy about the love of Jesus and His word, but she continues to teach me today.

Thanks, Mom, for not being afraid to stand up and show your appreciation of those who are helping us get through these trying times. Thanks for speaking up for the name of Jesus and praying for those who are on the front lines of this pandemic. Thank you that even though I have confined you to the house, you are still working tirelessly to share God's love through phone calls and care packages to those you love and care for.

You truly are living what Jesus said in Matthew 5:16, "Let your light shine before others, that they may see your good deeds and glorify your Father in heaven."

## "Right Place at the Right Time!
### Psalm 18:30

Sometimes, God has a way of making sure I'm at the right place at the right time. Twice, I have driven across town to see a church member in a rehab unit. The first time I went, I found out that he was on his way to the hospital. They were waiting for the ambulance. As I spent a few minutes with him and his wife, I realized how upset the wife was. I volunteered to drive her to the hospital. She finally relented and let me take her.

When we got there, one of her great-nephews was there and after about an hour I went in, prayed for them and left. They didn't keep the gentleman, but let him return to the rehab center.

A few days later, I went to see the same member. As I approached the door to the rehab center, I heard my name called. I turned, looked and saw his wife walking towards me. "He is in the ambulance. We are headed back to the hospital."

We waited for about 15 minutes before the ambulance finally headed to the hospital. As we waited, I asked her if she would like for me to go to the hospital with her. She said if I had the time that she would appreciate it. Of course, I made the time and this time we both drove to the hospital.

After we got there, we found out the gentleman was pretty sick and they got to work on him immediately. He was admitted to the hospital later that evening.

Now, arriving at the rehab center at just the right time has got me to Just Thinking! Some people would call it a coincidence that I happened to arrive when I did. Well, to those individuals I would say that they do not understand God like I do. I believe that God will put us at the right place at the right time if we seek Him and His will in our lives. If I am seeking to follow His ways, why would I end up in the wrong place? God understands me better than I understand myself and, if I listen to Him, He will guide me in the right paths.

As ministers of Jesus, we are not to wander around in circles, not really knowing where we are going. We have to have a plan. We are to have a purpose. The last place I want to be is where God is not. How many of us never seek God's leadership as we plan our day, week, month or year? How many of us get up each day and just say, "Whatever happens, happens!"?

That is such a sad way to look at life. I would much rather live a life where I know God is leading me to the people I need to see and the places I need to be. Life is not lived by chance if you are Jesus's disciple. It is lived by preparation in doing the will of God in all of your ways.

The Psalmist said, "As for God, his way is perfect: The Lord's word is flawless; he shields all who take refuge in him."

If you are focused on doing ministry for God then you will always be at the right place at the right time. God's way is perfect and He will always guide you to where He needs you to be. It's no coincidence!

## "A Prayer that Matters"
### 1 John 5:14-15

When visiting a rehab facility, you see many different people. One time, I was sitting in the cafeteria with some church members and before I left them, I stood close and offered a prayer. When

I left, a man sitting close asked them who I was. They told him I was their pastor and the man said, "I wish he would pray for me."

When I was visiting this couple another day, the wife told me about Jose. She said she wasn't sure where he was from, but he had an accent. She thought he may have been Greek. After she told me this and I visited for a little while, we walked down to Jose's room.

We walked in and I introduced myself. Jose was sitting in a wheelchair, He looked to be in his sixties, but sometimes I am not a good judge of age. I began asking him about himself. He was actually from Puerto Rico and had been in Greenville for four years. He had been married for 42 years. He tried to tell me why he was there, but at that time couldn't recall what had happened to him. I tried to guess, but we never hit on the exact problem. (My church member let me know later that he remembered and she texted me to tell me he had had three strokes.)

We talked a little and then I told him I had come to pray for him if he wanted me to. He said yes, if I wanted to. I assured him I wanted to pray for him and we bowed our heads and I placed my hand on his back.

I prayed for Jose that God would bless him and help him with his infirmities. I prayed for his family and his wife during these difficult days. As I continued to pray, Jose began to cry. His whole body shook and he began praying in a quiet fast-talking voice. I finished and said Amen. Jose continued on for a few seconds and then said Amen. He looked up with tears in his eyes and said thank you.

I asked him if he had a pastor and he assured me he did and that he came and visited him. I promised Jose that I would continue to lift him up in my prayers.

Now, meeting and praying for Jose has got me to Just Thinking! We never know how God is going to use us in ministry if we are available. The strokes look like they have put a very large dent into Jose's life. He acted if he was struggling with the whole concept of being unable to do for himself and being worthwhile.

# JUST THINKING!

As I looked around his room it was filled with pictures of family and you could tell that at one time, he had been a man of strength and ability. Now, his life had taken a complete turnaround and he was lost in his new normal.

Yet, one thing Jose was clinging to was prayer. I could tell as I prayed for him that this wasn't his first time. As he prayed softly and sweetly, he was calling on God to meet his needs and imploring Him to heal his body. I was blessed by my encounter with Jose. I was reminded how many people just want to know someone is praying for them and their situation. Just to know someone cares is a great relief.

The greatest asset we have in prayer is the fact that God listens. The fact that an almighty God, who is the creator of the universe and is all powerful and all-knowing, will take the time to listen to me and my petitions is one of the most amazing things that I know. God, who is greater than anything known to mankind, is willing to not only listen to, but grant our request if it is according to His will. In other words, He is not going to do things for us that we may think is best when He knows they are not.

I love the passage in 1 John that says, "This is the confidence we have in approaching God: that if we ask anything according to His will, he hears us. And if we know that He hears us – whatever we ask – we know that we have what we asked of Him."

That is one of the most amazing facts that I know. God listens when I pray. God seeks to answer my prayers and do what I ask when I am praying in His frame of reference.

So, God, I am not sure what your will is for Jose, but I ask that if he must suffer with the strokes and their side-effects that you will give him joy even in the midst of his storm.

## "God Supplies"
Philippians 4:19

I took a mission trip to West Virginia and visited Little Birch Baptist Church. When we arrived, we met Robin. Robin invited us into the church, where she had coffee and cookies laid out for us. We looked around and then sat down with Robin and began to talk to her. Robin is probably in her late 40s and is the pastor's wife. The pastor couldn't meet us because he works at a Toyota plant and drives 1 hour and forty-five minutes to get to work. That is 3½ hours a day driving to and from work!

He then pastors this church. He preaches on Wednesday night, Sundays and a third Saturday service where they invite their neighbors in and share food and clothes. Robin began to tell us about certain things that have been happening around the food pantry that the church keeps. She told us about dealing with some of the people who didn't want to give everything away because then they would have nothing to give away.

She told us about having 10 cakes to give away and one lady said let's hold on to half of them in case we don't get any more. Robin said she told her if we don't trust God enough to give us more cakes, then we shouldn't be doing what we are doing. Robin made sure that by the end of the day all 10 cakes were gone. The very next week the place where they get a lot of their food gave them enough cakes to stack on the floor and build a circle around the lady that wasn't sure they should give them away. Robin said, "I believe she now knows that we give it all away and believe God will supply enough for the next time."

As I sat and listened to Robin, I began to be ashamed of myself. Here is a pastor's wife living in a very rural area of West Virginia where she works to take care of the needs of her congregation and more while her husband is working. She takes senior adults to their doctor's appointments which are mostly an hour or more away from where they live. About once a week she drives a large delivery truck up and down winding mountain

## JUST THINKING!

roads about 90 miles to Charleston, W. Va., to pick up groceries to be ready to give them away on the third Saturday of every month. She has some people who help her, but you could tell she was tired.

Yet, she wasn't giving up. She was doing ministry, and her faith was brighter than anything you or I could imagine. Now, we are talking about a church that - on a good Sunday - will have 30 people in attendance and the offering published on the board was less than $200.

While we were there, the association's Director of Missions gave her a gift card to Walmart. He said that it had recently come in and he thought she could use it. She responded, "I sure can, we are not getting a great amount of canned goods these days and I will need to buy some if we are going to have enough for the third Saturday."

She was always looking out so that she can help someone, always trusting that God will supply her needs so she can bless others.

As I listened to Robin talk about all she did to minister in Jesus's name it got me to Just Thinking! Sometimes, I need to be reminded that my idea of having faith is not comparable to these folks up here who are not sure where their next meal is coming from. They don't have thousands of people living around them with the simple amenities of life at their disposal. The largest church congregation that we found in the area was no more than 50 on any given Sunday. Another church we went to has just recently started and they are excited when they have 10. There were five of us and five of them tonight. It was fun and worshipful to hear their preacher sing and play his guitar. Yet, they are just happy to be able to worship together, serve together, and reach the lost for Jesus.

We did not go into one building that didn't need some kind of immediate repair that can't be fixed because there is either not enough money or not enough people with skill to help. All the comforts that we complain about when it is too hot or too cold, they live without, but they don't stop trusting and believing.

Sometimes, I think I trust more in what I can provide for myself than I trust God for what He can supply for me.

So, thanks Robin! Thanks for reminding me to believe in God for everything. We say it a great deal and some people have it as their favorite verse, but the truth is often we only trust God when we can't do it ourselves.

The verse says, "God will supply all my needs through His riches in Christ Jesus." Yes, he will supply them even in rural and run-down Little Birch, West Virginia. If you don't believe it, just ask Robin.

## "What a Difference You Can Make!"
### 1 Samuel 3:9

So, there we were, 75 years since that church began its ministry. Today, that congregation ceases to exist. They sold their property to a Hispanic church.

I am grateful for the many lives from this church that helped to shape my spiritual life. I am grateful that my family was entrenched in this church and for all that I learned. I am grateful for all the people that I was able to meet and enjoy life with those earlier years in my journey.

This weekend, reminiscing the wonders of days gone by at Jasper Springs Baptist Church near Savannah got me to Just Thinking! Jasper Springs was never a large church. Yet, those few people made such an overwhelming impact on my Spiritual Life. Their faithfulness and commitment to worshiping and serving Jesus were what held me up during my "unfaithful" times. They were always there. They were so influential in my understanding of the very essence of God. They were not perfect, but no one tried harder to do it right.

Now, years later when I look back on my call to the ministry, it was these people who convinced me that God was calling me to the pastoral ministry. They were His spokesmen. Their support and encouragement helped convince me that it was God calling me to follow Him and His call on my life.

They were the ones who were my Eli, who told Samuel, "Go and lie down, and if he calls you say, 'Speak, Lord for your servant is listening.'"

My foundation of Christian experience is founded on the good men and women of Jasper Springs Baptist Church. Those dear people helped me to know that God did speak and we were supposed to listen and obey.

As I reflect on that aspect of my life, I can't help but wonder how we are doing when it comes to our influence on the younger generation today. Do they look at us as faithful and committed followers of Christ? Or do they just see people doing church? Everyone loves to see a full church, but remember, Jesus changed the world with just 12.

Is our faithfulness and commitment leading those younger than us to a faithful and committed lifestyle? If we are waiting for someone else to make a difference, then we will probably always be waiting. You can make a difference today! Let's start making a difference.

## "Following the Spirit's Leading"
### Hebrews 13:2

Peggy and I left church and rode to Chick-fil-A. I was going to buy a gift card for my doctor to buy herself a milkshake. As I was walking in the restaurant, a police officer also was walking up. I held the outer door for him and he held the inner door for me.

As he entered, I asked him if he would allow me to buy his supper in thankfulness for his service. At first, he refused, but after persuading him, he allowed me to do it. As I paid for his food and got my gift card and prepared to leave, I turned to him and told him thank you again.

He asked me my name and I told him that I was a pastor.

He grinned really big and said, "Well, that is interesting. I am a pastor also. I do this on the side." We had a big laugh about it and told each other God Bless You and went our separate ways. I got such a blessing out of speaking to him and buying his meal.

Now, the whole episode at the restaurant has got me to Just Thinking! It was such a small thing - buying supper for someone I didn't know. I felt the urging of the Holy Spirit to do it and I am glad I did. I think I made a friend. I'm sure if I see him again, I will recognize him and he me. Who knows what God may do with that relationship and what might come from it?

How many times are we so consumed with ourselves that we fail to see just the slightest opportunity to share the love of Jesus with someone? You know it doesn't have to be an officer. It can be a family or someone who looks lonely. You might even feel the need to go above the call of duty and do something out of the box that people might think you are losing your mind. All I am saying is that when the Holy Spirit prompts us, we should be ready and willing to respond.

I got back in the truck that night and I was smiling and had a joy that was very evident. I told Peggy all about what had happened while she was waiting in the truck. I almost had allowed her to go in and get the card, but I am so glad I didn't. God had a special blessing waiting for me and I got it because I was willing to listen to his guidance.

How many blessings are we missing because we are all about doing what we need to get done? How many blessings are we missing because we are in a hurry to finish what we started? How many blessings are we missing because all we want to do is do what we have to do and go home?

I want to encourage you to look around, tune in to the Holy Spirit and let God work through you. "Do not forget to show hospitality to strangers, for by so doing some people have shown hospitality to angels without knowing it."

Who knows what a blessing you might receive?

## "A Needed Rest"
Mark 6:31; Psalm 46:10

Vacations take on very different styles. Some vacations are filled with itineraries that have you going and doing the whole time you are on "vacation." Have you ever noticed that sometimes when people go on vacation they have to come home and recuperate from their vacation? They are so tired from going and doing. Not only do they pay for the vacation rental (whether it be hotel, camp site, or rental cabin), they also have the expense of entertainment and eating out. By the time they return home they are so worn out they need a vacation from their vacation. Pretty much, though, most people enjoy their vacation, no matter what sort of vacation they go on.

For several years we have rented a cabin for our whole family. One such cabin had a beautiful view of the mountains towards Grandfather Mountain. From the time we arrived on a Sunday afternoon until we left a week later, I left the cabin only four or five times: once to buy groceries on Monday, twice to pitch baseballs to the grandchildren as we played a semi-baseball game in a huge field, and, I think, I went twice to look for deer at dusk.

The thing I love about this cabin is that you don't have to spend money to have a good time. You can have a good time with your family. Our family loves to play games. Every day it was the same. We played games with the children. We played games with the adults. We hung out together and talked and, most of all, what we did was rest. We all have very busy lives. Both of my boys have families and jobs, as do their wives. Peggy and I stay busy and seldom have time just to rest. So, it is refreshing to just go up to this beautiful place and just rest.

Now, how we spend our time on vacation has got me to Just Thinking! Have you ever gauged your involvement in ministry and said something like, "I need a break"? Or maybe you are one of those who believe the more you do for Jesus, the more He will love you and reward you. Maybe when things are not going well in your life, you begin to think, "Well if I will just read my Bible more and pray more and do more ministry then God will work things out better for me."

In my many years in church work I have noticed those who are always trying to do more for more. I have also seen those who burn themselves out by doing too much. Maybe we need a serving God philosophy like I have adopted a vacation philosophy. Maybe every now and then, instead of doing more, I just need to rest.

After Jesus sends the disciples out to the towns and cities, He tells them when they get back, "Come with me by yourselves to a quiet place and get some rest."

Jesus knew then what we need to learn now. You cannot do your best work if you are tired and worn out. There are times when we don't need to work for Jesus, we just need to be still and get to know Jesus better.

How many times have you heard the Psalm, "Be still, and know that I am God"? That is very pertinent to our world today. We cannot do our best work if we are tired and worn out, but a little while with Jesus can empower us to do more than we could ever do alone.

So, the next time you get tired and want to take a break, just very sweetly decline the ministry invitation and go rest with Jesus. I can't think of a better vacation than one where you and Jesus spend some time together.

## "Ready to be Used"
### James 5:16

We had some new flooring put down in our home. One morning, about 10 o'clock, two young men showed up at the house. I let them in and met the first guy named Jason. Jason seemed to be in charge, so I was telling him what they could do if they left for lunch. I also told him that I would be back around 1 p.m. to eat. I explained I would stay out of their way, but I had

JUST THINKING!

to do it at home because I tube feed because of cancer. He asked me about the cancer I had and I told him. He also said that he lived in Travelers Rest and that his wife would probably bring him lunch.

I left for work at the church office. About 1 p.m. I headed home. When I got there no one was at the house. About five minutes after I got there, Jason walked in and following behind him were two children about the age of 10 to 12. Following the children was a very petite young lady. I said hello to the children and introduced myself to the lady. She told me her name was Kelly. I asked her if she home-schooled. She told me yes. I asked if they attended church anywhere and she said yes. I told her it was nice to meet her and excused myself to talk to Peggy on the phone.

After I finished talking to Peggy, I began to prepare my lunch. I heard my name called and looked over my shoulder to see Kelly sticking her head around the door. She said, "David, can I pray for you?" Stunned, I smiled and said why yes of course.

I dried my hands and walked to the den. Her husband was on the phone and she asked me if we could wait until he finished. I asked her if she knew of my situation. She said her husband had told her I had cancer. While he finished on the phone, I gave her a quick overview of my journey.

After Jason finished, she called him over and they placed their hands on me and she began to pray. Just to let you know, the Holy Spirit came down in my den. That little lady could pray. She called on God to do some amazing things. She said some things that there was no way she could have known that I was dealing with. The Spirit had to reveal it to her.

When she finished, I was in tears. I hugged both of their necks and thanked her for her prayer. She looked at me and said, "That's what we are to do - to lift up and pray for our brothers and sisters."

James wrote these words, "Therefore confess your sins to

each other and pray for each other so that you may be healed. The prayer of a righteous person is powerful and effective."

The rest of my day was great. I know for certain that God's Spirit came and visited me in the form of a petite, young, Godly woman.

Now, the fact that this stranger who entered my house would take it upon herself to pray for me has got me to Just Thinking! What has God planned for me that I am missing because I am afraid to step out like Kelly did? Now, you may say she didn't take much of a chance knowing that I was a pastor, but I'll bet you that she would have done it if I were a plumber or carpenter. She had it fixed in her mind that she wanted to pray for me and I believe it was the leading of the Holy Spirit that prompted her to ask. I could have said, "That's very nice of you to offer, but I have plenty of people praying for me." I could have done anything to put it off. Boy, am I glad I didn't.

She was tuned in to the Spirit of God. There is no question that she lives like this every day of her life. There was no doubt that she walks and talks with God all day long.

Too often in our lives, we shy away from this kind of living. Personally, I wish I knew more people like Kelly. As far as that goes, I wish I was more like Kelly. Why are we so afraid to stand up and call on the name of the most powerful source that we know, unless we are not sure we know Him well enough? There is no doubt in my mind that Kelly spends time with God in prayer even when she doesn't need anything. It is sad to say, but most of us only have a prayer life that consists of going through a list of wants and wishes. Yet, God just wants to spend time with us. He has a desire just to be in our presence and that we would be aware of Him.

I want more of His ever-enduring presence - not just when I bow my head in prayer, but every minute of every day. I want to be so aware of His presence that when I am in the presence of someone who needs prayer, that I would sense the Spirit calling me to pray for that individual no matter where I am or what I am doing.

God has a way of showing up to call us into His presence. God showed up and called on Noah, Abraham, Moses, David, Isaiah, Mary and Joseph, Peter and all the apostles, and Paul. These individuals had unique relationships with God. We have the same opportunities as these people did. We just need to be available and ready to hear the voice of God. Thank you, Kelly, for reminding me that God can, and will, use us wherever we are if we are willing. And thank you, Kelly, for a wonderful intercession on my behalf. I believe He will answer your prayer.

## "Waiting on the Lord"
### Psalm 27:14

One of the churches I pastored had a ministry to the homeless called Feed My Sheep. We prepared and took brown bag lunches to these individuals throughout the city twice a week.

It still saddens me to know there are that many individuals without a place to live and decent accommodations that I take for granted every minute of every day.

After being away from the ministry because of illness, I was able to resume helping. One of the other men showed me where they had been ending their route at a Salvation Army facility.

As my partner and I arrived at the Salvation Army, one morning we had one full container and a few bags left in another. I felt that we would have a great many left over because of my earlier experience. Well, as we pulled up, the men came to the back of the van. I began giving out bags and some of them asked for two. We accommodated, because we had so many left. As the line seemed to end, I gave out two bags to, probably, the last five men - just gave them without them asking.

I felt like we had finished when, all of a sudden, out of the door came three more men hustling to the van. It broke my heart to tell them we were out. I got one of the men with two to share one. I encouraged the other two guys to go inside and see someone with two and ask them to share.

I wanted to be like Jesus and just make the bags become more like He did at the feeding of the 5,000. We hung around for a few minutes and talked to a guy who was sharing with us how his life changed after he was saved. He was one of the men who shared one of his bags with another man. He thanked us several times for doing this for them. Finally, we headed back to the church.

Now, the experience of "jumping the gun" with the final bags and having to tell several of the men we were out has got me to Just Thinking! How many times in my life have I "jumped the gun" instead of waiting and listening to the Lord? How many times have I tried to decide what is best for me or the situation I am in instead of seeking the Lord and allowing Him to guide me? I am afraid the answer to those questions is many more times than I would like to admit. We get ahead of God. We think we are smart enough to figure things out on our own. Now, I'm not saying that God doesn't endow us with common sense and give us wisdom to discern. He does, but there are times when we need to stop and "wait on the Lord."

If I would have just given one bag like normal instead of trying to do it myself, I would have had plenty to share with everyone. I might have had one or two left over, but no one would have gone lacking. The man's face who I had to tell I was out is etched in my mind. He was disappointed and I felt like I let him down. I don't want that feeling anymore.

The Psalmist says, "Wait for the LORD; be strong and take heart and wait for the LORD." I want to trust in Him so much that I know He is going to work it out like He plans. I want to stay out of the way and allow the Lord to direct my paths.

I want to encourage all of us to wait more. We live in a society where we are always in a hurry. We are always going somewhere or just coming from somewhere. We need to slow down and listen to God speak.

Let's pray that we will wait on the Lord and watch what He is going to do.

## "Together We Can!"
### Ezra 3:8-9

You have heard the expression, "It's a small world." On a mission trip with the youth from our church, I met some interesting people. I want to share with you about a few of them.

First, I met a group from Albany, Ga., on Saturday where we ate lunch. They were headed to World Changers. I couldn't resist asking them if they knew where Ty Ty, Ga., was? Albany is located about 35 miles west of Ty Ty. Ty Ty is where Peggy and I got married. Most of them knew where this little town was located. It gave us a connection that reminded us each time we spoke that week that we knew a little about each other.

I met a church group from Moody, Al. Now, this was intriguing to me because Peggy's dad pastored in Moody when she was in junior high school. I began asking the older adults if they remember a pastor back in the early 70's named Harvey Taylor (Peggy's dad). I finally found one lady who remembered him. She said they had moved to town right after he left the church to move to Georgia. Glenda, one of the ladies from Moody, worked on my crew. As we got to know each other, I found out that Glenda worked at Samford University. I excitedly told her that I had graduated from Samford in 1982. She told me that her husband had attended Samford during those years and we began comparing whom we knew. I didn't remember her husband, but I was able to catch up on some old professors who have now retired and moved on, or are now deceased. It really is a small world. You just never know whom you will meet or whether they may have passed the same way you have passed.

Now, all of this familiarity has got me to Just Thinking! Have you ever noticed how God will put people in your life when you are doing ministry for Him? Here, I was some 750 miles from my home, yet I was able to connect with complete strangers and do ministry with them. We had some familiar connections, and together we worked to see God's ministry done in a town that none of us was from.

Why do you think it is like that? Well, I have a theory. When we go about doing God's work, He never expects us to do it alone. He provides others who love Him to come alongside us and help.

In the book of Ezra, these words are written when he talks about rebuilding the temple, "In the second month of the second year after their arrival at the house of God in Jerusalem, Zerubbabel, son of Sheaitiel, Joshua, son of Jozadak, and the rest of the people (the priest and the Levites and all who had returned from the captivity to Jerusalem) began the work. They appointed Levites twenty years old and older to supervise the building of the house of the Lord. Joshua and his sons and brothers and Kadmiel and his son (descendants of Hodaviah) and the sons of Henadad and their sons and brothers – all Levites – joined together in supervising those working on the house of God."

That is a great deal of people with one goal in mind: to complete the work of the Lord. No one is expected to do ministry alone. We are all to work together. So, let's join in and see God's Kingdom grow.

## "It's Not Room Service"
### Revelation 22:12

I was waiting in the hospital to see someone. They were involved, asked me to wait outside for a few minutes and I agreed to do so. As I waited, two individuals walked by me. They were both patients, but they responded to the same situation differently.

The first patient who walked by seemed to be in some discomfort and had a companion with him. They walked right past the nurse's station. They hadn't been in the room for more than a few minutes when I heard one of the nurses call out to another nurse. Would they please take two Pepsis down to their room. The nurse agreed, and I thought how odd it was that they didn't ask when they passed the nurse's station and it seemed to me they were acting as if the nurses were room service. It also bothered me that the companion would not go get the drinks without bothering the nurses.

The next patient who walked by me had no companion. She was in definite pain from an earlier surgery that had taken place. She walked by me and acknowledged my presence.

In a few minutes, she came back by me and went to the nurse's station. She asked for a Pepsi and some ice. They retrieved the drink for the young lady and she proceeded to walk back by me.

As she did, she remarked, "I wish I would have thought to ask for that before I made my way back to the room." I said something like, "Yes it looks as if you are in some difficulty." She said, "Yes, especially after surgery." We smiled at one another and she continued on her way with her Pepsi.

Now, you may be wondering what on Earth got me to Just Thinking! Well, you see, I feel that sometimes we use God like a room service attendant. We get ourselves comfortable in our situation and call on Him for our every want. We don't think once about doing for ourselves. We just figure that God is there and it is no harm for Him to just give us what we want.

Now, I know that the Bible doesn't specifically say this next statement: "God helps those who help themselves." I realize that you can't find that exact quote, but I believe that it is emphasized in theory, if not in an actual quote. God does want us to do our part. God does want us to get involved. God doesn't mind helping out, but He does expect us to do our best.

In the book of Revelation it says, "Look, I am coming soon! My reward is with me, and I will give to each person according to what they have done."

The reward of life only comes to those who have done

according to God's will. Now, I'm not talking about salvation. There is nothing we can do for our salvation but rely on Jesus. Yet, when we are saved there is something that God has for us to do.

Can you imagine Jesus just saying to His Father, "Well, I came down to earth Lord, what else do you want me to do?"

Yet, that is exactly what we say to God sometimes, "Well, God, I go to church, what else do you want me to do?"

And, then we think because we are a little righteous, God must perform to our benefit. I believe that we need to realize that God is calling us to be actively involved with our own lives. We just can't sit and cry out to God to meet our every need without trying to help ourselves. We have buzzed room service too long. We need to become servants, not the served.

## CHAPTER NINE

# JUST THINKING...
# ABOUT EVERYDAY LIFE!

### "How Green Are You?"
### 1 Peter 1:24-25

I have never liked cutting grass, but I have to do it. One of the places I used to cut grass was down at my father's lake house. We enjoyed going and spending time at the house and enjoying the lake, but one of the responsibilities was that we helped keep the yards cut and clean.

Well, one morning as I was riding the lawnmower and circling the yard, the wind was blowing ever so slightly. As I would plow through the yard, I would send the fresh cut clippings into the air and the breeze would sometimes blow them back into my face. As I finished up early that morning and began to do the trim work around the house and lake, I noticed that the clippings were laying in a neat-layered look all over the front yard. They were nice and green and smelled great.

I also noticed that as I exited the riding lawnmower that some of the clippings had settled on the mower deck and it turned that black color of the deck a nice green. As I finished the trim work and put up all the tools, I began to notice the lawn. That once-green-covered lawn with the now-not-so-recently-cut clippings was beginning to change colors. It was not basking in the bright and hot sunshine, but was changing into a dingy gray.

As I put up the weed eater and walked by the lawnmower, I saw the once-green-looking mower deck had also changed to a dingy brown. The grass that had been cut was either dead or dying and there was no more life in it. The green of the grass had been cut away and now the grass was withered into nothing.

The experience of actually noticing something that happens all of the time got me to Just Thinking! Sometimes, our faith takes a cutting like the grass. We can be lush and green and growing for our Lord and something will cut away at the very root of our faith and cause us to experience decay. We think for a while that the tragedy or hurt has only misplaced our trust and we think that we are still green and growing, but the truth is that we have placed our faith in something or someone who is not able to sustain us.

We rest on something that seems to grow our faith, but in actuality, we are being burned and dried up. Instead of having a lush, green, growing faith, our faith becomes withered and brown. We may have put our trust in a person, a religion, a church, or a special group. When any of those disappoint us, we fall on hard times and wonder why our faith has abandoned us.

It is important to make sure we have placed our faith in the right things. We must only put our faith in Jesus and His word. Anything else will only blow away and wither like the grass.

Remember the words of Peter, "For, 'All people are like grass, and their glory is like the flower of the field; the grass withers and the flowers fall, but the word of the Lord stands forever.'"

If you have placed your faith in anything other than the Lord and His word, you are standing on shaky ground. But if you are placing your faith in the word of the Lord you can be assured that He will stand with you forever.

## "What is Your Usual?"
### Isaiah 55:8

For many years I ate breakfast at a small café close to my home. I loved to eat breakfast there every morning when I had the opportunity. Not only is the breakfast good and the coffee hot, but the price is very reasonable. Every morning when I go there, I order the same thing. I have been ordering the same breakfast for many months.

I am what you call a regular at the café for morning breakfast. I enjoy going in and having my coffee delivered to my table. There are many mornings when someone I know or I have met at the café will join me for breakfast and there are many mornings that I eat alone and read the morning paper.

Now, the reason I tell this story is because I never order breakfast any more. The ladies will just walk up to me and say, "Are you eating the usual this morning?"

I will tell them "Yes," and without my saying a word they will recite, "Two eggs sunny side up, link sausage and wheat toast." I will nod in the affirmative and in a short while my breakfast will be served fresh and hot.

Now, I relate this story about my breakfast because it has got me to Just Thinking! I think we would all agree that God knows all about us. He knows our every thought and action. He knows what our needs are before we even ask.

The scripture says, "For your Father knows what you need before you ask him." So, we might then conclude that we don't need to ask. Yet, every once in a while, I will throw the ladies at the café a curve. I will splurge and order grits. Or, in a real weak moment, I might order pancakes and bacon. Now, I don't do it very often, but I always have the option. Well, in reality, although the ladies know my usual, they don't know my desires. They are different from God. Not only does God know my usual, He also knows my desires. There is nothing I can hide from God. Several times the scripture says that Jesus knew their thoughts.

Now, since God knows all about my every thought, maybe that should rearrange my thoughts and actions. Maybe that should help me to be more concerned about what I think and what I do. I do think that I should be more concerned about how God sees me and hears me. I know that God is a forgiving God and that He forgives me when I do wrong, but that doesn't give me a license to do wrong.

It is important that I seek to live in the way God wants me to live. Isaiah wrote, "'For my thoughts are not your thoughts neither are your ways my ways.' Declares the Lord."

I want God to help me see what He thinks so that I can be more like Him. It is my prayer today that God will see our usual as glorifying Him. I only hope that when God looks at me, He sees someone who usually is trying to please Him.

### "A Little Bump"
1 Corinthians 10:12

I bumped my hand on the door frame. I was carrying a box out of the house and accidentally slammed my hand into the catch where the storm door latches. I hollered out and it hurt for the moment, but I actually didn't think much of it.

The next day as I was sitting in a meeting, I looked down at my hand and it was about four times the size it is supposed to be. I worried for a few moments, but I realized it didn't hurt. I moved my hand and clinched it into a fist to see if it was painful or was causing discomfort. It was not, and upon touching it I could tell it was sore to the touch, but, once again, it wasn't hurting so I just kept a watch on it.

About two days later, I began to notice the bruise. My right hand is now a dark shade of brown with a small white center. The bruise is much larger than the initial bump I sustained. The interesting thing about the whole episode is that only one person has noticed the bruise. I have had to show and tell my family.

The person who noticed it didn't notice it until I had been in their presence for about a half hour. The bruise is still sore, but it looks a lot worse than it actually is.

The experience of this bruise got me to Just Thinking! Have you ever noticed how people think that just a little sinning won't do them any harm? Have you ever heard someone say, "Well it was just a little lie?"

Or, maybe even you have convinced yourself that something that you knew was wrong was OK because you had a good enough excuse to warrant the behavior? It is funny how we allow sin to creep into our lives and others don't even notice. It is sad that we allow ourselves to be trapped into sinful behavior and it usually only starts with a small insignificant act on our behalf.

We say things like, "I just can't love that person," and others will answer by saying, "Yeah, I know what you mean." We have just walked into a trap and someone has given us permission to feel that way. We tell a little bit of gossip and say, "Now, I'm not gossiping, but I do have a prayer concern about…" and then we tell the latest bit of news we heard about someone. We have just walked into a trap and someone has listened and we think it is okay.

We even use scripture to get us out of a jam. We miss something important at church that we know God would have wanted us to participate in and we say, "Well the ox was in the ditch and I just couldn't make it." Someone says, "Yea that has happened to me too."

Now, we feel justified and our guilt has been relieved. The fact is that anytime we allow sin to invade our lives, it leaves a bruise. It may not hurt at the time and we may not think it will cause a problem, but every time we do it there is a danger of becoming hard-hearted to God.

Paul cautions us to be careful in our Christian lives. He says, "So, if you think you are standing firm, be careful that you don't fall!" We must be careful that we do not allow sin to diminish our witness to others and our testimony for Christ. Remember, it is not the big stuff that often gets us in trouble. Most of the time it is the little stuff.

## "How's Your Road?"
### Romans 8:25; Proverbs 3:5

I'm sure you have been traveling down the road when all of a sudden, the traffic begins to back up. I know this has happened to me more times than I like to remember. The traffic just slowly moves along and you are sitting there wondering what is causing the holdup. You have places to go and things to do, yet there you are, stuck.

It happens on major freeways and, sometimes, in small town cities. There is no rhyme or reason behind it most of the time. Oh, I know sometimes it can be a wreck or road construction, but sometimes there are just so many people on the road that something or someone has caused a slowdown.

It can be very frustrating especially if you are on a time schedule. I really get frustrated if I get behind a large truck and can't see what is up ahead. I wonder if I should try a detour or just wait it out. Not being able to see ahead is just as bad as not being able to move along.

Now, traffic slowdowns and not being able to see what was holding me up has got me to Just Thinking! Have you ever noticed in your life when you are not traveling at the speed you would like to go? Maybe you are hoping for a better job and it just seems to never get here. Maybe you are waiting to hear from a doctor about a test and something seems to be blocking the way. Maybe you are creeping along in your spiritual life and your prayers just don't seem to be getting through.

You feel caught in traffic with nowhere to go and no way to tell what is causing the delay. You just keep moving along hoping for a break so that you can find your way and make it to your destination.

Well, I will tell you that God knows your way. He has mapped out a plan for your life and has your destination in sight. All we need to do is trust and have faith and he will carry us through to the end.

I encourage you to remember the words of Paul when he wrote to the church in Rome. He says, "But if we hope for what we do not yet have, we wait for it patiently."

We trust in a God who has our life in His hands, and so we wait patiently for what is to come. We believe in Him and know that He has our best interest at heart.

"Trust in the LORD with all your heart and lean not on your own understanding; in all your ways acknowledge him, and he will make your paths straight."

I hope your travel days will be full of uncluttered roads.

## "No Tail Lights"
### Genesis 35:3; Psalm 119:105

I borrowed a boat from a friend of mine. We have been great friends for many years and he allowed us to borrow the boat to go to the lake. We visited a little while, then went out and hooked the boat up to our SUV. We checked the lights and everything was working well. We visited for a while longer and decided we needed to head on back to home. We loaded up and began to go down their long driveway.

As we headed down the driveway, we all smelled a distinctive burning smell. We stopped the car just short of the highway and went to check things out. We noticed that now none of the trailer lights or the taillights of the car were working. We had headlights, turn signals and brake lights on the car, but none on the trailer. We figured a fuse had burnt out.

We tried for more than an hour to figure out what had taken place with no success. Finally, I backed the boat back into the yard and left it. We traveled home with no tail lights on the SUV. We made it home safely, but every time I would see a car approaching from behind, I would tap my brakes or put on the flashers to alert them I was up ahead. I didn't want anyone hitting me from behind because they couldn't see me. I could see where I was going, but was afraid no one could see where I'd been.

Now, the fact that I didn't have any taillights got me to Just Thinking! When was the last time you considered where you have been? Doesn't our past have a great influence on our future? Many times, we focus more on our past than we do on our future. We allow our past to affect us in our everyday life and cripple us into doing and being things, that God never intended. We allow our past to shape us and handicap us from the bright future that God has for us.

Do you remember the story of Jacob? He returns from his journeys and is directed by God to return to Bethel. Jacob is listening to God as He explains what Jacob is to do. God directs him to return to the place where he and God made a covenant.

Listen to the words of Jacob as he explains why God is sending him back to Bethel, "Then come, let us go up to Bethel, where I will build an altar to God, who answered me in the day of my distress and who has been with me wherever I have gone."

Jacob knew that God had been with him in his past and would be with him in his future. Jacob could have allowed his past to cripple his present, but instead he acknowledged that God had been with him in the past and would guide him in the future. Jacob didn't allow the past to affect his future.

My friend initially wanted me to drive his car home. He said I probably didn't need to drive without taillights. He was probably right technically, but I decided that I wasn't backing up all the way home, I was driving forward. I had headlights and knew that they would direct my path. Too many of us want to back up into life instead of traveling head-first into it.

The Psalmist said, "Your word is a lamp to my feet and a light for my path."

I am glad God knows where I have been, but I am happier that He shines a light where I am going.

## "Are You Working on It?"
### 1 Corinthians 3:1-2; Ephesians 3:14-19

I get my hair cut about once a month. For the last 10-plus years I like it to be very short, a change from when I was younger. It is funny how people react when you have your hair cut. Some people notice right away and others have to have it pointed out to them. Some like it and some don't.

I have noticed over my years as a pastor that some people like me to wear my hair longer and some like it cut shorter. Of course, you know the old saying, "The only difference between a good haircut and a bad one is two weeks." The thing that is amazing about having a haircut is that you consistently have to do it. There is an amazing thing about hair (or let me say about my hair): it continues to grow back. I will get it cut and, in a few weeks, I have to get it cut again.

Now, my hair knows how I like it and you would think it would just stay the same all the time, but it doesn't. In spite of what I think the perfect length of my hair is, it continues to grow back. When it gets too long, I have to get it cut. Now, if it was up to me, I would just freeze my hair at a certain length and then I would never have to have a haircut again.

Now, the fact that I got my haircut and the fact that it grows back got me to Just Thinking! How cool would it be if our spiritual maturity grew like our hair? What if without me even thinking about it my life in Christ would be growing every day? What if without even trying I could see a difference in how I treated others in my everyday life? What if without even concentrating on it I began to reflect Christ more in my life?

You know, I don't think about my hair growing. It just does it. But to be more spiritually mature, I have to work on it constantly.

Yet, most people think that their spiritual maturity just happens. They never work at growing as a Christian. They never try to treat others differently because of their faith. They don't concentrate on reflecting Christ more in their life. And, unless you try, you will not succeed at being more Christ-like. Some believe that just by coming to church, serving on a committee or singing in a choir they are becoming spiritual.

It just doesn't happen that way. It takes a constant effort on our part to grow in Christ. Paul addressed the Christians in Corinth and proclaimed their immaturity. Listen to his words, "Brothers and sisters, I could not address you as people who live by the Spirit but as people who are still worldly - mere infants in Christ. I gave you milk, not solid food, for you were not yet ready for it."

To be able to grow spiritually, you must lend yourself to knowing more about Christ. Listen to the prayer of Paul for the followers of Christ, "For this reason I kneel before the Father, from whom every family in heaven and on earth derives its name. I pray that out of his glorious riches he may strengthen you with power through his Spirit in your inner being, so that Christ may dwell in your hearts through faith. And I pray that you, being rooted and established in love, may have power, together with all the Lord's people, to grasp how wide and long and high and deep is the love of Christ, and to know this love that surpasses knowledge - that you may be filled to the measure of all the fullness of God."

If you want to be filled to the measure of all fullness of God, you must work at it. Unlike hair, it doesn't happen automatically.

## "That Special Look!"
### John 1:12-13

One of the joys of being a pastor is when I get to visit with a mom and dad after the birth of a child. One day, I traveled to see a new baby and the new parents in the hospital. It was unique, because soon after I arrived it was just me, the baby and the parents in the room. All of the grandparents, aunts and uncles had gone home for a while.

As I sat talking to the new parents I was awestruck as the new mother held her little girl and kept staring at her. She would look down at this new baby and then look up at her husband and me and just smile. Every now and then she would say, "I just can't believe she is mine."

I told the dad that he had better get a picture of that mom looking at her child because it was just about the sweetest thing I had ever seen. There was just the most peaceful and pleasant look on that mom's face as she looked at her little girl. Matter of fact, I don't know if love has a look to it or not, but if it does, I know I saw love on the face of that mom as she looked into the eyes of her little girl.

Now, the fact that a baby was born is not that unusual, but the love expressed in the look of a mother got me to Just Thinking! Can you imagine just how much God must look at us with the eyes of love? I believe that every time a child is born that God shows that very same look of love on His face. I believe that His desires, dreams and purposes for each person born are steeped in love. He looks at us with the eyes of love and just can't believe that we are His. I also believe that when we make that step and get born again by the spirit that He also smiles the smile of satisfaction because He knows we have made that step from this life to the next. We have been born not just of water, but also of the Spirit.

It is exciting when I get to visit these new babies and see the joy and love expressed on the face of the parents, but it is even more exciting when I get to see the birth of a Christian, when I get to feel the love of God in the life of someone who has accepted Jesus as their personal savior. I know that God looks upon each of His children with the look of love that the new mother looks upon her daughter.

The apostle John wrote in the opening words of his gospel

these words, "Yet to all who received him, to those who believed in his name, he gave the right to become children of God - children born not of natural descent, nor of human decision or a husband's will, but born of God."

I pray today that God is looking at you with the love of satisfaction on His face because you have been born into His kingdom.

### "Bad Messages"
Hebrews 4:2

Have you ever operated a copy machine? Copy machines, or as we sometimes call them, Xerox machines, can be the most useful and the most aggravating pieces of office equipment that you can have access to.

When they are working, they are great. You can do so much with the copy machine. You can create identical copies in a matter of minutes. You can reduce or enlarge an original copy and help some of us out who can't read all of the small print. You can copy on both sides of the paper for things like bulletins or newsletters. I will admit that a copy machine is a wonderful piece of equipment to have in your office and I don't think we could operate without it. Although it is a necessary piece of equipment, it is also the most aggravating piece of equipment when it is broken.

The office copy machine was broken. Now, everything seems to be alright, except that there is a message telling us to close the side door. The strange thing about this message is that the side door is not open. We turn off the machine and turn it back on and we get the same message. I open and shut the side door and we get the same message. The machine looks the same, but it is not operating the same because of a bad message.

Now, the bad message being given by the copy machine got me to Just Thinking! We get a great deal of bad messages in this world. We read in the paper and hear on the news about people who make mistakes in life because they have believed a bad message. They have been told to live for themselves. They have been told that they need to watch out for No. 1. They are told to "live and let live." They are told to step on anyone, walk over everyone, and don't respect others in climbing the ladder to success. They are told that the more they have in their bank account, the better standing they will have in society.

I don't know about you but I believe those are bad messages. Someone needs to come in and change the messages and get the machine running right. I tried to fix our copy machine and I was unable to get the message to go away because I am not a service technician. We try to fix our bad messages by working on our lives by ourselves and most of the time we make a bigger mess.

We need the service technician for our lives to come in and readjust our thinking. Most of the people we know have heard the correct message - they just ignore it. They only hold to the part of the message that makes them comfortable.

Listen to the writer of Hebrews as he directs us about the message, "For we also have had the good news proclaimed to us, just as they did; but the message they heard was of no value to them, because they did not share the faith of those who obeyed."

The message that changes lives and clears up the problems in our lives is the message of faith in the life technician. Jesus Christ is that life technician, and if you are having trouble with your equipment, copy His example and you will have life more abundantly.

## "Me, Forget?"
### Deuteronomy 4:9

Do you ever forget? I am always amused by the people who tell me that they have senior moments. They will forget something that you have told them or that you remind them of.

Yet, I have discovered that you don't have to be a senior in age to forget. I forget sometimes. I forget to bring something home from the office or I will tell someone that I will call them back, and then I remember about 10 p.m. that I didn't call them back. I once made an appointment with a couple on a Sunday afternoon and forgot to meet them. I apologized for days. They were very understanding, but I felt awful.

Sometimes, I forget a name that I know I'm supposed to remember or a telephone number that I memorized long ago. Forgetfulness is not a trait that I brag about or claim to be proud of, but I do forget.

Being forgetful has got me to Just Thinking! Do you think God ever forgets about you? Do you think He forgets to listen to your prayers or pay attention to your needs? Do you think God forgets to keep the earth rotating or the sun to shine? I know God doesn't forget, but sometimes we forget God. Sometimes we get so busy that we forget that God wants us to pay Him the attention that He deserves. Sometimes we get so preoccupied with our lives that we forget that God has a purpose and a plan for our lives. Sometimes we get so wrapped up in our family and our problems and our wants that we forget that God knows all about us and our family and our problems and our wants.

There is a problem when we forget God! There is a problem with who we have become. When we forget God, we depend on what we can do and forget who created us and what He does.

Moses reminded the people of Israel that we need to be careful that we do not forget God. Listen to his words, "Only be careful, and watch yourselves closely so that you do not forget the things your eyes have seen or let them slip from your heart as long as you live. Teach them to your children and to their children after them."

We too quickly forget that God is the giver and sustainer of life. We forget the majesty of what we see God do and what we have felt Him do. We are too quick to ask the question, "What has He done for me lately?"

Too often, I have seen a committed Christian silently walk away from their commitment because they forget God. I encourage you to not forget God. Be careful. Watch, and keep God in your heart as long as you live.

## "Doing the Right Thing"
Galatians 3:28

Peggy and I went to see the musical "Big River." This is the story of Huckleberry Finn and his escapades down the Mississippi River. Accompanying him on his trip is a runaway slave named Jim. During a talk that they have, Jim tells Huck of his family and how he hopes to see them one day. For the first time in his life, Huck sees Jim as a person, not as a possession.

The story continues and, in the end, Huck risks his life to help Jim escape. Before they escape, Huck is battling with the theological issue of doing right and going to heaven or doing wrong and going to hell. Finally, he decides if helping a slave escape is wrong, he will just have to suffer the consequences. Jim is his friend no matter the color of his skin.

As I watched the story unfold on stage it got me to Just Thinking! How often do you and I act on tradition taught to us versus what is right and wrong? I know we live in a world that teaches prejudice.

My surroundings as a white male growing up in the South exposed me to prejudices that I struggle with every day. Yet, as I watched the musical and saw these two figures on stage - one white and one black - embrace as brothers, I was struck with a heavy feeling of guilt. Do I treat others as I want to be treated, no matter the skin color? And it is not just the black-white issue. Our world now has interactions among all ethnicities. Are we going to live by tradition, or by right and wrong?

Jesus was asked who is our neighbor? He answered by telling the story of the good Samaritan. He told this story not because it was traditionally right for a Jew to have anything to do with a Samaritan, but because it was the right thing to do.

Paul said, "There is neither Jew nor Greek, there is neither bond or free, there is neither male nor female: for you are all one in Christ Jesus."

Let's pray that we will all seek to defeat the traditional wrongs and live by what Jesus said was right: "Love Your Neighbor as Yourself."

### "Make the Call!"
Acts 1:8

Here is my count to the best of my knowledge:

- one call to solicit my membership in the National Rifle Association;
- one call to solicit a subscription to a deer hunting magazine;
- One call to get my name on a political watchdog list;
- One that asked if I was over 50 years old to please stay on the line;
- Three offers to stay in Myrtle Beach, Daytona Beach, and Fripp Island if I would only listen to their offer one afternoon for about three hours;
- Seven opportunities to receive a no-obligation credit card over the phone, and, finally;
- Eight offers by mail and numerous other offers from people I don't even know. You can double the mail offers, because for everyone I got, Peggy got a duplicate.

Well, those are offers either by phone or mail trying to sell me something I didn't ask for or solicit in any way. I guess you get those same types of offers at your house, too.

Now, all of these offers have got me to Just Thinking! Do you remember how Christians are often labeled as pushy about telling others about Jesus? We are often told to mind our own business. We are told that if someone wants to find out about Jesus, they will ask.

Yet, we are overwhelmed with these telemarketers over the phone and through the mail. They get away with it and spend our valuable time trying to sell us things that, most of the time, we don't need or will only get us into debt. Well, I for one am tired of it. I made a commitment that for every person who calls me on the phone to get me to buy something, I will make a deal to listen to their sales pitch if they promise to allow me to tell them about Jesus before they hang up. (Most don't make the deal.) I was just hoping we could find the zeal of giving away our Savior as the telemarketer gives away their product. Our gift is worth more, costs less and will last a lifetime.

Jesus said, "You will be my witnesses!"

In the day and age of people trying to get you to listen to their advice about how you can have more freedom and a better life if you will just purchase their product, why are we so timid about sharing the greatest product of all that is already paid for? Why are we allowing the "Good News" to become obsolete?

We need to become as bold as the disciples were in the first century. We need to speak out and speak up about Jesus. He is the greatest answer to all of our needs. Go ahead, give someone a call and make your pitch. Jesus will do the convincing; you and I won't have to!

## "Who Do You Call?"
### Psalm 121:1-4

Have you ever had to call 911? I did once when the house next to the church caught on fire. I found the fire, rushed back to my office and actually dialed 911. Guess what? It really works!

Immediately, someone answered and asked, "What is the nature of your emergency?" I quickly told them where the fire was and in about three minutes the firemen and the trucks began to pull up to the house. Now, it was not that I doubted the 911 service, but even though I knew it was there, I never actually saw it function until I called. I hope you never have to use this service, but if you do, I can confirm that it works.

Now, seeing the response of calling 911 has got me to Just Thinking! Isn't it good to know that God is always there? Whether in an emergency or not, He is always available to us. He is never too sick or too busy to listen to us when we call. He is never on vacation or away from His desk. He never turns on His voicemail for me to leave a message. He listens to me when I call. He will speak if I listen. He always responds in the right way and takes care of me whatever my needs.

In life we need to depend on God more. Call Him when you need Him. Call Him just to talk and tell Him how your day has been. God is always available to us if we just call. Remember what the Psalmist said, "I lift up my eyes to the hills - where does my help come from? My help comes from the Lord, the Maker of heaven and earth. He will not let your foot slip - He who watches over you will not slumber; indeed, He who watches over Israel [me and you] will neither slumber nor sleep."

The God who created us is ready and willing to hear us when we call. He cares about us and wants what is best for us. Don't worry, just trust and believe. God will not let you down. Call on Him; it really works.

## "Do It Now!"
### Romans 13:11

Have you ever waited too long before doing something you needed to do? One morning after Christmas, the family and I left my parents' home to travel to Alabama to celebrate Christmas with Peggy's family.

After stopping for breakfast in Macon, I was able to persuade Peggy to drive for a little while. As she left Macon heading for Atlanta, it began to rain. We both immediately realized that we needed a new set of windshield wipers on the car. I suggested we get to the other side of Atlanta and stop when we would need gas. She agreed and drove on.

About two hours later, we pulled off the interstate and got gas. It was still raining. I stopped at an auto parts store and purchased a set of wiper blades for the car. After some 15 minutes, standing in the sprinkling rain, I was able to change the wiper blades. I got back in the car, turned the wipers on and got the windshield really clean.

The wipers wiped the windshield clean only once because it stopped raining almost immediately. Peggy had driven through rain for two hours with bad wiper blades. I changed the blades and the rain stopped.

Now, putting off what I needed to do has got me to Just Thinking! Why is it that we put off doing what we know needs to be done? What have you put off lately? Do you need to visit that special friend that you haven't seen in a while? Do you need to make amends for something that you've done wrong? Do you need to restore a friendship that has gone sour because of a misunderstanding? Do you need to take your spouse out on a date? Do you need to ask your children to forgive you for not spending enough time with them? Do you need to ask God to forgive you for not being the Christian person you know you should be? Do you need to accept Christ as your personal Savior? Why wait to do something that you know needs doing right now?

Paul said, "And do this, understanding the present time. The hour has come for you to wake up from your slumber, because our salvation is nearer now than when we first believed."

Don't wait, do it now!

## "Are You Scared to Death?"
### John 10:10

I was sitting in my truck, minding my own business while waiting for a friend to return from the store from buying a Pepsi. We were in a small town at a convenience store next to a post office.

I saw this lady run around the building and into the store. In just a moment, my friend came out of the store with another man. The other man, who I later found out was the store owner, had a gun in his hand. My friend called for me to get out of the truck. He told me that the lady inside had just been robbed and was hysterical. I went inside and identified myself as a pastor. I tried to calm the lady down. She was beside herself. She was crying and screaming, "I just begged him not to kill me. I know you are not supposed to run, but I just had to get out of there."

We finally realized that the assailant had left in a car. We walked the lady back into the post office and helped her call for help. We stayed with her until some family members and the police arrived. It was a very scary situation for the lady.

Now, this encounter has got me to Just Thinking! This lady was distraught with fear and pain, even after the situation was under control. I could not even imagine how she felt. She was faced with the fear of losing her life.

In reality, we are all faced with the loss of life every day. Maybe not by having a gun waved in our face, but don't we all take simple risks every day? If you drive or ride in a car, you are taking a risk. None of us knows when the doctor will say we have cancer and only a short time to live. We don't like to think about it, but it is true. None of us knows when our life will be taken from us. None of us is promised tomorrow.

Jesus Himself talked about the thief that comes to steal, kill and destroy. Are we ready to face that time in our life? We can be if we allow Jesus to be the Savior and Lord of our life.

He also said, "But I have come to give you life and give it more abundantly."

Even when we face death, we can have assurance that we will live forever. We can live abundantly because Jesus lives in us through the Holy Spirit. Why should you go around "scared to death?" You can have this same assurance in Jesus. I hope you have the abundant life promised by Jesus. It helps to take away some of the fear and dread of death.

## "Enjoy the Food!"
Psalm 66:5

There are some restaurant drive-thru windows that I actually hate going to. You are supposed to be getting "fast food," but sometimes it is anything but fast. The first thing I struggle with sometimes is trying to figure out what the person is saying over the static and interference through the intercom. Then, if you are lucky, they finally get the order right.

Then comes my biggest complaint of all. I hate it when I drive up to the window and they take my money and then they say, "Will you please drive up to the yellow line and we will bring your order right out."

I even had that happen once when no one was behind me. I can't stand it. For one thing, they will serve two other cars while you are waiting. I believe they forget you are out there. And then, what happens to me is, they hand me the order, it is wrong - or they have left something out - and I have to get out anyway and go into the restaurant for them to get things straight. I get frustrated just thinking about it. And it is all because I am in a hurry. I don't have time to wait and I have another agenda on my mind.

Now, having this happen to me at the drive-thru has got me to Just Thinking! We do church like we do the drive-thru. We are in a hurry to get in and get out. We come prepared to leave.

We don't have time to sit and absorb what is being done. We are too caught up in ourselves to hear God if He does speak. We get frustrated when we are delayed or have to wait or the service goes long.

Church should be like a fine restaurant. We should go in and take our time. We shouldn't be in a rush. We should tune our hearts and ears to God and listen for the specials He has to offer us. We should savor every morsel that is on our plate. The Psalmist said it best when he said, "Come and see what God has done, his awesome deeds for mankind!"

Let me encourage you to go to church and allow God to fill you with life-giving food. Allow God to give you food for your spiritual soul and enjoy each mouthful. Take time to hear God and be filled with His goodness. Don't be in a hurry! Come to church and experience God.

## "Do You Have It Right?
### Mark 1:15

Can you spell? I can't. One of the really important things to me on my computer is my spell-check. Each time I write a letter or type an article, it goes through spell-check. Yet, inevitably, (spell-check got this word spelled right) I will stump the spell-checker. That's right. I will spell something how I believe it sounds and the computer will come back with "No Suggestion Found."

That's why I have my little black book beside my computer. It is The New Webster's Spelling Dictionary. I can thumb through and find just about any word and how it is spelled. It is difficult sometimes when you are not sure even if you have the right word. Like the other day, I was trying to say convenient, and the spell-check gave me the option of conveyance. I selected that word and then got to thinking it was incorrect. I wanted to say "the act of making something comfortable," yet I was about to say "the act of transporting, transmitting, or communicating."

I was glad I checked my little black book. I am in the business of making sure people understand what is said. I have learned that the simpler I can make it, the better off I am.

Now, getting something right has got me to Just Thinking! How true that is with the gospel. Jesus didn't say that He came so that we would all be able to theologically differentiate (had to check on that word) between Augustine's theory of original sin and Pelagius's theory of choice before we could become a born-again Christian. He didn't say we needed to be able to parse the many understandings of the Greek word for salvation (soteria) to receive His grace. He didn't say we needed to understand the theology of the Pharisees and the Sadducees before we could understand the crucifixion.

He did say, "The time is fulfilled, and the kingdom of God is at hand, repent and believe the gospel."

Let us be careful that we do not make trusting Jesus harder than it really is. Let's not make it hard for those who do not know Jesus to come to know him. The gospel is simple. Jesus did all the work. We just need to confess and believe.

Always remember: when in doubt always check that little black book, not the spelling dictionary, but THE BIBLE.

## "Have You Received the Right Directions?"
### Acts 2:21

I was a chaperone with the fourth, fifth and sixth-graders for a trip. We took three days and went up to Virginia. We spent two nights in a hotel in Williamsburg. The first night we finally arrived at about 8:30. After getting our boys settled down in their rooms, a friend and I decided to watch a movie. The drinks in the Coke machine were costing more than we wanted to pay. Not willing to continue paying the price, we decided that I would go to a local convenience store and buy a 2-liter coke.

I asked the hotel clerk how far away was the nearest convenience store. She remarked that there was one only a block or two over the overpass directly in front of the hotel. I thanked her and began walking.

The 7-Eleven was not in sight after I crossed the overpass. I asked another lady and she assured me that the 7-Eleven was just around the corner. The 7-Eleven was a good half-mile from the hotel. I finally reached my destination, made my purchases and returned to the hotel 45 minutes after my excursion began.

When I finally got on the fourth floor, my friend was getting ready to come look for me. What was intended to be a 10-minute trip turned into forever.

Now, this little trip to the store got me to Just Thinking! Have you ever been misled by someone's directions? Now, I was not mad at the clerk, but I decided to never ask her for directions again. Sometimes we are misled by salespersons, insurance companies, investment opportunities, real estate purchases and even TV products that are money back guaranteed. It is easy to be misled.

Yet, there is some news that has been the same since its inception. That is the good news of Jesus Christ. The message is the same no matter when or how you share it. The Old Testament prophets spoke of its coming. John the Baptist preached it to the masses. Jesus solidified the claim and made it so. Paul and all the apostles preached the reality of the event.

And you and I still have the opportunity today to revel in the glory of the news, "For everyone who calls upon the Name of the Lord, will be saved."

No misleading instructions for the directions to an abundant life. Have you taken the direction of the Savior, or are you still being misled?

## "Are You Waiting in Line?"
Galatians 6:7

We all have to stand in lines, whether it is at the grocery store, the DMV, the post office, the restaurant or a theme park. Well, have you ever noticed people when they have to stand in line? Most of us do not like to wait. We will sometimes do anything to gain an unfair advantage. I guess one of my pet peeves is people who break in line. I try (Do you hear my confession?) not to do it.

On a family outing, we had to stand in line and wait for a tube ride down a hill. It was part of the fun we had in Snowshoe, W. Va. I was amazed at all of the people who were unwilling, or too rude, to wait their turn. They would intentionally break in line. One boy, thinking he would receive an advantage because he was small, even asked with a sneering grin, "Can I break in front and not have to wait?"

I guess some people around me thought I was rude. I said no - not because I'm a bad person, but because it is not right to try and gain an unfair advantage over others who have been waiting.

It also happens when I'm driving and the sign says "Right Lane closed, ahead move to the left." Yet, people will travel far down the right lane, pass others and expect someone up ahead to let them in. They are jumping the line and making others wait - again, getting an unfair advantage.

Now, all of this breaking in line has got me to Just Thinking! Do we try to gain an unfair advantage with God? Do we try to manipulate God's commands and laws so that we can do what we want to do and not go by God's rules? Do we try to justify our wrongs and make them right?

Paul said, "Do not be deceived. God is not mocked. Whatsoever a person sows, that shall they also reap." I don't want an unfair advantage with God. I want to be the best I can be. I want to learn to stand in line and wait my turn. I want to obey God and reap the benefits of His blessings. Remember the old saying, "Good things come to those who wait."

## "Are You Judging?"
Matthew 7:2

Have you ever joked about winning the lottery, the Publisher's Clearing House Sweepstakes, the Reader's Digest Sweepstakes or numerous other instant-win games? You know, the excitement of having your name drawn out of a box and being declared the winner of lots and lots of money, or maybe even a neat gift. I guess everyone at one time or another has had that dream.

Well, there was a time when I was hoping that I wouldn't win. You see, I watched a man pick names out of a round box. He would spin the box, stop it and pick out a name. He did this 14 times on five different occasions. Each time, he would give the names to a group of lawyers and they would decide on eight people to serve on a jury to decide a case. I sat all day long in Federal Court hoping that I wouldn't win.

Instead of people wanting to hear their name called, most people were cringing every time the clerk would call out a name. When she would finish calling out the names, there was a collective sigh among those not called. It is really the first time I have ever observed people wanting to lose.

Now, watching this whole process take place got me to Just Thinking! What is it that has us so afraid of being on a jury? Some people do not want the inconvenience of serving. Some people feel as though they do not have time. Some people do not believe in the system. Most of the people I talked to did not want to be the judge of someone else's problems.

Yet, we judge people all of the time. We judge people by what they say, do, wear, where they work and how they look. Yet, we say we do not want to be the ultimate judge of someone's fate. We need to be careful how we judge others and the things we say. Often our remarks about someone can cause others to judge them falsely. Remember God is the ultimate judge of our lives. Jesus reminds us, "For in the same way you judge others, you will be judged, and with the measure you use, it will be measured to you."

We need to be fair and just in all of our dealing with others. We need to judge others in the love and forgiveness that our Savior judges us.

## "Red Light, Green Light"
### Psalm 27:14

I took Dad and Mom to a few doctor's appointments. As we traveled from their house, we encountered a great many traffic lights. Now, if you drive you understand the concept of traffic lights. Red means stop, yellow means to get ready to stop and green means go. As I traveled down the road, traffic lights had a great deal to do with how quickly I got to my destination.

For example, if I get fortunate enough to catch a lot of green lights, I make good time. Yet, if I get caught by a great many red lights, my travel is slowed down. There is one truth about traffic lights: you had better obey them. To not obey them can cause great harm to you and someone else.

As I drive down the road, I find myself hoping for green lights so I can make good time. When I am delayed by red lights, I spend a great deal of time going nowhere. And, I find myself watching the other light to find out when it will turn red so that I may continue on my journey. It is amazing how much these simple traffic controls can help or impede my progress.

Now, as I consider these traffic lights, it has got me to Just Thinking! What are the red and green lights in your spiritual life? Do you find times you are stuck in your spiritual progress by some bad attitude or situation that has taken place in your life? Do you struggle with everyday events that seem to bog you down and hinder your way?

We can get caught in the ways of life that will hinder our spiritual advance. We can get behind the red light and feel like we are going nowhere. When these times happen, we need to remember that the light will eventually turn green. We need to wait on God and do those things that He desires for us to do. The Psalmist said, "Wait for the Lord, be strong and take heart and wait for the Lord."

He wants us to stay connected through Bible study and prayer. He wants us to worship Him and be reminded that He is all powerful and great. When we stay connected, God will reveal Himself, we will find the light turns green and we can move on in our lives. We will find the path open and we will see progress in our journey. God wants to provide green lights for our life, but when the occasional red light gets in your way, stop and take notice. Wait on the Lord to reveal His path for you to take.

My prayer for all of us is that we will encounter very few red lights in our Christian walk. But when we do, my prayer is that we will wait patiently on the Lord and allow Him to guide us when the light turns green. Pay attention to the red lights and learn from them. It makes the green lights much nicer in your life.

## CHAPTER TEN

# JUST THINKING...
# ABOUT SOMETHING FUNNY!

### "Find It!"
Matthew 25:29

Have you ever lost something? Out of the clear blue one day, I asked Peggy about a beautiful silver candelabra we once owned. I asked her where it was. She told me that she thought it got broken. And then she said we may have misplaced it in one of the three moves we had made after we were married. I expressed sorrow because it had been a wedding gift and it was very lovely. I was considering using it for a sermon illustration I was thinking about.

Well, many months went by and I thought of it no more. Later that year, the very first church I was pastor of called to see if I would preach at their homecoming. I was delighted, and we made arrangements to travel back to Kentucky and see old friends and remember those who had already gone on to heaven.

We got to the church that Sunday morning and were talking to different individuals. There was a lull in the conversation, and Peggy nudged me and said in a quiet whisper, "Look over there on top of the library cabinet."

I did, and guess what I saw? You're right; it was the

candelabra. Both of us broke into soft laughter. It was not broken at all; it had been left behind. Well, needless to say, I did not have the courage - or the guts - to walk up to the pastor and say, "By the way I left this here nine years ago and I have come to collect it." I guess you could say we have donated it to the church.

Now, discovering the candelabra and realizing it wasn't lost after all has got me to Just Thinking! Have we ever left something behind in our lives that is precious to God? Maybe at one time you were involved in a Sunday School class. Hey, maybe you were even teaching the class. Or, maybe at one time you sang in the choir or played an instrument. Maybe there was a time when you were very active serving on teams and committees and helping out in the activities of the church. Maybe when we think of it we have a soft laugh and then go on.

Well, God wants us to know that all of our talents are precious in His sight. He wants us to know that it is OK to come to Him and say, "Hey, I left this and want to reclaim it and start again."

Remember, if we do not use our talents, we will lose them. Remember the parable of the talents in Matthew. The one who hid his talent lost it, "For whoever has will be given more, and they will have an abundance. Whoever does not have, even what they have will be taken from them."

Let us find the courage and the guts to say to God, "Here I am Lord, use me."

## "Laugh!"
### Psalm 126:2

Did you ever try to get things just perfect? It was the Saturday before Easter and we were preparing for baptism. The church was decorated with beautiful Easter lilies and we had placed some of them around the baptismal pool. The florist had advised me that we might want to pull the yellow pollen out of the center of the lilies to keep the highly potent smell down. The baptismal

# JUST THINKING!

was about one-third full of water when Peggy and I ventured up to that area to "fix" the flowers.

As I reached to pick up the last of the lilies, my elbow bumped another. Yes, you guessed it: the lily fell into the baptismal pool. Black dirt completely muddied the water. I let out a disgusted sigh and Peggy began to laugh. I saw nothing funny at the moment until I saw her laughing uncontrollably. Of course, you know I had to drain the water out of the baptistery, clean up the mess and start the water all over again. I made Peggy help.

We think back on that night and laugh. (Even I can't help but laugh.) We wanted everything to be just perfect, but something (my elbow) got in the way.

Now, the fact that it didn't go perfectly has got me to Just Thinking! Life can be like that incident. We can either let our mistakes and misgivings cause us pain, or we can look at them and laugh. I am glad Peggy helped me to see the humor on that Saturday night.

How do you respond when things don't go your way? How do you respond when something you have planned ends up being turned upside down? Is your frustration and demeanor one that exemplifies Jesus or one that exemplifies the world?

I am convinced that when we learn to laugh at those things that don't go exactly right, we have a better attitude about all things. Jesus can help us to move past ourselves and remember that it is just things.

The Psalmist said this, "Our mouths were filled with laughter, our tongues with songs of joy. Then it was said among the nations, 'The Lord has done great things for them.'"

I could have allowed the dirt in the baptistery to ruin my night, but instead it has become a time of laughter and joy. We still share that story today and it goes to show the greatness of a God who changes us from the inside.

Laugh. Being angry will not change a thing. Laughter is contagious.

## "Keep Practicing!"
### Jude 1:24-25

Most people reading this know me. You will probably get a good laugh when I tell you that one Christmas the boys gave me a pair of roller blades. For those of you who do not know, roller blades are skates that have four wheels in a line. Some people call them in-line skates.

When most people found out that I received these skates as a gift they immediately began to laugh, my wife being one of the first. She could not wait for me to try them on and see if I could skate. Well, I was no Scott Hamilton, but then I didn't fall right away, either. I was learning. My sons even said that I was getting better. I took that as a compliment from an 11-year-old and a 7-year-old who could skate rings around me.

As I continued practicing, I was not as wobbly as I was at first. And every time I put them on, I was becoming more comfortable. I am still a little afraid to try some of the neat tricks my boys are doing. I have a little more to pick up off the ground when I fall and at my age - which was 36 at the time - I will not heal as quickly as they would. All and all, my courage was getting stronger.

Now, learning how to use these new skates has got me to Just Thinking! For most of us, learning about God is a lot like learning how to skate for the first time. We really want to learn how to trust God in everything. When we try to believe His promises to us the first time, we are a little afraid. We think we might fall. We are shaky in our beliefs and our faith is weak.

Yet, the more we put our trust in Him, the more He proves Himself faithful. We become stronger in our faith. We trust His word more. We spend more time in prayer believing that He will answer. Before long, we can even recommend Him to others as the greatest friend we have ever had.

What about those who never try? They are afraid they might fall. Let me remind you of this scripture, "To Him who is able to keep you from falling and to present you before His glorious presence without fault and with great joy to the only God our Savior be glory, majesty, power and authority, through Jesus Christ our Lord, before all ages, now and forevermore! Amen."

You can see that Jesus has already taken care of your falling. You will fall. You will have to get up. You will have doubts and wonder. The truth is that Jesus is ready to keep you from falling if you will learn how to put your total trust and faith in Him.

Remember, the more you practice, the better off you will be.

### "No Bargaining!"
### John 14:6

Now, sometimes being a preacher has its advantages. One year I was asked by a young couple to officiate at their wedding. I immediately said yes, and then they said we are getting married on a cruise ship going to the Bahamas. I looked a little quizzical. The fiancé added "if you come down and do the wedding, we will pay for you and Peggy to go on the cruise." My puzzled look left very quickly and I said yes.

After the wedding – which took place while we were still in United States territory - we headed to the Bahamas with the couple and many of their friends. We enjoyed the relaxed atmosphere and a time to just get away from the real world. I probably had more fun in the Straw Market than anywhere else.

The Straw Market is a place in Nassau, the capital of the Bahamas, where the local people set up their wares to sell to the tourists. You can buy practically anything there. Mostly, they sell things made of straw and shells.

The great thing about the Straw Market is that you never pay the asking price. The correct term for what you do is haggle. We always called it bargaining. I just love it. I would bargain with those ladies just for the sake of bargaining. I sometimes wouldn't even buy what I was bargaining for. We discovered one man who was not in the bargaining mood. He told us he didn't want our compliments or a bargain. The merchandise cost $40; he needed bucks not compliments. We all laughed at his retort and moved on.

Now, all of the bargaining has got me to Just Thinking! I was thinking about how much we try to bargain with God. He has given us the truth and we are always trying to compromise the truth. We are asking for him to give us a little more leeway. We need another chance or a better deal if we are going to be Christians.

Yet, Jesus said it best to his disciples, "I am the way, the truth, and the life. No one comes to the Father but by me."

There is no bargaining with that statement and there is no bargaining with God. Either you accept Him or reject Him. Jesus has given us His best. What more could we want? We need to stop bargaining with God and just accept what He has for us. What God has for us is better than we could ever expect from anyone or anything else in the world.

So, He doesn't need our compliments, He just needs our commitment.

## "Do You Believe?"
### Mark 11:24

One summer I preached a revival at my college roommate's church in Georgia. Darin and I were very good friends. He was a bi-vocational pastor. That means he holds down two full-time jobs, one as a pastor. His primary job is that of a parole officer. He was trying to get into the FBI and had been for the past two years.

Traveling back and forth to his church, we went through the various little towns in Georgia. In one such town there was a church with a marquee in front. Darin and I were talking about the fact that the FBI had not been in touch with him for two years. He had almost given up hope. I told him not to fret, that God would give him direction if that is what God wanted him to do in his life.

On the way home that Monday night, the sign in front of the church said, "If you are looking for a sign from God, This is it!" We laughed about the message and jokingly Darin said, "Well there is my answer."

The next day at about 12:30 p.m., the FBI called to let him know that he had an interview. Wow, did we ever get shook up! I pressed the answering machine and there is a message that Darin is supposed to go for an interview. We couldn't believe it.

Now, the sign and what it said and what happened afterward has got me to Just Thinking! Why is it when we ask God for something in our lives, we are so surprised when we receive it? Could it be because we do not actually believe that he has anything to do with the answer? I mean, really. It seems like when a prayer is answered we are always amazed.

The key word is "believe." To believe something is more than just saying or repeating something. Jesus told his disciples, "Therefore I tell you, whatever you ask for in prayer, believe that you have received it, and it will be yours."

So, let us quit marveling at the answers and start believing that Jesus means what He says.

And by the way, "If you are looking for a sign, this is it!"

## "Ask For Help!"
### Matthew 11:28-30

I stopped in for breakfast at a local restaurant. As I was waiting for my order, I noticed a nicely dressed family sitting not far from me. Now, it was before 9 a.m., so I wondered where they might be going, all dressed up so early in the morning.

One of the young men was trying desperately to tie his necktie. I noticed that he was looking down at his phone. I guessed he was watching a YouTube video of how to tie a tie. The older gentleman sitting across from him at the table had a tie on, but I did not see him giving any helpful instructions. I guessed, and could have been wrong, that the father was allowing the son to learn for himself. The young man was still trying to get his tie tied when his meal arrived. He stopped long enough to eat his breakfast and then continued to go through the motions of getting the tie tied. He was having no success.

Finally, as the family moved away from the table to go pay the bill, the young man stood up, continued to watch the video and attempted to tie his tie - with no success.

As the lady passed by (I guessed it was the mom) I said, politely, "Guess he is having a hard time." She replied that yes, they were going to the grandmother's funeral and they couldn't get it tied. I asked the young man if he would like for me to tie his tie and he jumped at the opportunity. In less than a minute, I had the tie tied around his neck and the young man just shook his head in awe. He thanked me over and over and I told him it was my pleasure. I had tied many ties in my life - most on me, but many on others. They quickly exited the restaurant and headed for the funeral.

Now, the experience of tying the tie has got me to Just Thinking! Have you ever tried to do something on your own with no success? Have you even sought help, but the instructions you received did not seem to help you get the job done?

Often, we get frustrated and quit whatever it is we don't seem to accomplish. I watch people do this with their relationship with God. They try to figure God out, or at least understand Him to their satisfaction. They seek others' opinions of God and try to fit them into their own structure. They become frustrated, aggravated, and angry at the prospect of not being able to work the "God" thing out. They remind me of this young man trying to tie his tie. As soon as we drop our ways of doing something and go to an expert, we get satisfaction.

One of the biggest struggles we have is allowing God to fix

our struggles. We want to handle them our way, or we want to read a self-help book and follow the easy steps to conquering the problem. We want the quick and easy way so that it doesn't take too much time from the other things we really want to do.

Jesus seemed to have the solution if we will just listen and follow: "Come unto me all you who are weary and heavy laden and I will give you rest. Take my yoke upon you and learn from me, for I am gentle and humble in heart, and you will find rest for your souls. For my yoke is easy and my burden is light."

If you are struggling with a problem, a relationship or a decision, maybe you need to go to an expert. My prayer for all of us as individuals is that we would allow God to "tie our ties."

## "What Do You See?"
1 Peter 2:9

What does a preacher look like? Does he look any different than a doctor or lawyer? Does he look any different than a factory worker, electrician or plumber? Now, I am a people watcher. I like to go to the mall not to shop, but to watch people. I like to see what eccentric outfits people are wearing, or how they wear their hair differently.

I must confess that I don't sit around wondering about their profession. I don't recognize certain traits in them because they are dressed a certain way or because they go into a certain store or because they carry on a certain conversation.

Just this week, I have encountered several people who have just walked up to me and asked, "Are you a pastor?" I think one man overheard me talking in a restaurant and got the clue that way. One lady was visiting a friend in the hospital and she just guessed maybe because it was a Sunday and I came in dressed in slacks and a nice shirt. One man thought he knew me and I looked like a preacher he knew.

So, what does a preacher look like?

Now, all of this "looking like a preacher" has got me to Just Thinking! Do you and I look different to God? Does He take into consideration our profession when He deals with our lives? Does He consider education as a prerequisite to being able to serve Him and promote His Kingdom? Does He look at how we are dressed or how we wear our hair in deciding whether to gift us with a Godly talent?

I submit to you that God does not look for certain qualifications when searching for His disciples. Look at the group He chose in the Bible. There were fishermen, tax collectors, a rebel rouser, a prejudiced Hebrew, a prostitute, and various other clientele. Paul was a man of high esteem, but Peter was a commoner. Jesus used them both.

You probably have heard it said, "Jesus doesn't call the qualified, He qualifies the called." It doesn't really matter what we "look like." It matters who we "look to!" I may "look like a preacher," but that doesn't make me any more usable for God's Kingdom than you.

Peter declared, "But you are a chosen people, a royal priesthood, a holy nation, a people belonging to God, that you may declare the praises of him who called you out of darkness into his wonderful light."

## "He is the Rock!"
### Psalm 40:2

You may have heard it said that, "The best things in life are free." Well, I am not so sure about that, but I can tell you that some of the cheapest entertainment can be found near Brevard, N.C.

Peggy and I rode the motorcycle up to our son Joshua's one afternoon. We took a nice ride through the mountains and stopped by Sliding Rock in Pisgah National Forest outside of Brevard. You pull into the recreation area and are stopped by a friendly park ranger who takes up the entry fee: One dollar per person. I do not know anywhere you can have as much fun for $1.

We parked the bike and walked to the "rock." There we saw many people. They were all shapes and sizes. They all had a smile on their face. I did not see one person in the group who was unhappy. No one seemed to be uninterested or forced to be there. People were standing in line, young and old, to sit down in cold mountain water and slide down a rock to land in a pool of cold water. There was laughter and just a feeling of belonging.

Peggy and I didn't participate in the jaunt down the rock, but we just enjoyed watching others making memories as we enjoyed remembering some of our own.

Now the short stopover at Sliding Rock has got me to Just Thinking! It has been years since Peggy, the boys and I visited Sliding Rock, yet the "rock" looked the same. I am not sure, but I would imagine that several thousand people have slid down the rock since we visited it many years ago, but I could not see one change in the "rock." The water rushed down the "rock" the same as it did the first time, I saw it. The overall attitude of the people, although they were different people, was the same. Laughter abounded and there was good humor all around.

It reminds me of who God is and how I would hope we would be in His presence. We can come to God with nothing and leave His presence with joy and gladness in our hearts. We can come time and time again and, no matter how long it has been since we were in His presence, we will find Him unchanged. I know where I've been and am excited about where God has placed me. He is my "Rock!" I hope He is yours!

The Psalmist proclaimed, "He lifted me out of the slimy pit, out of the mud and mire; he set my feet on a rock and gave me a firm place to stand."

If you are tired of a world that has nothing solid to offer, I invite you to come to the "Rock" of Jesus Christ.

## "It Is the Same!"
### Hebrews 13:8

My mom called one night and asked me to stop by the store and pick up a half-gallon of buttermilk before coming to their house. I readily agreed to do so. As I approached the milk counter, I was overwhelmed with the choices. You see, I don't buy milk. I don't drink it so I don't buy it.

Oh, every once in a while, I will get Peggy a-half gallon for her cereal, but most of the time she buys it. Well, to say the least, I had trouble finding the buttermilk. I found soy milk, almond milk, goat milk, powdered milk, silk milk, whole milk, 1% milk, 2% milk, low-fat milk, skim milk and lactose-free milk.

Now, when I was a child, my mom would put chocolate flavoring in milk to get me to drink it. Boy, has that changed. Now there is blueberry milk, strawberry milk, vanilla milk and several other flavors. I finally found the buttermilk, but they didn't have low-fat buttermilk, only no-fat buttermilk. I got a-half gallon and finally left the store.

Now, all of these different varieties and flavors has got me to Just Thinking! Do you remember when you just told the milkman how much to leave at the door? (Some of you reading this probably didn't even know that happened at one time.) I remember having home delivery and having to put the empty glass bottles from the previous delivery outside. He would leave the amount you specified. He would leave how many half-gallon bottles you needed.

I remember when Mom started ordering a gallon jug that sat in the fridge and was dispensed through a turn nozzle. Oh, by the way, there was only one kind of milk. We called it white milk.

Have you ever looked around and seen how different it can be to reach people with the good news of Jesus? At one time it was so simple; you just opened the door, invited your friends and neighbors, and they came. People went to church and learned about God because it was the only "kind" in town.

Well, just like milk, that has changed – drastically. We have to work at getting people to look our way and stop long enough to listen. We try all types of service projects. We seek to reach people where they are and meet their needs. It would be nice if there was only one "kind," but that is just not the case.

Thankfully, the good news of Jesus Christ has not changed. "Jesus Christ is the same yesterday, today, and forever." We just need to make sure we are giving it out where people will hear it.

## "Get Ready for the Turn!"
### Isaiah 55:8

Blinkers! You know, those annoying little flashing lights that are to warn you of an impending turn. OK, some of you call them their appropriate name, turn signals. Well, I grew up in the South where we called them blinkers!

Have you ever noticed how many people do not use their blinkers? There I am driving along, following a car, when all of a sudden - out of nowhere -the car's brake lights come on and they turn. I have to brake suddenly and hope the car behind me is not following too closely. (Peggy would say I wouldn't have had to brake so suddenly if I were not following too closely.)

Anyway, I guess my question here is, why do people not use their turn signals? It is not like they were installed on the car for decorations. I just wish people were more conscious of the need for using blinkers.

I know people forget - well, I'm not so sure we forget as much as we don't have another hand to initiate the little arm that controls the blinker. We have one hand on the steering wheel (unless we are busy using both hands and we are driving with our knee); we have one hand on the cell phone; we might be finding another radio station or changing CD's. Or, as I have witnessed, we may be putting on makeup, reading the newspaper, or 100 other interesting things to do while driving. The poor blinker doesn't have a chance.

Well, you can imagine that all this blinker talk has got me to Just Thinking! Don't you wish sometimes that God had a blinker? You know, so you could know which way to turn in your life so you could be everything He wants you to be. Maybe when you are praying or seeking His will, He could just initiate the blinker and you would know that He is about to make a turn in your life. You could prepare for it, be expecting it, and plan how you will react to it. Life very often catches us by surprise, and I would really love it if God would just signal that a turn is about to happen.

Well, I am reminded that God doesn't play by my rules. He has set up the rules, and I must abide by them. Maybe if I were a little less interested in what I wanted to do and more interested in what He wanted me to do, I would be less surprised and more prepared.

Let us not forget what God told His people through the prophet Isaiah, "For my thoughts are not your thoughts, neither are your ways my ways," declares the LORD." So let's plan on being ready with or without a blinker. If we trust and believe, God will never lead us down the wrong path.

## "Pay Attention to the Buggies!"
### Luke 10:29

Well, it has happened to me several times in the past few months. Maybe I need to learn something from it. I will leave a store with my purchases in the buggy, arrive at my truck and place the items in the truck. As I push the buggy to the collection area there will be a person there who is gathering the buggies to take them back inside for others to use. (I would love to know what the official title is for someone who does this.)

Anyway, I politely offer my buggy to the person who is

collecting the buggies out of the rack and they take my buggy and push it into the empty rack. They do not add it to the ones they have already gathered. They do not take the time to place it in the row of buggies that they have prepared to return to the store. They just push it into the empty rack.

The other thing that strikes me about these people is they look very frustrated. It is like they were told to go and do this job, but they really didn't want to. I believe that I am helping them by offering them my buggy, but they look at me as if I have caused them great distress. There is no smile on their face, no thank you for not just ramming them with the buggy, no appreciation of the fact that I just didn't leave the buggy in the parking space. They just look at me as if I am the one who caused them the pain of having to retrieve the buggies, that I could solve their problem if I just didn't use a buggy or I would at least bring it back to the store when I am finished.

All of this buggy stuff (I realize while I am writing this that most of you probably want me to call the buggy a shopping cart) got me to Just Thinking! I wonder how many people I leave at an empty rack because I am only focused on what I have to do, not what I need to do. I wonder as I go about living my life for Jesus and go about my daily task if I look frustrated. I wonder if I look at people without a smile. I wonder if I look like they are in my way. We can get so wrapped up in our lives and how Jesus wants us to live that we miss the people that He puts in our path each and every day.

One day, an expert of the law asked Jesus this question: "But he wanted to justify himself so he asked, 'And who is my neighbor?'"

Jesus told the story of the Good Samaritan to remind us that it is our responsibility to "love our neighbor as ourselves." It is sad that even in Jesus's day that the very people who were not willing to help were the religious people.

How can you help out someone in need this month? How can you spare a few minutes of your busy schedule to make a difference in someone's life? If we look like we don't care, who will? As you go out each day and collect the buggies of your life, don't overlook that one buggy (person) that Jesus sends your way. He put them there for a reason!!!

## "Which Door Do You Choose?"
### Matthew 7:13-14

Have you ever noticed the signs above the automatic doors at Walmart? Over the left door it says "Enter" and over the right door it says "Exit." Have you ever noticed that most people pay no attention to those two words? What is really upsetting is when you are trying to go through the proper door and you can't get in because people are exiting the wrong door.

Now, don't get upset with me if you are one of those people who don't go through the proper door. I also know that Walmart is not the only place this happens. I watch people who drive in the exit and drive out the entrance. And, what is really confusing is when they look at you as if you are in the wrong because you are blocking their way out.

I sure hope all this in-and-out, entrance-and-exit stuff is not confusing to you, but I really wouldn't be surprised if it is. It seems to be confusing to most people who enter or exit a building or parking lot where there are markers telling them where to enter and exit.

Now, I also know that there are some generic doors. There is neither an entrance nor an exit sign above the door. It is just a door to get into the place of business and the same door to leave. Do you know what I have noticed about those types of doors? People are always standing to the side, allowing others to go first. They are always being polite and saying, "After you!"

Do you think that is strange? I do! You may have guessed that one of my "pet peeves" - and something I watch with anticipation - is people who go in and out the wrong doors.

Now, all of this talk about doors has got me to Just Thinking! In the grand scheme of things, no one is going to jail for entering or exiting the wrong door. And, other than a small fender bender, no one has been seriously injured by driving the wrong way in an entrance/exit lane.

As of yet, (maybe we should not give any ideas) no one has been shot at Walmart for entering the exit or exiting the enter door. So why all the fuss? I just want to make sure we all understand that it does make a difference on how we enter the Kingdom of Heaven.

May we never propagate the belief that there are many doors to heaven. May we never give credence to the idea that we don't have to worry about how we come and go in the Kingdom of God. May we never get so worried about acceptance that we just invite people to come in any door they choose.

Remember the words of Jesus, "Enter through the narrow gate. For wide is the gate and broad is the road that leads to destruction, and many enter through it. But small is the gate and narrow the road that leads to life, and only a few find it." Praying you find the "right" door and invite others to enter it also.

## "Where Do You Put Your Money?"
### 1 Peter 4:10

I went on a mission trip to West Virginia. There were five of us, and we traveled in a big Ford truck owned by the director of missions from our association. Because I have a rod in my leg, I was the lucky one and got to ride in the front. The other three guys got in the back, but had plenty of room.

We traveled well together and didn't miss too many rest areas on the way. As we entered West Virginia we came to our first toll road. The director of missions approached the toll booth and stopped to give the lady the $4 toll to continue riding on the road. We didn't have too much further to travel before we got off the road and when we did, we had another toll booth and this time the fee was only 75 cents. Well, none of us had 75 cents. So, we pulled into a toll booth where there was no one working. As we got ready to back out, the toll worker at the other booth stopped us and I rolled down my window and gave him a dollar. He gave me four quarters and I handed them to the director of missions, who was right next to the door where the toll booth worker enters the booth. The director of missions rolled down his window and threw the three quarters out of the window into the door. The other four of us just stared at him and then he realized what he had done. We all broke out in a guffaw laugh. Right ahead of where he threw the coins was a huge white funnel basket with the words, "Put the money here," and a huge arrow pointing downward. For some reason, he either didn't see it or for a moment just lost his focus.

As we were laughing, I looked and the young man who was working the booth was looking at me with a disturbed look on his face. He must have seen what happened and already had four more quarters ready for me. I handed him another dollar and this time we made sure they got put in the right place.

The rest of our time together one of us would think about what happened and we would all begin to laugh together. Matter of fact, I guess we will never let the director of missions live down this act of trying to pay the toll in the wrong place.

When the director of missions reflected back on why he did it, he really wasn't sure. He tried to say that the door had a little skirt around it and made him think the money went there, but even as he tried to make excuses, he would laugh at himself. It was just a really random act that happened where we lost 75 cents and it cost us $1.50 because we put the money in the wrong place. I doubt it will ever happen again.

Now, this throwing money at the wrong place has got me to Just Thinking! I've thought a great deal about how quick this incident happened and how little it cost considering it was only 75 cents. Yet, I have wondered back over my life and wondered when I lost focus and spent money that I didn't have to spend. I wondered if I have been a good steward of all that God has given me.

We realize that we have received nothing on our own merit. Yes, we may have worked hard for it, but without our own God-given abilities we would not have been able to work. Yes, we may have invested wisely, but let us remember that God is the "giver of all good and perfect gifts."

Peter speaks of how we use our gifts. He says, "Each of you should use whatever gift you have received to serve others, as faithful stewards of God's grace in various forms." When we give a gift, it should be because we have been given a gift. When we share those gifts, we share the very grace of God.

I guess what I really want us to remember is that when we give, let's do it responsibly. Let's make sure that as good stewards of God's resources we do what He would do and take care of the widows and orphans, the hurting and homeless, the children with no parent and the senior with no children. Go out of your way to give a gift that makes a difference and watch God as he multiplies that gift in more ways than you could ever imagine. And the greatest joy for you and I will be when we see the smile on the face of that person or persons that we reach out to and minister too.

When we receive the gift that God gave at Christmas, not only does it put a smile on God's face, but the Bible says that all the angels in heaven rejoice. As we give and share with others let's make sure they know the reason is because of Jesus the greatest gift that was ever given to us.

And one last work of caution. Make sure you read the signs so you know where to put your money.

## "He was Right!"
### Psalm 119:144

One weekend I took Dad and Mom to Macon, Ga., so we could celebrate their son-in-law's 50th birthday. On the way we made several stops. We were blessed to stop and see a dear lady's new home in Washington, Ga. She had been a member of our church before she left to be close to her daughter. We then traveled to Jackson, Ga., to see some old friends of Dad and Mom who work for Truckstop Ministries, Inc. As we got to Jackson, Dad told me to go a certain way to find a restaurant. They were having training for chaplains and they would all be at the restaurant. Well, I went the way he told me and looked where he told me the restaurant was and it wasn't there. We circled the block and retraced our path, but it wasn't there.

Now, all of this time, I'm beginning to think that Dad (and Mom, too) was losing it. It is funny now, but I'm believing they are totally mistaken about where the restaurant is supposed to be. We finally found the place, and as we went in, Dad asked his friend if the restaurant had always been there. He said yes. Dad was confused. He said he didn't remember it always being in this location. His friend told him yes it had.

Finally, someone overheard the conversation and said, "No, the original restaurant burned down a few years ago and they moved it here." "That's right," my Dad's friend said, "I had forgotten about that."

Go figure. Dad was right all along. He wasn't losing it after all.

This excursion up and down the street in Jackson has got me to Just Thinking! Have you ever played that same game with God? You know, where you try to tell God that He left something out, or forgot to do something, or just plain forgot about you? You argue with God about how something should always be or should always happen and it doesn't. We find ourselves in a dilemma when we try to convince God we know better than He does.

We may not always say it, but we are like I was when I was

listening to the conversation between Dad and his friend. I was like Dad is wrong, and yet he will not accept it. Yet Dad was right.

It reminds me that God is never wrong either. He is always right. The Psalmist said, "Your statutes are always righteous; give me understanding that I may live."

He is always looking out for our best interests, even when we doubt it or don't understand it. He is always paving the way for something good to happen, even though the path is plagued with hardships and problems. As I approach life each day, I just want to find myself always trusting, always believing and always confident that my God knows what He is doing. Life sure gets easier when we just believe.

Don't worry, Dad. I don't know why I ever doubted you!

## "Just Talk!"
### 1 Thessalonians 5:16-18

The other day I was in the lobby of the hospital waiting for an elevator. There was a young woman with her back to me and I heard her talking away to no one. I wondered for a moment if she had wandered down from the psychiatric ward. She was just talking and there was no one around her. I began to think that this was most unusual.

Finally, as we were waiting for the elevator she turned around and I saw the reason she was talking. Although she did not have a phone in her hand, I recognized that she had an earpiece and a microphone that connected to the phone in her pocket. All the time I thought she was talking to the wall. She had been conversing with someone on the phone. I was very relieved and smiled at her to say, "I'm glad you are OK."

As we entered the elevator, she told the person on the phone she was probably going to be cut off and would call her back after she exited the elevator. As the elevator doors closed, she made small talk with the few who got on the elevator. As she exited the elevator, I saw her grab her phone and begin to make a call and I perceived that she was calling the person back she had just disconnected with. As the doors of the elevator closed, I saw her walking away once again as if she was talking to the air.

Now, all of this talking to no one got me to Just Thinking! This lady was not the least worried about someone thinking she was strange. She just talked away and was oblivious to the fact that those around her may be wondering if she had lost her mind. I wish that we, as Christians, would feel that good about praying to God. I wish that we could feel as comfortable with just talking to God and letting Him know of our every thought and feeling. For most of us, we will talk on the phone to anyone at any time, but for a great deal of people, praying in public is something they would never do. They feel insecure or uncomfortable with speaking to God in public, but they will interrupt a conversation with someone else to answer a phone call and begin a completely different conversation with someone else in public.

I'm not sure I completely understand the concept of being afraid to talk to God in public. I guess we are worried about what people will say about our conversation, but most of us are not concerned about what we say on the telephone when someone is listening to only one side of the conversation. Maybe we don't feel comfortable talking to God because He is almost unreal. Because we have never seen him or talked to him in person, He almost feels inhuman. And because He feels that way to us, we feel inadequate to converse with Him.

I guess my wish for all of us is that we could feel as comfortable talking to God anywhere at any time as we do talk to someone on the phone. I believe that Paul had that attitude. Here is how he put it, "Rejoice always; pray continually; give thanks in all circumstances, for this is God's will for you in Christ Jesus."

And if it makes you feel better, put a phone to your ear and let people think you are talking on the phone. No one will be the wiser and you can carry on a good long conversation with the one who loves and knows you best.

## "Where is My Ticket?"
### Psalm 16:5

I helped my wife, Peggy, with a fundraiser for a foundation that she used to work for. They sold BBQ plates at three restaurants. One of the places they sold plates was in a little town close to where we lived.

My job every year was to handle the drive-up cars and the take-out plates. I had a great time making sure everyone has their plates and talking to those who generously purchase these plates for a good cause. Matter of fact, we had the fastest pick-up service anywhere. Many times, people would talk about how good the service was as we greeted them at their window and then brought their plates to them. They never had to wait or be inconvenienced. We had a great day and raised money for a good cause.

Now, the thing that always gave me great joy for the day was asking the people how many plates they had come to get. They purchased their tickets ahead of time. It almost never failed that they would say, "Wait, let me find my tickets." People put tickets in the most unusual places. One person found them stuck in the bottom of her purse. Another stuck them behind their checkbook. One man had them in his glasses case. One lady had to get out of her car and she found them in her trunk. And of course, there was the lady who said, "I promise I bought the tickets; I just can't find them."

Now, all of this searching for tickets got me to Just Thinking! Where do we, as Christians, place Jesus on an everyday basis? He is our ticket to a greater life and abundant living. Yet, where do we keep Him? Is He fresh and new every day? Or, do we throw Him around and when we need Him, we have to search our lives to find out where He is? Have we put Him somewhere so when it's time to show our ticket we won't forget where we put Him? Or, do people know what place He holds in our life because they can see Him every moment, every day?

I am convinced that if you are a Christian your ticket is secured. The Psalmist said, "Lord, you alone are my portion and my cup, you make my lot secure."

Don't be looking for your ticket, know Jesus has secured your plate.

## "Good Intentions"
### James 4:17

On the first Sunday in April, I finished preaching and while someone was praying the benediction I walked to the back door, as always, to greet the people as they exited the sanctuary. Having noticed my watch, I saw it was 12:01 pm. As I opened the door, I noticed a young couple that I knew making their way up the steps. The young man began by saying hello and inquired why I was at the door when church should already be started. "Startled," I remarked. "We have just finished."

I wish you could have seen the look on both of their faces. He was not only surprised by my answer, but he was also confused. He looked down at his watch and said, "But it's only 11 o'clock." I said, "No, today is the first day of daylight savings time."

It was as if a light came on. He realized I was right and he and his friend began to exit quickly to his car. He called out over his shoulder, "David, keep them inside until we get away, I don't want anybody to know what we've done."

The three of us laughed as they hurried to their car and escaped without anyone else knowing of their mistake.

Now, my friend being late for church that Sunday got me to Just Thinking! Have you ever noticed how we have good intentions, but sometimes we miss out on the right thing because our intentions are not what counts. He wanted to be at church, but for some reason he missed out on the message that everybody else got that it was time to change the clocks.

We sometimes want to read our Bible more, but we are too

busy watching our favorite show on TV. We want to pray more, but we are tired and just can't stay awake when we go to bed. We want to go to church more, but our family keeps planning other things to do on Sunday. The truth of the matter is that we miss out on the things God wants us to do because we are too busy doing what we want to do.

It was interesting to me that my friend wanted to hide his mistake from everybody. Yet he could not hide it from God. We are like that with our mistakes and good intentions. When they don't turn out like we hoped they would, we want to hide them and hope no one notices.

The truth of the matter is that it doesn't matter what others think or feel, but it does matter what God thinks or feels about it. I am reminded about what the writer of James says about sin, "If anyone, then, knows the good they ought to do and doesn't do it, it is sin to them."

That's pretty straightforward to me. I pray that you aren't depending on your good intentions to make you present when the time comes for God to call your name? I pray that if you know what is right to do, you will do it.

## "Guaranteed for Life"
### Hebrews 7:23; John 11:25

I was talking to some friends the other day and they were telling me about a website on the Internet that sells frogs. You heard me correctly, frogs. She was telling me about her little girl and the fact that they bought a frog off of this website. It comes as a tadpole and you grow the frog. You feed it and it has a little house that it stays in. You feed it and it jumps up and eats the food.

The name of the website, if any of you are interested, growafrog.com. I was just astounded that someone could sell frogs over the Internet - and that someone would buy them.

Believe it or not, they are not that expensive and after having got on the Internet just to look at the site, it is unbelievable what you can buy to grow a frog.

The most interesting part of growing a frog is that they give a lifetime guarantee on the frog. Now, everybody knows that frogs don't live forever, but this company says that if your frog dies for any reason, they will replace it for free. You just have to call them up and tell them what stage of life your frog was in. If your frog is 2 years old, they will send you a 2-year-old frog to replace it. If your frog is still in the tadpole stage, they will send you another tadpole. All you have to do is send $3 for shipping and handling and they will send you another frog.

Now, I hope you are staying under better control than I did when the young lady was telling me this story. To tell you the truth I was laughing uncontrollably. Who would ever believe you could buy a frog and keep it forever – well, at least keep some type of frog forever.

By the way, the website does say that the normal life span of one of their frogs is 5 years, but they do get emails that people tell them their frogs have been living as long as 20 years.

Now, not necessarily the frogs, but the guarantee on the frogs, has got me to Just Thinking! Would you like to have a guarantee on your life with no shipping and handling charge? Just think about it, if anything goes wrong and your life should end prematurely or by natural causes, you can get a new life for no charge. You don't have to pay for anything, you just need to make sure you have made arrangements.

All you have to do is accept Jesus Christ as your personal Lord and Savior and you will have everlasting life. It will not matter how long the average life expectancy for others is, it will only depend on the provisions you make while you are alive. You can either accept the guarantee or reject it.

I know if there is a company that can guarantee a frog for life, that I can trust God, who guarantees me for life. God says that He wants us to live abundantly and the writer of Hebrews says, "Jesus has become the guarantee of a better covenant."

That covenant is that if we accept Jesus as our Lord and Savior, God will guarantee that we will never die. Listen to the words of Jesus as He talks to Martha at the graveside of Lazarus, "I am the resurrection and the life. He who believes in me will live, even though he dies; and whoever lives and believes in me will never die. Do you believe this?"

Do you hear the guarantee? Listen once again, "He who believes in me will live, even though he dies...!!"

I think I will put my faith in trust in a God who makes a promise like that instead of the guarantee of a frog company. How about you?

## "Can You Read?"
### Psalm 119:36

I went to West Virginia with my family to go skiing. I went down the mountain, but I wouldn't call it skiing. Anyway, while we were there, I kept Peggy company in the ski lodge. On Saturday, the place was packed with people. I began to notice that either people can't read very well or they just don't care. On the glass doors to the ski lodge there is written in large white letters these words, "SORRY, NO SKIS ALLOWED IN THIS BUILDING."

I realized after just a short while that there is a great deal of skiers who are illiterate. They just couldn't read. Every time I would see people come into the lodge some person would be carrying their skis with them. I even heard two young ladies use this excuse before they entered the lodge:

Young Lady #1, opening the door with skis in the other hand, "Oh, we aren't supposed to carrying our skis in."

Young Lady #2, after a short pause where I am sure she was

thinking, "Oh, well, that means we aren't supposed to wear them in." Then the girls proceeded to go into the area with their skis.

One man actually dropped his skis on my back. Of course, he apologized, but as I said to him, "That's probably the reason it says not to bring them into the lodge." Of course, he ignored me and the sign.

I told Peggy that we should put up a sign that says, "Don't Give the Big Man in the Camouflage Bibs $20." We could get rich. I will bet 20 or 30 people would have given me the money.

Now, this incident has got me to Just Thinking! What if we told people they couldn't come to church? What if we told people they couldn't read their Bible? What if we told people they couldn't pray? We would probably find more people doing it.

Those statements are sad to me. Are we a nation who seeks to ignore the rules? Have we become a nation that needs to be rebellious? I have a feeling that most of those people ignored the sign because it didn't satisfy their own selfish needs. I have a feeling that most people don't go to church, or read their Bible, or pray because it doesn't satisfy their own selfish need.

The Psalmist said, "Turn my heart toward your statutes and not toward selfish gain."

I tend to agree with the psalmist. I want to read and be attentive to the Lord's statutes. I do not want to ignore them. Together let us read and obey the signs of God.

## "Do You Have a Clear Conscience?"
### Acts 24:16

I was returning from the hospital one afternoon. As I was headed back to the church, I had to travel through two small towns. The speed limit is strictly enforced in these towns, so I was being careful to watch my speed.

As I was headed into one of these small towns, I saw the city policeman head north in his patrol car. He went past me at

## JUST THINKING!

a high rate of speed. I figured he had caught some unexpecting motorist. After he passed me, I noticed that he turned on his blue light and did an about face in the middle of the road; you know, one of those turns you see the police do on TV.

I began to move over to the side of the road so he could pass me. You see, I knew there was no way he could be coming after me. Just about the time I was going to pull over, I noticed a white automobile in my rear-view mirror. He was traveling very fast and I was afraid he would rear-end me. I moved on ahead to avoid contact, still, to the best of my ability, trying to get out of the policeman's way.

We had just moved over to the right lane because there was some road construction taking place. I finally drove my truck up on the sidewalk, trying to avoid getting into the policeman's way. I glanced into my mirror and saw the policeman pulling in behind the white car. I finally figured out that he was after him all the time.

I started to move back onto the highway, when all of a sudden, a black GMC Jimmy was coming right at me. Before I could think of what to do next, the white car ran into the rear of my truck and another police officer in plain clothes stepped out of the Jimmy, pulled his revolver and pointed it towards me.

Well, he was really pointing it towards the car behind me, but at that range who could tell the difference? I'm not exactly sure what happened next, because I was looking at the brake pedal, the gas pedal and the clutch. In other words, I was in the floorboard.

Finally, I snuck a peak to find the officers apprehending the man in the other car. A nice police officer came up and apologized for the delay. He asked if I was OK and told me the truck didn't look as if it had been hurt. I said thank you and if he would close the door to his car I would be on my way. He told me he would have to detain me for a few more minutes as a witness. I was obliged to help in any way.

As I sat in the truck waiting for the officer to return, I began to think someone was playing a trick on me. After it was all over, I got a good laugh out of it.

Now, all of this excitement got me to Just Thinking! You know, it really does feel good to know you've done nothing wrong. I must say, for a few seconds I was scared to death, but I knew I had done nothing wrong. I knew they couldn't be after me. Oh, I thought maybe I had a vehicle that matched a description they were looking for, or maybe this was a Candid Camera (a 1960s TV show) or practical jokes stunt, but my conscience was clear.

What a good feeling to have a clear conscience. The apostle Paul knew how it felt. Before Felix, the governor, he spoke these words, "So I strive always to keep my conscience clear before God and man."

What an honorable goal: to have a clear conscience, to know the things I do and say are righteous and good. I don't always reach my goal, but we must always press towards a mark.

# BEFORE YOU GO!

I would be amiss if I didn't take a few minutes to thank some people who helped make this project possible.

First of all, let me thank any and all of you that I have had the privilege to be your pastor over the 40 years. The fact that you shared your life with me is very much appreciated and helped to make me a better person.

To any of you who happen to make it into one of my stories, thank you for allowing me to learn and grow through God's guidance. Doing life with you was a blast and helped to shape me into the person I am.

To my friend and fellow Hurricanes fan, Rudy Jones. Your editorial expertise was invaluable. Peggy and I are blessed to call you and Doris our friends. Thank you for your hard work and all of the help in making necessary corrections.

To my friend Rachel Greene Bass. You always impress me with your vision and attention to detail. The front cover of my book was everything I thought it would be. It has been a joy and privilege to see you grow into the person God has called you to be.

To Randy Bradley, thanks for writing the forward. I treasure the moment that we met and still consider you to be a very valuable friend. You have been a wonderful mentor and guide through some of my toughest days. I will always be indebted.

To Heath Davis, thanks for reading the manuscript. Your inspiration and words mean a great deal to me. I look forward to continuing to hear God speak through you every week as you remain my pastor.

To Steve Taylor, an accomplished author in your own right. Thank you for your input and encouragement as I journeyed through this process. It means a great deal to me that you took the time to read and respond to the manuscript.

To my parents, Larry & Palma Simmons. I as so grateful that you raised me in a home that loved God. Your teaching and example have helped to guide me in the right paths. Your love and support in this project have been an inspiration and a source of strength.

To my sons and their families: Joshua, Laura, Foster & Corbin Simmons; Caleb, Sally Ann, Reid & James Simmons. Your love and support keep me moving forward every day. I am blessed to be your Father and Papa. You make everyday special and I am glad to be able to do life with you.

To my very special wife, Peggy, the Pearl. Your love and support have inspired me in ways you will never understand. You have encouraged me and pushed me to finish this project. For that I am grateful. Thank you for loving me and putting up with my inabilities and quirks. I love you more!!

And finally, to my Savior and Lord Jesus Christ. Without you the life I live would be fruitless and bland. I cannot imagine what life would be life without you as my friend and guide. Thank you for loving me and forgiving me. I give you all the praise and glory for all that is accomplished and for all that I have done in my life. To God Be The Glory!!

David M. Simmons
January 2024